Introductory
Microsoft® ACCESS 2.0
for Windows™

Introductory
Microsoft® ACCESS 2.0
for Windows™

Joseph J. Adamski
Grand Valley State University

Course

TECHNOLOGY

Course Technology, Inc. One Main Street, Cambridge, MA 02142
An International Thomson Publishing Company

Introductory Microsoft Access 2.0 for Windows is published by Course Technology, Inc.

Managing Editor	Mac Mendelsohn
Series Consulting Editor	Susan Solomon
Product Manager	David Crocco
Director of Production	Myrna D'Addario
Production Editor	Donna Whiting
Desktop Publishing Supervisor	Debbie Masi
Composition	Gex, Inc.
Production Assistant	Christine Spillett
Copyeditor	Jenny Kilgore
Proofreader	Elyse Demers
Indexer	Alexandra Nickerson
Product Testing and Support Supervisor	Jeff Goding
Technical Reviewers	Brenda Domingo
	Mark Vodnik
Prepress Production	Gex, Inc.
Manufacturing Manager	Elizabeth Martinez
Text Designer	Sally Steele
Cover Designer	John Gamache

Introductory Microsoft Access 2.0 for Windows © 1995 by Course Technology, Inc.
An International Thomson Publishing Company

Trademarks

Course Technology and the open book logo are registered trademarks of Course Technology, Inc.

I(T)P The ITP logo is a trademark under license.

Microsoft is a registered trademark and Windows and Access for Windows are trademarks of Microsoft Corporation.

Some of the product names and company names used in this book have been used for identification purposes only and may be trademarks or registered trademarks of their respective manufacturers and sellers.

Disclaimer

Course Technology, Inc. reserves the right to revise this publication and make changes from time to time in its content without notice.

ISBN 1-56527-148-3 (text)

Printed in the United States of America

10 9 8 7 6 5 4 3 2

From the Publisher

At Course Technology, Inc., we believe that technology will transform the way that people teach and learn. We are excited about bringing you, college professors and students, the most practical and affordable technology-related products available.

The Course Technology Development Process

Our development process is unparalleled in the higher education publishing industry. Every product we create goes through an exacting process of design, development, review, and testing.

Reviewers give us direction and insight that shape our manuscripts and bring them up to the latest standards. Every manuscript is quality tested. Students whose backgrounds match the intended audience work through every keystroke, carefully checking for clarity and pointing out errors in logic and sequence. Together with our own technical reviewers, these testers help us ensure that everything that carries our name is error-free and easy to use.

Course Technology Products

We show both *how* and *why* technology is critical to solving problems in college and in whatever field you choose to teach or pursue. Our time-tested, step-by-step instructions provide unparalleled clarity. Examples and applications are chosen and crafted to motivate students.

The Course Technology Team

This book will suit your needs because it was delivered quickly, efficiently, and affordably. In every aspect of our business, we rely on a commitment to quality and the use of technology. Every employee contributes to this process. The names of all of our employees are listed below:

Tim Ashe, David Backer, Stephen M. Bayle, Josh Bernoff, Ann Marie Buconjic, Jody Buttafoco, Kerry Cannell, Jim Chrysikos, Barbara Clemens, Susan Collins, John M. Connolly, Kim Crowley, Myrna D'Addario, Lisa D'Alessandro, Howard S. Diamond, Kathryn Dinovo, Joseph B. Dougherty, MaryJane Dwyer, Chris Elkhill, Don Fabricant, Kate Gallagher, Laura Ganson, Jeff Goding, Laurie Gomes, Eileen Gorham, Andrea Greitzer, Catherine Griffin, Tim Hale, Roslyn Hooley, Nicole Jones, Matt Kenslea, Susannah Lean, Suzanne Licht, Laurie Lindgren, Kim Mai, Elizabeth Martinez, Debbie Masi, Don Maynard, Dan Mayo, Kathleen McCann, Jay McNamara, Mac Mendelsohn, Laurie Michelangelo, Kim Munsell, Amy Oliver, Michael Ormsby, Kristine Otto, Debbie Parlee, Kristin Patrick, Charlie Patsios, Jodi Paulus, Darren Perl, Kevin Phaneuf, George J. Pilla, Cathy Prindle, Nancy Ray, Marjorie Schlaikjer, Christine Spillett, Michelle Tucker, David Upton, Mark Valentine, Karen Wadsworth, Anne Marie Walker, Renee Walkup, Donna Whiting, Janet Wilson, Lisa Yameen.

Preface

Course Technology, Inc. is proud to present this new book in its Windows Series. *Introductory Microsoft Access 2.0 for Windows* is designed for a first course on Microsoft Access. This book capitalizes on the energy and enthusiasm students naturally have for Windows-based applications and clearly teaches students how to take full advantage of Access' power. It assumes students have learned basic Windows skills and file management from *An Introduction to Microsoft Windows 3.1* or *A Guide to Microsoft Windows 3.1* by June Jamrich Parsons or from an equivalent book.

Organization and Coverage

Introductory Microsoft Access 2.0 for Windows contains six tutorials that present hands-on instruction. In these tutorials students learn how to plan, create, and maintain Access databases. They learn to retrieve information by creating queries and developing professional-looking reports. Students also learn to create customized forms to access and enter data in a database.

The text emphasizes the ease-of-use features included in the Access software: toolbar and toolbox buttons, Shortcut menus, graphical relationship tools, graphical query by example (QBE), Cue Cards, and Wizards. Using this book, students will be able to do more advanced tasks sooner than they would using other introductory texts; a perusal of the table of contents affirms this. By the end of the book, students will have learned "advanced" tasks such as creating input masks, importing data, creating parameter queries, linking multiple tables, and creating custom forms and reports.

Approach

Introductory Microsoft Access 2.0 for Windows distinguishes itself from other Windows textbooks because of its unique two-pronged approach. First, it motivates students by demonstrating why they need to learn the concepts and skills. This book teaches Access using a task-driven rather than a feature-driven approach. By working through the tutorials—each motivated by a realistic case—students learn how to use Access in situations they are likely to encounter in the workplace, rather than learn a list of features one-by-one, out of context. Second, the content, organization, and pedagogy of this book make full use of the Windows environment. What content is presented, when it's presented, and how it's presented capitalizes on Access' power to perform complex database tasks earlier and more easily than was possible under DOS.

Features

Introductory Microsoft Access 2.0 for Windows is an exceptional textbook also because it includes the following features:

- **"Read This Before You Begin" Page** This page is consistent with Course Technology, Inc.'s unequaled commitment to helping instructors introduce technology into the classroom. Technical considerations and assumptions about hardware, software, and default settings are listed in one place to help instructors save time and eliminate unnecessary aggravation.

- **Tutorial Case** Each tutorial begins with a database-related problem that students could reasonably encounter in business. Thus, the process of solving the problem will be meaningful to students.

- **Step-by-Step Methodology** The unique Course Technology, Inc. methodology keeps students on track. They click or press keys always within the context of solving the problem posed in the Tutorial Case. The text constantly guides students, letting them know where they are in the process of solving the problem. The numerous screen shots include labels that direct students' attention to what they should look at on the screen.

- **Page Design** Each *full-color* page is designed to help students easily differentiate between what they are to *do* and what they are to *read*. The steps are easily identified by their color background and numbered bullets. Windows' default colors are used in the screen shots so instructors can more easily assure that students' screens look like those in the book.

- **TROUBLE?** TROUBLE? paragraphs anticipate the mistakes that students are likely to make and help them recover from these mistakes. This feature facilitates independent learning and frees the instructor to focus on substantive conceptual issues rather than common procedural errors.

- **Reference Windows** and **Task Reference** Reference Windows provide short, generic summaries of frequently used procedures. The Task Reference appears at the end of the book and summarizes how to accomplish tasks using the mouse, the menus, and the keyboard. Both of these features are specially designed and written so students can use the book as a reference manual after completing the course.

- **Questions, Tutorial Assignments, and Case Problems** Each tutorial concludes with meaningful, conceptual Questions that test students' understanding of what they learned in the tutorial. The Questions are followed by Tutorial Assignments, which provide students with additional hands-on practice of the skills they learned in the Tutorial. Each Tutorial Assignment (except Tutorial 1) is followed by four complete Case Problems that have approximately the same scope as the Tutorial Case.

- **Exploration Exercises** Unlike DOS, the Windows environment allows students to learn by exploring and discovering what they can do. The Exploration Exercises are Questions, Tutorial Assignments, or Case Problems designated by an E that encourage students to explore the capabilities of the computing environment they are using and to extend their knowledge using the Windows on-line Help facility and other reference materials.

The CTI WinApps Setup Disk

The CTI WinApps Setup Disk, bundled with the Instructor's copy of this book, contains an innovative Student Disk generating program that is designed to save instructors time. Once this software is installed on a network or a standalone workstation, students can double click the "Make Access 2.0 Student Disk" icon in the CTI WinApps icon group. Double clicking this icon transfers all the data files students need to complete the tutorials, Tutorial Assignments, and Case Problems to a high-density disk in drive A or B. These files free students from tedious keystroking and allow them to concentrate on mastering the concept or task at hand. Tutorial 1 provides complete step-by-step instructions for making the Student Disk.

Adopters of this text are granted the right to install the CTI WinApps group window on any standalone computer or network used by students who have purchased this text.

For more information of the CTI WinApps Setup Disk, see the page in this book called "Read This Before You Begin."

Supplements

■ **Instructor's Manual**   The Instructor's Manual is written by the author and is quality assurance tested. It includes:
  - Answers and solutions to all of the Questions, Tutorial Assignments, and Case Problems. Suggested solutions are also included for the Exploration Exercises
  - A disk (3.5-inch or 5.25-inch) containing solutions to all the Questions, Tutorial Assignments, and Case Problems
  - Tutorial Notes, which contain background information from the author about the Tutorial Case and the instructional progression of the tutorial
  - Technical Notes, which include troubleshooting tips as well as information on how to customize the students' screens to closely emulate the screen shots in the book
  - Transparency Masters of key concepts
■ **Test Bank**   The Test Bank contains 50 questions per tutorial in true/false, multiple choice, and fill-in-the-blank formats, plus two essay questions. Each question has been quality assurance tested by students to achieve clarity and accuracy.
■ **Electronic Test Bank**   The Electronic Test Bank allows instructors to edit individual test questions, select questions individually or at random, and print out scrambled versions of the same test to any supported printer.

Acknowledgments

I want to thank the many people who contributed to this book. I thank the many reviewers of this book, in particular: Dr. Michael Paul, Barry University; James M. Kraushaar, University of Vermont; and Minnie Yen, University of Alaska Anchorage.

I also thank the dedicated and enthusiastic Course Technology, Inc. staff, including the excellent production team: Donna Whiting, Production Editor; Christine Spillett, Production Assistant; the student testers: Brenda Domingo and Mark Vodnik.

My special thanks to Susan Solomon for her friendship, advice, and support and to David Crocco, Product Manager, for his assistance, suggestions, and positive nature.

Joseph J. Adamski

Brief Contents

Contents

TUTORIAL 4   **Querying Database Tables**

TUTORIAL 5   **Designing Forms**

TUTORIAL 6   Creating Reports

Index

Task Reference

Reference Windows

Introductory
Microsoft Access® 2.0
for Windows™ Tutorials

1 **Introduction to Database Concepts and Access**

2 **Creating Access Tables**

3 **Maintaining Database Tables**

4 **Querying Database Tables**

5 **Designing Forms**

6 **Creating Reports**

Read This Before You Begin

To the Student

To use this book, you must have a Student Disk. Your instructor will either provide you with one or ask you to make your own by following the instructions in the section "Your Student Disk" in Tutorial 1. See your instructor or technical support person for further information. If you are going to work through this book using your own computer, you need a computer system running Microsoft Windows 3.1 and Microsoft Access 2.0, and a Student Disk. *You will not be able to complete the tutorials and exercises in this book using your own computer until you have a Student Disk.*

To the Instructor

Making the Student Disk To complete the tutorials in this book, your students must have a copy of the Student Disk. To relieve you of having to make multiple Student Disks from a single master copy, we provide you with the CTI WinApps Setup Disk, which contains an automatic Student Disk generating program. Once you install the Setup Disk on a network or standalone workstation, students can easily make their own Student Disks by double-clicking the "Make Access 2.0 Student Disk" icon in the CTI WinApps icon group. Double-clicking this icon transfers all the data files students will need to complete the tutorials, Tutorial Assignments, and Case Problems to a high-density disk in drive A or B. If some of your students will use their own computers to complete the tutorials and exercises in this book, they must first get the Student Disk. The section called "Your Student Disk" in Tutorial 1 provides complete instructions on how to make the Student Disk.

Installing the CTI WinApps Setup Disk To install the CTI WinApps icon group from the Setup Disk, follow the instructions inside the disk envelope that was bundled with your book. By adopting this book, you are granted a license to install this software on any computer or computer network used by you or your students.

README File A README.TXT file located on the Setup Disk provides additional technical notes, troubleshooting advice, and tips for using the CTI WinApps software in your school's computer lab. You can view the README.TXT file using any word processor you choose.

System Requirements

The minimum software and hardware requirements for your computer system are as follows:
- Microsoft Windows Version 3.1 or later on a local hard drive or a network drive.
- A 386 or higher processor with a minimum of 6 MB RAM (8 MB RAM or more is strongly recommended).
- A mouse supported by Windows 3.1.
- A printer supported by Windows 3.1.
- A VGA 640 × 480 16-color display is recommended; an 800 × 600 or 1024 × 768 SVGA, VGA monochrome, or EGA display is acceptable.
- 19 MB free hard disk space.
- Student workstations with at least 1 high-density disk drive. If you need a 5.25-inch CTI WinApps Setup Disk, contact your CTI sales rep or call customer service at 1-800-648-7450. In Canada call Times Mirror Professional Publishing/Irwin Dorsey at 1-800-268-4178.
- If you wish to install the CTI WinApps Setup Disk on a network drive, your network must support Microsoft Windows.

Introduction to Database Concepts and Access

Planning a Special Magazine Issue

 CASE

Vision Publishers   Brian Murphy is the president of Vision Publishers, which produces five specialized monthly magazines from its Chicago headquarters. Brian founded the company in March 1970 when he began publishing *Business Perspective*, a magazine featuring articles, editorials, interviews, and investigative reports that are widely respected in the financial and business communities. Using the concept, format, style, and strong writing of *Business Perspective* as a model, Brian began *Total Sports* in 1975, *Media Scene* in 1978, *Science Outlook* in 1984, and *Travel Vista* in 1987. All five magazines are leaders in their fields and have experienced consistent annual increases in circulation and advertising revenue.

Brian decides to do something special to commemorate the upcoming 25th anniversary of *Business Perspective* and schedules a meeting with four key employees of the magazine. At the meeting are Judith Rossi, managing editor; Harold Larson, marketing director; Elena Sanchez, special projects editor; and Helen Chung, print production director. After reviewing alternatives, they agree that they will create a special 25th-anniversary issue of *Business Perspective*. The issue will include several articles reviewing the past 25 years of the magazine and of the business and financial worlds during those years. Most of the special issue, however, will consist of articles from previous issues, a top article from each year of the magazine's existence. They expect to sign up many advertisers for the issue and to use it as an incentive bonus gift for new and renewing subscribers.

Brian instructs Judith to select past articles, Elena to plan for the special issue, Harold to contact advertisers and plan the marketing campaign, and Helen to prepare the production schedule. Brian will decide on the concept for the new articles and will communicate assignments to the writers.

Judith begins her assignment by using the Vision Publishers database that contains all articles ever published in the five magazines. From this Access for Windows 2.0 database, Judith will scan the articles from *Business Perspective* and select the top articles.

Elena will also use Access for Windows 2.0 for her assignment. Once Judith and Brian determine which articles will be in the special issue, Elena will use Access for Windows 2.0 to store information about the selected business articles and their writers.

In this tutorial, you will follow along as Judith completes her task. You will also learn about databases and how to use the features of Access for Windows 2.0 to view and print your data.

Using the Tutorials Effectively

The tutorials will help you learn about Access for Windows 2.0. They are designed to be used at your computer. Begin by reading the text that explains the concepts. Then when you come to the numbered steps, follow the steps on your computer. Read each step carefully and completely before you try it.

As you work, compare your screen with the figures in the tutorials to verify your results. Don't worry if your screen display differs slightly from the figures. The important parts of the screen display are labeled in each figure. Just be sure you have these parts on your screen.

Don't worry about making mistakes; that's part of the learning process. **TROUBLE?** paragraphs identify common problems and explain how to get back on track. You complete the steps in a **TROUBLE?** paragraph *only* if you are having the problem described.

After you read the conceptual information and complete the steps, you can do the exercises found at the end of each tutorial in the sections entitled "Questions," "Tutorial Assignments," and "Case Problems." The exercises are carefully structured to help you review what you learned in the tutorials and apply your knowledge to new situations.

When you are doing the exercises, refer back to the Reference Window boxes. These boxes, which are found throughout the tutorials, provide you with short summaries of frequently used procedures. You can also use the Task Reference at the end of the tutorials; it summarizes how to accomplish tasks using the mouse, the menus, and the keyboard.

Before you begin the tutorials, you should know how to use the menus, dialog boxes, Help facility, Program Manager, and File Manager in Microsoft Windows. Course Technology, Inc. publishes two excellent texts for learning Windows: *A Guide to Microsoft Windows 3.1* and *An Introduction to Microsoft Windows 3.1*.

From this point on, the tutorials refer to Access for Windows 2.0 simply as Access.

Your Student Disk

To complete the tutorials and exercises in this book, you must have a Student Disk. The Student Disk contains all the practice files you need for the tutorials, the Tutorial Assignments, and the Case Problems. If your technical support person or instructor provides you with your Student Disk, you can skip this section and go to the section "Introduction to Database Concepts." If your instructor asks you to make your own Student Disk, follow the steps in this section.

To make your Student Disk, you need:

- a blank, formatted, high-density 3.5- or 5.25-inch disk
- a computer with Microsoft Windows 3.1, Microsoft Access 2.0, and the CTI WinApps icon group installed on it

If you are using your own computer, the CTI WinApps icon group will not be installed on it. Before you proceed, you must go to your school's computer lab and find a computer with the CTI WinApps icon group installed on it. Once you have made your own Student Disk, you can use it to complete all the tutorials and exercises in this book on any computer you choose.

To make your Access 2.0 Student Disk:

❶ Launch Windows and make sure the Program Manager window is open.

   TROUBLE? The exact steps you follow to launch Microsoft Windows 3.1 might vary depending on how your computer is set up. On many computer systems, type WIN then press [Enter] to launch Windows. If you don't know how to launch Windows, ask your instructor or technical support person.

❷ Label your formatted disk "Access 2.0 Student Disk" and place it in drive A.

   TROUBLE? If your computer has more than one disk drive, drive A is usually on top or on the left. If your Student Disk does not fit into drive A, then place it in drive B and substitute "drive B" anywhere you see "drive A" in the tutorial steps.

❸ Look for an icon labeled "CTI WinApps" like the one in Figure 1-1, or a window labeled "CTI WinApps," like the one in Figure 1-2 on the following page.

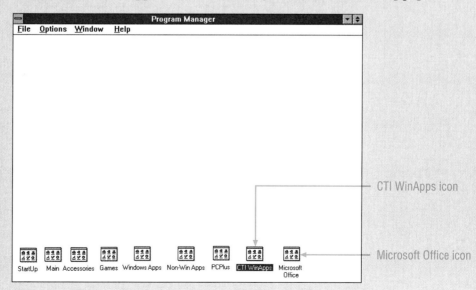

Figure 1-1
The CTI
WinApps icon

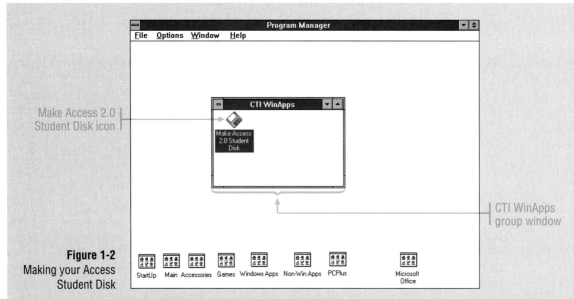

Figure 1-2
Making your Access
Student Disk

TROUBLE? If you can't find anything labeled "CTI WinApps," the CTI software might not be installed on your computer. If you are in a computer lab, ask your instructor or technical support person for assistance. *If you are using your own computer*, you will not be able to make your Student Disk. To make it, you need access to the CTI WinApps icon group, which is, most likely, installed on your school's lab computers. Ask your instructor or technical support person for further information on where to locate the CTI WinApps icon group. Once you create your Student Disk, you can use it to complete all the tutorials and exercises in this book on any computer you choose.

❹ If you see an icon labeled "CTI WinApps," double-click it to open the CTI WinApps group window. If the CTI WinApps window is already open, go to Step 5.

❺ Double-click the icon labeled "Make Access 2.0 Student Disk." The Make Access 2.0 Student Disk window opens. See Figure 1-3.

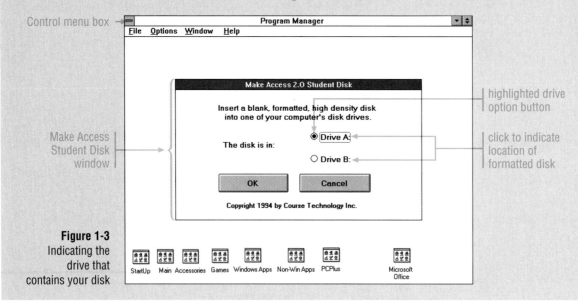

Figure 1-3
Indicating the
drive that
contains your disk

❻ Make sure the drive that contains your formatted disk corresponds to the drive option button that is highlighted in the dialog box on your screen.

❼ Click the **OK button** to copy the practice files to your formatted disk.

❽ When the copying is complete, a message indicates the number of files copied to your disk. Click the **OK button**.

❾ To close the CTI WinApps window, double-click the **Control menu box** on the CTI WinApps window.

Introduction to Database Concepts

Before you work along with Judith on her Vision Publishers assignment, you need to understand a few key terms and concepts associated with databases.

Organizing Data

Data is a valuable resource to companies. At Vision Publishers, for example, writers' names and payments and past magazine article titles and publication dates are data of great value. Organizing, creating, storing, maintaining, retrieving, and sorting such data are important activities that lead to the display and printing of information useful to a company.

When you plan to create and store new types of data either manually or on a computer, you follow a general three-step procedure:

- Identify the individual fields.
- Group fields for each entity.
- Store the field values for each record.

You first identify the individual fields. A **field** is a single characteristic of an entity. An **entity** is a person, place, object, event, or idea. Article title and article length are examples of two fields that Vision Publishers tracks for the entity magazine articles. The company also tracks the fields of writer name and writer address for the entity writers. A field is also called a **data element**, **data item**, or **attribute**.

You next group together all fields for a specific entity into a structure called a **table**. Among its many tables, Vision Publishers has a MAGAZINE ARTICLES table and a WRITERS table, as shown in Figure 1-4. The MAGAZINE ARTICLES table has fields named Article Title, Magazine Issue, Magazine Name, and Article Length. The WRITERS table has fields named Writer Name, Writer Address, and Phone Number. By identifying the fields for each entity and organizing them into tables, you have created the physical structure for your data.

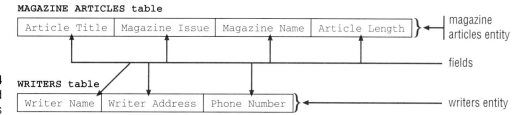

Figure 1-4
Fields organized
in two tables

Your final step is to store specific values for the fields of each table. The specific value, or content, of a field is called the **field value**. In the MAGAZINE ARTICLES table, for example, the first set of field values for Article Title, Magazine Issue, Magazine Name, and Article Length are, respectively, Trans-Alaskan Oil Pipeline Opening, 1977 JUL, Business Perspective, and 803 (Figure 1-5). This set of field values is called a **record**. Each separate stored magazine article is a separate record. Nine records are shown in Figure 1-5; each row of field values is a record.

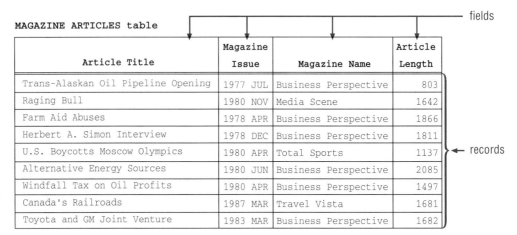

Figure 1-5
Data organization
for a table of
magazine articles

Databases and Relationships

A collection of related tables is called a **database**, or a **relational database**. Two related tables at Vision Publishers, for example, are the WRITERS table and the MAGAZINE ARTICLES table. Sometimes you might want information about writers and the articles they wrote. To obtain this information you must have a way to connect records from the WRITERS table to records from the MAGAZINE ARTICLES table. You connect the records from the separate tables through a **common field** that appears in both tables. Each record in the MAGAZINE ARTICLES table has a field named Writer ID, which is also a field in the WRITERS table (Figure 1-6). For example, Leroy W. Johnson is the third writer in the WRITERS table and has a Writer ID field value of J525. This same Writer ID field value, J525, appears in the first and third records of the MAGAZINE ARTICLES table. Leroy W. Johnson is therefore the writer of these two articles. Tables are also often called **relations**, because records can be connected to form relationships between tables.

MAGAZINE ARTICLES table

common field

foreign key

Article Title	Magazine Issue	Magazine Name	Article Length	Writer ID
Trans-Alaskan Oil Pipeline Opening	1977 JUL	Business Perspective	803	J525
Raging Bull	1980 NOV	Media Scene	1642	S253
Farm Aid Abuses	1978 APR	Business Perspective	1866	J525
Herbert A. Simon Interview	1978 DEC	Business Perspective	1811	C200
U.S. Boycotts Moscow Olympics	1980 APR	Total Sports	1137	R543
Alternative Energy Sources	1980 JUN	Business Perspective	2085	S260
Windfall Tax on Oil Profits	1980 APR	Business Perspective	1497	K500
Canada's Railroads	1987 MAR	Travel Vista	1681	H655
Toyota and GM Joint Venture	1983 MAR	Business Perspective	1682	S260

two articles by Leroy W. Johnson

WRITERS table

primary key

Writer ID	Writer Name	Phone Number	Last Contact Date	Freelance?
C200	Kelly Cox	(204)783-5415	11/14/82	Yes
H655	Maria L. Hernandez	(916)669-6518	4/9/94	No
J525	Leroy W. Johnson	(209)895-2046	1/29/91	Yes
K500	Chong Kim	(807)729-5364	5/19/94	No
R543	Adam Reynolds	(211)457-9811	10/30/88	No
S253	Myra Schneider	(819)534-6785	2/28/89	No
S260	Wilhelm Seeger	(306)423-0932	12/24/93	Yes

Figure 1-6
Database relationship between tables for magazine articles and writers

Each Writer ID value in the WRITERS table must be unique, so that we can distinguish one writer from another and identify the writer of specific articles in the MAGAZINE ARTICLES table. We call the Writer ID field the primary key of the WRITERS table. A **primary key** is a field, or a collection of fields, whose values uniquely identify each record in a table.

When we include a primary key from one table in a second table to form a relationship between the two tables, we call it a **foreign key** in the second table. For example, Writer ID is the primary key in the WRITERS table and is a foreign key in the MAGAZINE ARTICLES table. Although the primary key Writer ID has unique values in the WRITERS table, the same field as a foreign key in the MAGAZINE ARTICLES table does not have unique values. The Writer ID values J525 and S260, for example, each appear in two records in the MAGAZINE ARTICLES table. Each foreign key value, however, must match one of the field values for the primary key in the other table. Each Writer ID value in the MAGAZINE ARTICLES table, for instance, appears as a Writer ID value in the WRITERS table. The two tables are related, enabling us to tie together the facts about magazine articles with the facts about writers.

Relational Database Management Systems

To manage its databases, a company purchases a database management system. A **database management system (DBMS)** is a software package that lets us create databases and then manipulate data in the databases. Most of today's database management systems, including Access, are called relational database management systems. In a **relational database management system**, data is organized as a collection of tables. These tables are formally called relations, which is how the term relational databases originated.

A relationship between two tables in a relational DBMS is formed through a common field. A relational DBMS controls the physical databases on disk storage by carrying out data creation and manipulation requests. Specifically, a relational DBMS has the following functions (Figure 1-7 summarizes these functions):

- It allows you to create database structures containing fields, tables, and table relationships.
- It lets you easily add new records, change field values in existing records, and delete records.
- It contains a built-in query language, which lets you obtain immediate answers to the questions you ask about your data.
- It contains a built-in report generator, which lets you produce professional-looking, formatted, hardcopy reports from your data.
- It provides protection of databases through security, control, and recovery facilities.

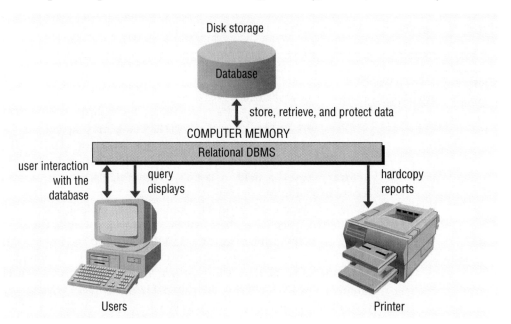

Figure 1-7
A relational database
management system

A company like Vision Publishers additionally benefits from a relational DBMS because it allows several people working in different departments to share the same data. More than one person can enter data into a database, and more than one person can retrieve and analyze data that was entered by others. For example, Vision Publishers keeps only one copy of the WRITERS table, and all employees use it to satisfy their specific needs for writer information.

Finally, unlike other software tools, such as spreadsheets, a DBMS can handle massive amounts of data and can easily form relationships among multiple tables. Each Access database, for example, can be up to 1 gigabyte in size and can contain up to 32,768 tables.

Launching and Exiting Access

Access, marketed by Microsoft Corporation, is rapidly becoming one of the most popular relational DBMSs in the Windows environment. For the rest of this tutorial, you will learn to use Access as you work with Judith Rossi on her project.

You first need to learn how to launch Access, so let's launch Access from the Program Manager window.

To launch Access:

❶ Make sure you have created your copy of the Access Student Disk. The Microsoft Office group icon should be visible in the Program Manager window, as you saw in Figure 1-1.

TROUBLE? If you don't have a group icon labeled Microsoft Office, then look for a group icon labeled Microsoft Access and use it instead. If you do not have either of these group icons, ask your technical support person or instructor for help finding the proper icon. Perhaps Access has not been installed on the computer you are using. If you are using your own computer, make sure you have installed the Access software.

TROUBLE? If you don't have a Student Disk, then you need to get one. Your instructor will either give you one or ask you to make your own by following the steps earlier in this tutorial in the section called "Your Student Disk." See your instructor for information.

❷ Double-click the **Microsoft Office group icon** in the Program Manager window. The Microsoft Office group window opens. See Figure 1-8.

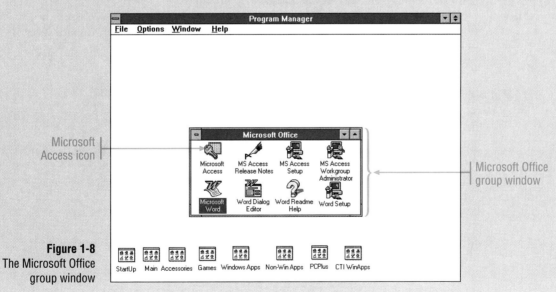

Figure 1-8
The Microsoft Office group window

❸ Double-click the **Microsoft Access icon** in the Microsoft Office group window.
After a short pause, the Access copyright information appears in a message box
and remains on the screen until Access is ready for use. See Figure 1-9.

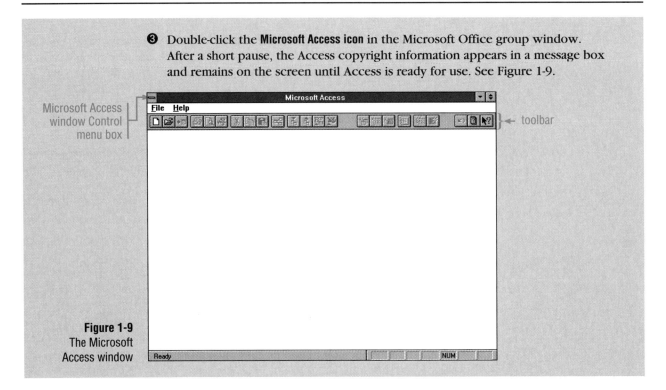

Microsoft Access
window Control
menu box

toolbar

Figure 1-9
The Microsoft
Access window

Access is now loaded into your computer's memory. Although Judith wants to work
with an existing database, it's always a good idea to know how to exit a software package
when you first start working with it. In case you need to end your working session with
the package to do something else or if you want to start all over again, you should feel
comfortable that you can exit the package at any time.

The Reference Window called "Exiting Access" lists the general steps for exiting
Access. Don't try these steps now. Just read the Reference Window to get a general idea
of what you are going to do. Specific steps for you to follow will be provided in the next
section of numbered steps.

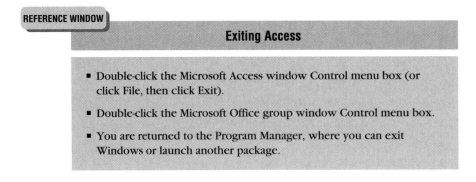

REFERENCE WINDOW

Exiting Access

- Double-click the Microsoft Access window Control menu box (or
  click File, then click Exit).

- Double-click the Microsoft Office group window Control menu box.

- You are returned to the Program Manager, where you can exit
  Windows or launch another package.

Practice exiting Access by completing the following set of steps. You can exit Access almost any time, no matter what you are doing, by following these steps. If you ever try to exit Access and find you cannot, your active window is likely to be an open dialog box. An open dialog box will prevent you from immediately exiting Access. Simply cancel the dialog box, and you will then be able to exit Access.

To exit Access:

❶ Double-click the Microsoft Access window **Control menu box** (or click **File**, then click **Exit**).

❷ Double-click the Microsoft Office group window **Control menu box** to close it. You are returned to the Program Manager.

After exiting Access, you should follow the steps to launch Access when you continue with the next section of the tutorial.

Opening a Database

To select the anniversary issue articles, Judith will work with an existing database, so her first step is to open that database. When you want to use a database that was previously created, you must first open it. When you open a database, a copy of the database file is transferred into the random access memory (RAM) of your computer and becomes available for your use. You can then view, print, modify, or save it on your disk.

REFERENCE WINDOW

Opening a Database

- Click the Open Database button on the toolbar in the Microsoft Access window. The Open Database dialog box appears.

- Change the drive and directory information, if necessary, to the disk location of the database.

- Scroll through the File Name list box until the database name appears and then click it. The name appears in the File Name text box.

- Click OK or press [Enter] to accept the changes in the Open Database dialog box.

You open a database by using the Open Database button on the toolbar. The **toolbar buttons** on the toolbar represent common operations you perform with your database. For example, the Help button is used to ask for help about Access tasks. When you switch to different windows in Access, both the toolbar and menu bar change to provide you with the appropriate common operations relevant to that window.

When you first view the toolbar, you will probably be unsure of the function associated with each toolbar button. Fortunately, when you stop the mouse pointer on a toolbar button, Access displays a ToolTip under the button and a description of the button in the status bar at the bottom of the screen. A **ToolTip** is a boxed caption showing the name of the indicated toolbar button.

Let's display the ToolTip for the Open Database button. If you exited Access earlier, launch Access before you follow the next step.

To display a ToolTip:
❶ Move the mouse pointer to the toolbar and stop the pointer on the second button from the left. After a short pause, Access displays a ToolTip under the button and the button's description in the status bar. See Figure 1-10.

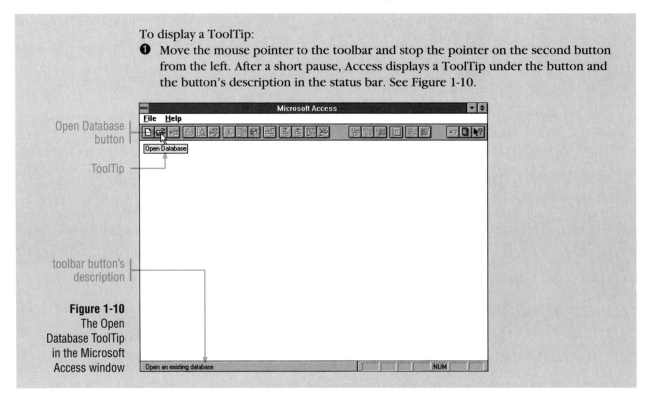

Open Database button

ToolTip

toolbar button's description

Figure 1-10
The Open Database ToolTip in the Microsoft Access window

Some toolbar buttons appear dimmed because they are not active now. They will become active later, after you have opened a database or taken some other action. You can spend a few moments stopping at each toolbar button to view its ToolTip and status bar description.

Let's now open the database for Vision Publishers.

To open an existing database:
❶ Make sure your Access Student Disk is in the appropriate drive—either drive A or drive B.
❷ Click the **Open Database button** 🖻 in the Microsoft Access window. Access displays the Open Database dialog box. See Figure 1-11.

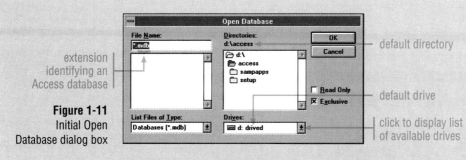

extension
identifying an
Access database

Figure 1-11
Initial Open
Database dialog box

default directory

default drive

click to display list
of available drives

❸ Click the **down arrow button** on the right side of the Drives box. A list of available drives drops down. Click the letter of the drive in which you put your Student Disk. Notice that the Directories section of the dialog box also changes as you change your selection in the drop-down Drives box.

❹ Click **vision.mdb** in the File Name list box. The name of the selected file now appears in the File Name text box. See Figure 1-12.

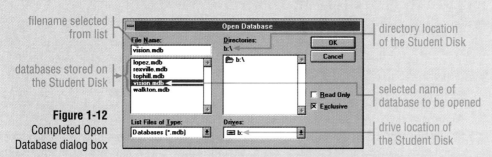

filename selected
from list

databases stored on
the Student Disk

Figure 1-12
Completed Open
Database dialog box

directory location
of the Student Disk

selected name of
database to be opened

drive location of
the Student Disk

TROUBLE? If you can't find a file named vision.mdb, check that the Drives box indicates the location of your Student Disk. If the Drives box shows the correct drive, perhaps you are using the wrong disk in the drive. Check your disk to be sure it's your Student Disk. If it is the correct disk, check with your technical support person or instructor. If it is not the correct disk, place the correct Student Disk in the drive and resume your work from Step 3.

❺ Click the **OK button** to let Access know you have completed the Open Database dialog box. Access opens the Vision.mdb database and displays the Database window.

After opening the Vision Publishers database, Judith checks the window on the screen to familiarize herself with her options. After making this check she will begin her assignment for Brian. Judith wants to review magazine article titles to select past articles for the special edition of *Business Perspective*.

The Database Window

After a database is opened, Access displays the Database window. Because you have experience with the Windows graphical user interface (GUI), you already recognize these components of the Database window: the Microsoft Access window Control menu box, the title bar, the Microsoft Access window sizing buttons, the menu bar, the toolbar, the toolbar buttons, the Database window Control menu box, the Database window sizing buttons, the status bar, and the Microsoft Access window. These are labeled in blue in Figure 1-13 on the following page. Components of the Database window that are new to you appear in red in Figure 1-13.

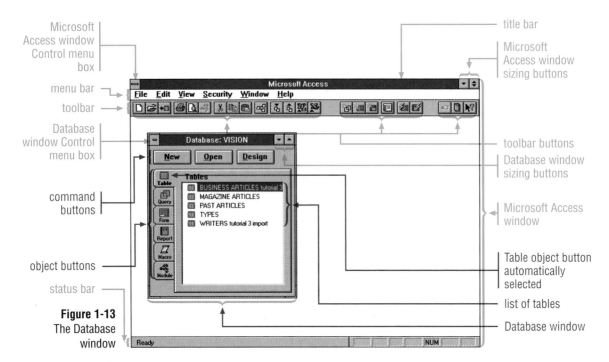

Microsoft Access window Control menu box

menu bar

toolbar

Database window Control menu box

command buttons

object buttons

status bar

Figure 1-13
The Database window

title bar

Microsoft Access window sizing buttons

toolbar buttons

Database window sizing buttons

Microsoft Access window

Table object button automatically selected

list of tables

Database window

- The Database window appears on top of the Microsoft Access window and represents the main control center for working with a database.
- The object buttons represent the six types of objects you can create for an Access database. Unlike most other DBMSs, Access stores each database in a single file. The database contains all the tables you define for it, along with all queries, forms, reports, macros, and modules; these collectively are the objects that make up the database. Each separate query and each separate report, for example, is a separate object so that, if Vision Publishers has three tables, five queries, and four reports in a database, Access treats them as 12 separate objects.

You already know what a table is, so let's consider the other five objects. You use the built-in Access query language to create a query (or question) about data from your tables. For example, if Judith needs to find records from the MAGAZINE ARTI-CLES table for a specific writer she can use a query for this purpose. You use a form to store, display, and view records from your tables. For example, Judith can create a form for others to use that displays one record at a time from the WRITERS table. You use a report to print data from tables in a customized format. For example, Brian might need a printed list that shows all writer information; a report can be used to generate this list. A **macro** is a saved list of operations to be performed on data. Access carries out the operations when you run the macro. Judith can use a macro, for example, to open a special form automatically whenever someone opens the company database. Finally, Access has a built-in programming language called Access Basic. A **module** is a set of one or more Access Basic programmed procedures. Vision Publishers uses a module, for example, to calculate payments to its writers for the articles they write.

- The three command buttons represent the major operations performed on tables. You can create a new table by clicking the New button. For an existing table, click the Open button to view table records or click the Design button to change the table structure.
- Notice that the Table object button is automatically selected when you first open a database, and a list of available tables for the database appears. When you click one of the other object buttons, that object button becomes the one that is selected; a list of available objects of that type then appears.

Viewing and Printing a Table

Now that you have opened a database and familiarized yourself with the components of the Database window, you are ready to view and print an existing Access table. If you are interested in looking up information from a small number of records in a table, you usually view them on the screen. However, if you need information from a large number of records or need to present the information to other people, you usually print a hardcopy of the table.

Datasheet View Window

Vision Publishers has a table named MAGAZINE ARTICLES that contains data about all the magazine articles published by the company. Judith opens this table to start her selection of top articles from *Business Perspective* magazine.

REFERENCE WINDOW

Opening the Datasheet View Window for a Table

- Scroll through the Tables list box until the table name appears and then click it.
- Click the Open command button.

Let's open the MAGAZINE ARTICLES table for Vision Publishers.

To open the Datasheet View window for the MAGAZINE ARTICLES table:
❶ Click **MAGAZINE ARTICLES**, then click the **Open command button**. The Datasheet View window for the MAGAZINE ARTICLES table appears on top of the previous windows. See Figure 1-14 on the following page.

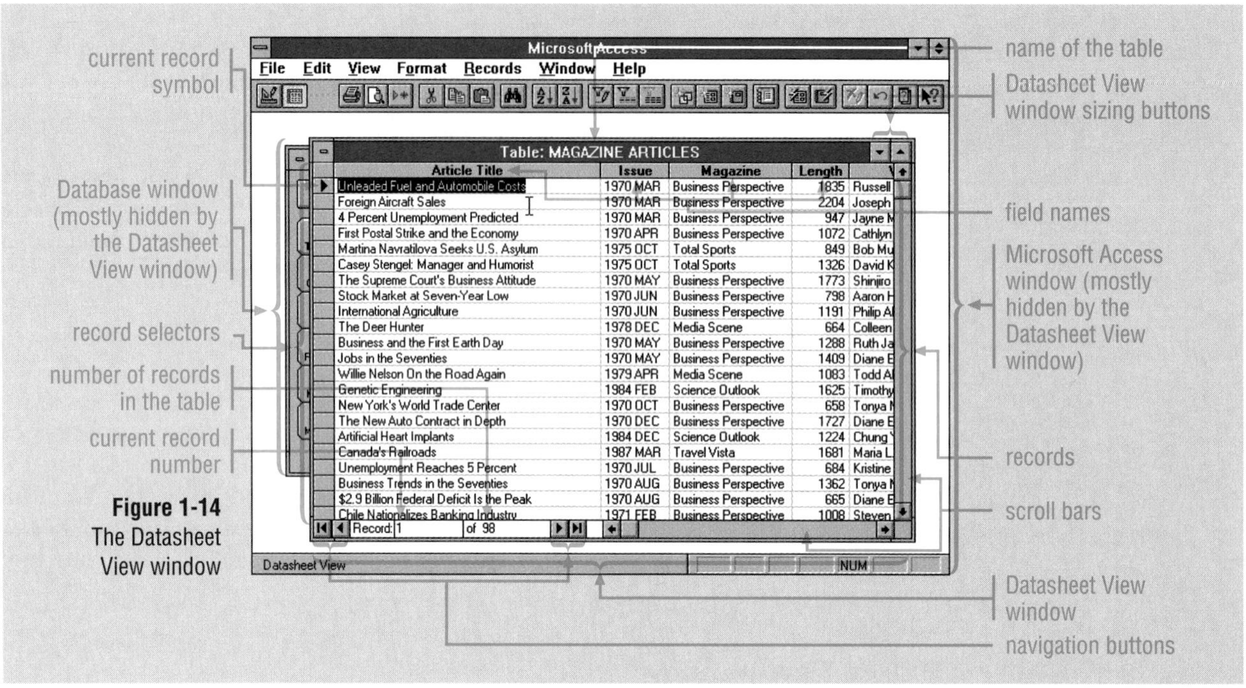

Labels around the figure:

- current record symbol
- Database window (mostly hidden by the Datasheet View window)
- record selectors
- number of records in the table
- current record number
- name of the table
- Datasheet View window sizing buttons
- field names
- Microsoft Access window (mostly hidden by the Datasheet View window)
- records
- scroll bars
- Datasheet View window navigation buttons

Figure 1-14
The Datasheet View window

Table: MAGAZINE ARTICLES

Article Title	Issue	Magazine	Length	
Unleaded Fuel and Automobile Costs	1970 MAR	Business Perspective	1835	Russell
Foreign Aircraft Sales	1970 MAR	Business Perspective	2204	Joseph
4 Percent Unemployment Predicted	1970 MAR	Business Perspective	947	Jayne N
First Postal Strike and the Economy	1970 APR	Business Perspective	1072	Cathlyn
Martina Navratilova Seeks U.S. Asylum	1975 OCT	Total Sports	849	Bob Mu
Casey Stengel: Manager and Humorist	1975 OCT	Total Sports	1326	David K
The Supreme Court's Business Attitude	1970 MAY	Business Perspective	1773	Shinjiro
Stock Market at Seven-Year Low	1970 JUN	Business Perspective	798	Aaron H
International Agriculture	1970 JUN	Business Perspective	1191	Philip Al
The Deer Hunter	1978 DEC	Media Scene	664	Colleen
Business and the First Earth Day	1970 MAY	Business Perspective	1288	Ruth Ja
Jobs in the Seventies	1970 MAY	Business Perspective	1409	Diane E
Willie Nelson On the Road Again	1979 APR	Media Scene	1083	Todd Al
Genetic Engineering	1984 FEB	Science Outlook	1625	Timothy
New York's World Trade Center	1970 OCT	Business Perspective	658	Tonya N
The New Auto Contract in Depth	1970 DEC	Business Perspective	1727	Diane E
Artificial Heart Implants	1984 DEC	Science Outlook	1224	Chung Y
Canada's Railroads	1987 MAR	Travel Vista	1681	Maria L
Unemployment Reaches 5 Percent	1970 JUL	Business Perspective	684	Kristine
Business Trends in the Seventies	1970 AUG	Business Perspective	1362	Tonya N
$2.9 Billion Federal Deficit Is the Peak	1970 AUG	Business Perspective	665	Diane E
Chile Nationalizes Banking Industry	1971 FEB	Business Perspective	1008	Steven

Record: 1   of 98

Datasheet View   NUM

The **Datasheet View window** shows a table's contents as a **datasheet** in rows and columns, similar to a spreadsheet. Each row is a separate record in the table, and each column contains the field values for one field from the table. Each column is headed by a field name. When you first open a datasheet, Access automatically selects the first field value in the first record for processing. Notice that this field is highlighted and that a darkened triangle symbol, called the current record symbol, appears in the record selector to the left of the first record. The **current record symbol** identifies the currently selected record. If you move your mouse pointer over any field value, it changes to I. If you then click the I on a field value in another row, that field value becomes the currently selected field. Although the entire field value is not highlighted, the insertion point stays where you clicked, the new record becomes the current record, and the current record number, between the navigation buttons at the bottom of the screen, changes. Practice clicking the I on different fields and records and notice the changes that occur in the datasheet.

Although the MAGAZINE ARTICLES table has only five fields, the Datasheet View window isn't large enough to display the entire writer name field. Similarly, you see only the first group of records from the table. One way to see different parts of a table is to use the vertical and horizontal scroll bars and arrows on the right and bottom of the datasheet. Practice clicking these scroll bars and arrows to become comfortable with their use.

Using the lower-left navigation buttons is another way to move vertically through the records. From left to right respectively, the **navigation buttons** advance the selected record to the first record, the previous record, the next record, and the last record in the table (Figure 1-15). The current record number appears between the two pairs of navigation buttons, as does the total number of records in the table. Practice clicking the four navigation buttons and notice the changes that occur in the datasheet, in the current record number, and in the placement of the current record symbol.

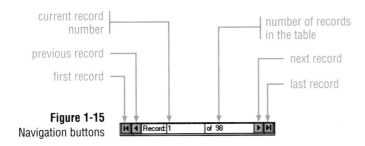

Figure 1-15
Navigation buttons

Judith decides to print the records from the first datasheet page of the table to study their contents more closely, but first she maximizes the Datasheet View window.

To maximize the Datasheet View window:

❶ Click the **maximize button** for the Datasheet View window to expand the window. See Figure 1-16. Notice that a restore button replaces the minimize and maximize buttons and that the table title appears in the Access title bar.

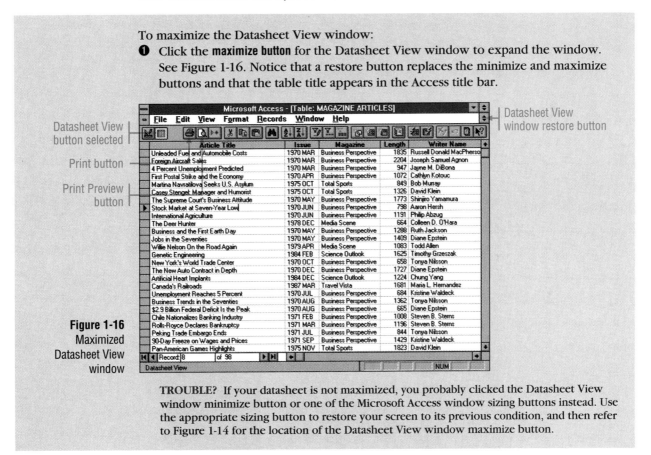

Figure 1-16
Maximized
Datasheet View
window

TROUBLE? If your datasheet is not maximized, you probably clicked the Datasheet View window minimize button or one of the Microsoft Access window sizing buttons instead. Use the appropriate sizing button to restore your screen to its previous condition, and then refer to Figure 1-14 for the location of the Datasheet View window maximize button.

You might have noticed that one toolbar button, the Datasheet View button is selected, as shown in Figure 1-16. You can click the Datasheet View button to switch to the Datasheet View window of your table whenever you see this button on the toolbar. To the right of the Datasheet View button are the Print and Print Preview buttons. You click the Print Preview button whenever you want to review the appearance of a datasheet on screen before you print a hardcopy of it. Use the **Print button** instead, if you want to print a hardcopy without reviewing it on screen.

REFERENCE WINDOW

Printing a Hardcopy of a Datasheet

- Click the Print Preview button on the toolbar to display the Print Preview window. Click the Print button on the toolbar. The Print dialog box appears.

- Select the Copies box if you want to change the number of copies you want to print.

- Click Pages in the Print Range section if your want to print only a portion of your datasheet. Specify the beginning page in the range in the From box and the ending page in the range in the To box.

- Click All in the Print Range section if you want to print all the pages in your datasheet.

- Click the OK button or press [Enter].

Let's print preview Judith's datasheet and then print its first page.

To print preview and print a datasheet:

❶ Click the **Print Preview button** 🔍 on the toolbar. The Print Preview window appears. See Figure 1-17.

Zoom button —

miniaturized
datasheet page —

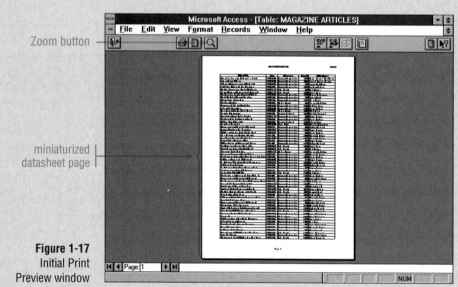

Figure 1-17
Initial Print
Preview window

When you move the mouse pointer over the datasheet page, it changes to 🔍. You can click the 🔍 or click the toolbar Zoom button to see a close-up of the datasheet page. Judith decides to preview a close-up of the page.

❷ Click the **Zoom button** 🔍, or click the 🔍 when it is positioned over the miniaturized page. A close-up of the page appears. See Figure 1-18. Depending on whether you clicked the 🔍 or the 🔍, your screen might differ from the illustration.

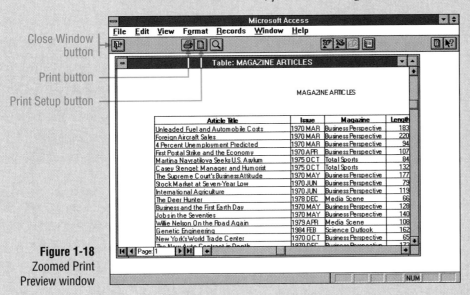

Close Window button

Print button

Print Setup button

Figure 1-18
Zoomed Print
Preview window

If you click the 🔍 or the 🔍 a second time, the page returns to its original miniaturized view. Practice clicking the 🔍, the 🔍, and the navigation buttons. When you are done practicing, you are ready to print the datasheet page.

❸ Make sure your printer is on-line and ready to print. Click the **Print button** 🖶 on the toolbar. The Print dialog box appears. See Figure 1-19. Check the Printer section of the dialog box to make sure your printer is selected.

prints entire datasheet

prints specified range of pages within the datasheet

Figure 1-19
Print dialog box

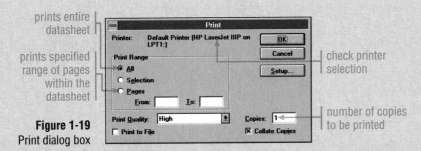

check printer selection

number of copies to be printed

TROUBLE? If the correct printer is not selected, click the Setup... button in the Print dialog box, select the correct printer from the Specified Printer list, and click the OK button.

❹ Because you want to print just the first datasheet page, click the **Pages option button**, type **1**, press **[Tab]**, type **1**, and click the **OK button**. A dialog box appears to inform you that your datasheet page is being sent to the printer. See Figure 1-20 on the following page.

Figure 1-20
Printing
dialog box

⑤ After the dialog box disappears, click the **Close Window button** in the Print Preview window toolbar to return to the Datasheet View window.

TROUBLE? If your document hasn't printed yet, check the print status in the Windows Print Manager by pressing [Alt][Tab] until the Print Manager title bar appears, and then release. Remove your document from the print queue before returning to your datasheet and then print the first datasheet page again. If it still doesn't print, check with your technical support person or instructor.

Judith is ready to close the Datasheet View window. Whenever you finish your work with a particular window, you should close the window. This frees up memory, speeds up processing, and removes unnecessary clutter from your screen. Any object—a table using a datasheet, a query, a form, a report, a macro, or a module—is closed in a similar way.

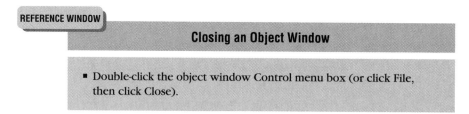

REFERENCE WINDOW

Closing an Object Window

• Double-click the object window Control menu box (or click File, then click Close).

Let's close the Datasheet View window you have been using.

To close the Datasheet View window (or other object window):
① Click **File** to open the File menu. See Figure 1-21.

Datasheet View
window Control
menu box

Close window
command

Figure 1-21
Closing the
Datasheet View
window

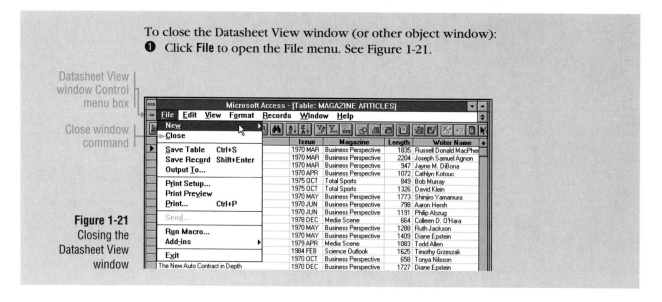

❷ Click **Close**. Access closes the Datasheet View window and returns you to the Database window. See Figure 1-22. Because you previously maximized the Datasheet View window, the Database window now appears maximized.

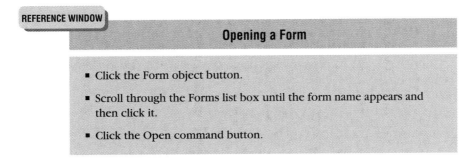

Form object button

Figure 1-22
Maximized Database
window

TROUBLE? If Access displays a message box asking if you want to save changes, click the No button. You accidentally changed the datasheet and do not want to save the modified version in your table.

If you want to take a break and resume the tutorial at a later time, you can exit Access by double-clicking the Microsoft Access window Control menu box in the upper-left corner of the screen. When you resume the tutorial, place your Student Disk in the appropriate drive and launch Access. Open the database vision.mdb, maximize the Database window, and then continue working on the next section of the tutorial.

Form View Window

Judith now opens an existing form to view the records from the MAGAZINE ARTICLES table. A form gives you a customized view of data from a database. You use a form, for example, to view one record from a table at a time, to view data in a more readable format, or to view related data from two or more tables. The way you open a form is similar to the way you opened a datasheet and the way you open all other database objects.

Opening a Form

- Click the Form object button.
- Scroll through the Forms list box until the form name appears and then click it.
- Click the Open command button.

Let's now open the form named Magazine Articles.

To open a form:

❶ Click the **Form object button**. A list of available forms appears in the Forms list box. See Figure 1-23.

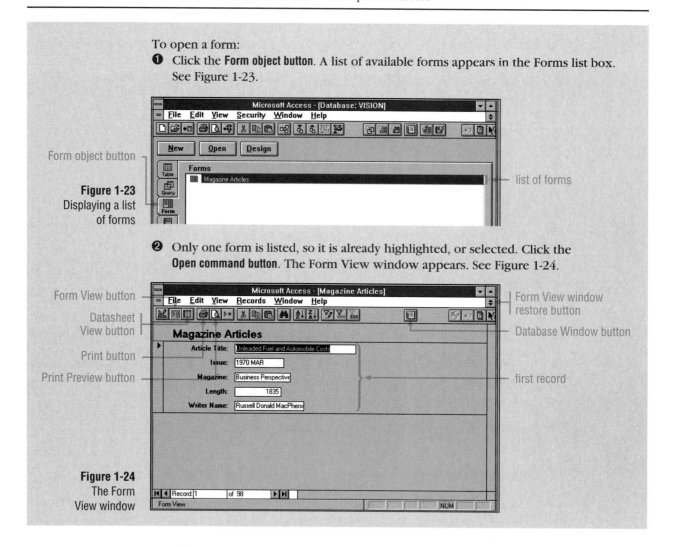

Figure 1-23
Displaying a list
of forms

Form object button — list of forms

❷ Only one form is listed, so it is already highlighted, or selected. Click the **Open command button**. The Form View window appears. See Figure 1-24.

Form View button

Datasheet
View button

Print button

Print Preview button

Form View window
restore button

Database Window button

first record

Figure 1-24
The Form
View window

The **Form View window** shows a table's contents in a customized format, usually one record at a time. The form, as shown in Figure 1-24, displays all five fields from the MAGAZINE ARTICLES table vertically, one record at a time. Each field has a label on the left and a boxed field value on the right. The label is the field name.

Some of the same window components you saw in the Datasheet View window also appear in the Form View window and have the same functions. Notice the location of the Form View window restore button and the navigation buttons. Practice clicking the navigation buttons and clicking different field values. Then notice the changes that occur in the form.

You should also practice clicking the Datasheet View and Form View toolbar buttons. Clicking the Datasheet View button switches you from the Form View window to the Datasheet View window. Clicking the Form View button switches you from the Datasheet View window to the Form View window.

Judith prints the first page of records from the Form View window but does not first use the Print Preview option. Access prints as many form records as can fit on a printed page. The steps you follow to print from the Form View window are similar to the steps you followed when you printed from the Datasheet View window.

To print a form page:

❶ Before continuing, be sure you are in the Form View window with the first record appearing in a maximized window. Click the **Print button** 🖶 on the toolbar. The Print dialog box appears.

❷ Make sure your printer is on-line and ready to print. Check the Printer section of the dialog box to make sure the correct printer is selected. Click the **Pages option button**, type **1**, press **[Tab]**, type **1**, and then click the **OK button**. A dialog box informs you that your datasheet page is being sent to the printer. After the dialog box disappears, Access returns you to the Form View window.

Closing a Database

Judith is done working on both the form and the database, so she closes the database. She could close the Form View window, as she previously closed the Datasheet View window, and then close the database. However, whenever you close a database without closing the Form View window or any other open object window, Access automatically closes all open windows before closing the database.

REFERENCE WINDOW

Closing a Database

- Click the Database Window button in an open object window to make the Database window visible and make it the active window.
- Double-click the Database window Control menu box.

Let's close the Vision Publishers database that you have been using.

To close a database:

❶ Click the **Database Window button** 🖳 on the toolbar to activate the Database window on top of a smaller-sized Form View window. See Figure 1-25.

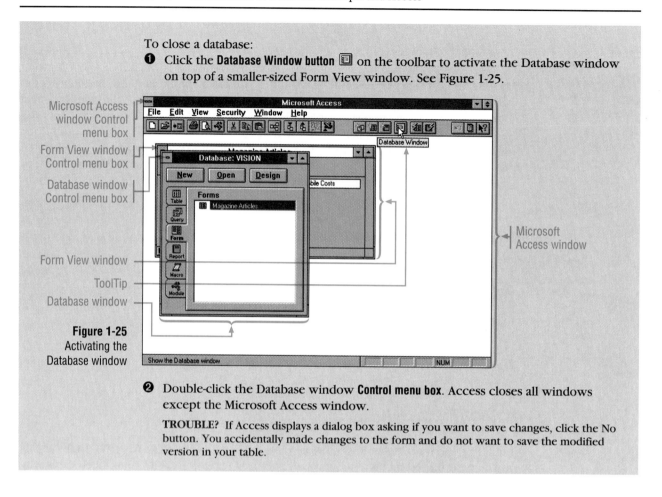

Microsoft Access window Control menu box

Form View window Control menu box

Database window Control menu box

Microsoft Access window

Form View window

ToolTip

Database window

Figure 1-25
Activating the
Database window

❷ Double-click the Database window **Control menu box**. Access closes all windows except the Microsoft Access window.

TROUBLE? If Access displays a dialog box asking if you want to save changes, click the No button. You accidentally made changes to the form and do not want to save the modified version in your table.

Getting Help

While you are using Access on your computer, there might be times when you are puzzled about how to complete a task. You might also need to clarify a definition or Access feature or investigate more advanced Access capabilities. You can use Access's Help system to give you on-line information about your specific questions. There are four ways you can get on-line help as you work: by using the Help Contents, the Search feature, the Glossary feature, or the context-sensitive Help system. Let's practice using the Access Help system.

Starting Help and Using the Help Contents

Judith has some questions about moving the toolbar and about shortcut menus and uses the Access Help system to find answers. One way to use the Access Help system is to click Help and then click Contents.

To start Help:

❶ Click **Help** and then click **Contents**. The Microsoft Access Help window becomes the active window and displays the Microsoft Access Help Contents topic. See Figure 1-26.

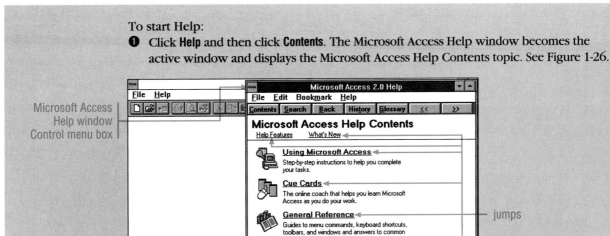

Microsoft Access Help window Control menu box

jumps

Figure 1-26
The Microsoft Access Help window

TROUBLE? If the size or position of your Microsoft Access Help window is different from what is shown in the illustration, don't worry. Continue with the tutorial.

The underlined words and topics in the Microsoft Access Help window serve as a top-level table of contents. You can get detailed information on each of these words or topics by clicking one of the words or topics. The mouse pointer changes to 🖑 when you move it over any of the words or topics. Underlined words or topics are called jumps. A **jump** provides a link to other Help topics or to more information or a definition about the current word or topic.

Judith wants to find out how to use Help and decides that clicking Help on the Microsoft Access Help menu bar might tell her how to do this.

To get help on using Access Help:

❶ Press **[F1]** while the Microsoft Access Help window is active (or click **Help** within the Microsoft Access Help window, then click **How to Use Help**). See Figure 1-27 on the following page. Judith wants more information about the scroll bar jump.

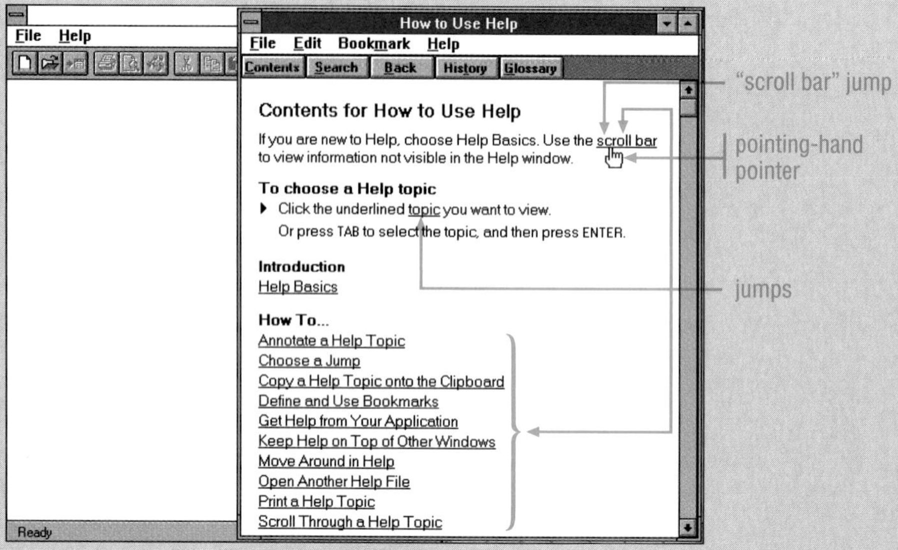

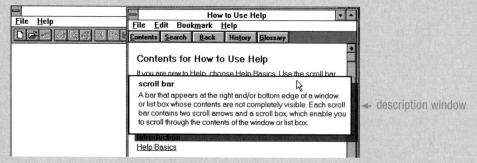

Figure 1-27
The How to Use
Help window

❷ Click the words **scroll bar** when the mouse pointer changes to 🖑 over them. Access Help displays a description of the term. See Figure 1-28. The pointer changes back to ▷.

Figure 1-28
Description
of "scroll bar"

TROUBLE? If you get the message "Help topic does not exist," you might not have the complete Access Help system installed on your system. Ask your technical support person or instructor for assistance.

❸ Click the words **scroll bar** again. The description window disappears.

❹ Read the material under the heading Contents for How to Use Help. Use the scroll bar to view the entire topic.

Judith sees the Search for a Help Topic jump as she scrolls through Contents for How to Use Help and decides to view that jump.

To view the Contents for How to Use Help jump:
❶ Find and click the jump **Search for a Help Topic.**
❷ Read the information under Search for a Help Topic, using the scroll bar to view the entire topic.

Using the Search feature of Help appears to be what Judith needs to use to get answers to her questions. Because the How to Use Help window is active, however, she must switch back to the Microsoft Access Help window before she can use the Search feature. If she does not switch back, she will be searching for Help topics rather than Access topics.

To return to the Microsoft Access Help window:
❶ Click the **Back button** in the Help button bar two times. Notice that the title bar changes to Microsoft Access Help.

Using Search

Having read about the Search feature in Access Help, Judith uses that feature to search for information about moving toolbars.

To use the search feature in Access Help:
❶ Click the **Search button** on the Help button bar. The Search dialog box appears. See Figure 1-29.

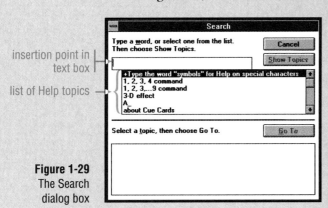

insertion point in text box

list of Help topics

Figure 1-29
The Search dialog box

❷ Type **m** in the text box. The list of topics shown changes to those topics starting with *m*.
❸ Type **oving t** after the *m* in the text box. The list of topics shown changes to those starting with the letters "moving t" and the topic moving toolbars is visible in the list box.
❹ Click **moving toolbars** in the list box and then click the **Show Topics button.**
See Figure 1-30 on the following page.

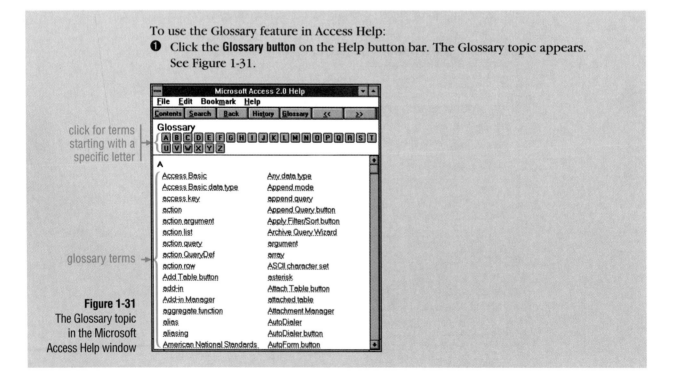

enter topic to
be searched for ┤

click to see
├ related topics

select related topic ┤

Figure 1-30
The Search
dialog box with
topic selected

click to go to topic

❺ Click the **Go To button** or press **[Enter]**. The Moving Toolbars topic appears. Read the information under Moving Toolbars, using the scroll bar to view the entire topic.

Judith has the answers she needs to her questions about moving toolbars and next looks up the definition of the term Shortcut menu in the glossary.

Using the Glossary

The Glossary contains Access terms and their definitions. Judith uses the Glossary feature to read the definition of Shortcut menu.

To use the Glossary feature in Access Help:

❶ Click the **Glossary button** on the Help button bar. The Glossary topic appears. See Figure 1-31.

click for terms
starting with a
specific letter ┤

glossary terms →

Figure 1-31
The Glossary topic
in the Microsoft
Access Help window

❷ Click the **S button**. Access displays the beginning of the list of terms beginning with the letter S.

❸ Scroll until the term Shortcut menu appears. Click the words **Shortcut menu**. Access displays the corresponding definition window. Read the definition.

❹ Click the words **Shortcut menu** again. The definition window disappears.

Judith has the answers to her questions and is ready to exit Help.

To exit Help:
❶ Double-click the Microsoft Access Help **Control menu box**. The Help window closes.

Using Context-Sensitive Help

When you start Help by pressing [F1] instead of using the Help menu, the Microsoft Access Help window you see is **context sensitive**, which means that Access displays information that is relevant to the window or operation that is active when you start Help. If you want Help information about a particular component of an Access window, click the Help button on the toolbar instead of pressing [F1]. The mouse pointer changes to 🕮, which is the Help pointer. You then click the 🕮 on the window component you want information about, and Help opens a window specific to that component.

Judith learns more about the Access toolbar by clicking the Help button.

To use context-sensitive Help on a specific window component:
❶ Click the **Help button** 🔯 on the toolbar. The mouse pointer changes to 🕮. See Figure 1-32.

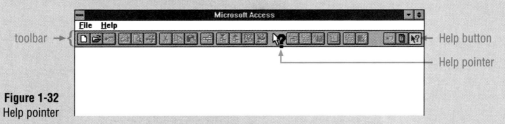

Figure 1-32
Help pointer

❷ Do not click any of the toolbar buttons. Instead, click anywhere else in the toolbar with the Help pointer. Help opens the Database Window Toolbar topic window. See Figure 1-33 on the following page.

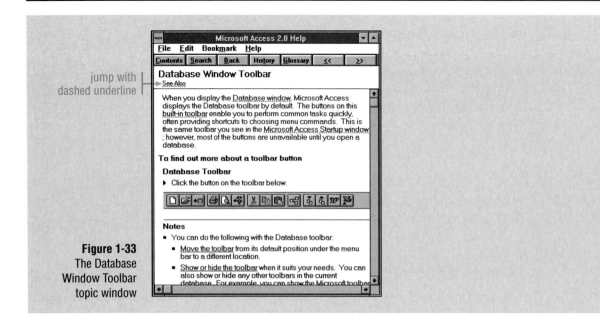

jump with dashed underline

Figure 1-33
The Database
Window Toolbar
topic window

Judith notices the See Also jump, wonders what it means, and clicks it.

To view the See Also jump:

❶ Click the words **See Also**. Access Help displays a window containing other topics that are related to the Database Window Toolbar topic. See Figure 1-34.

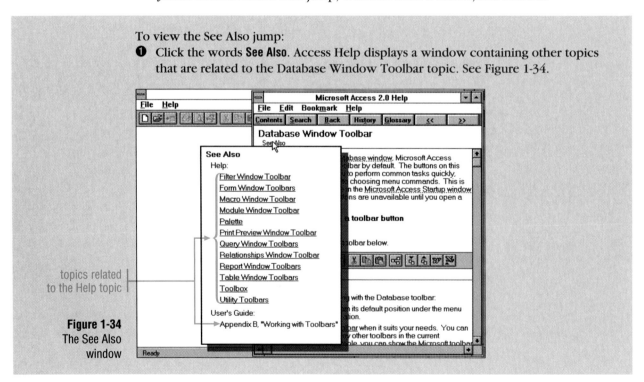

topics related
to the Help topic

Figure 1-34
The See Also
window

Her curiosity satisfied, Judith is done using Help and follows up by experimenting with Shortcut menus and moving the toolbar.

Shortcut Menus

As described in the Help glossary, a **Shortcut menu** contains a list of commands that relate to the object you click. To display a Shortcut menu window, you position the mouse pointer on a specific object or area and click the right mouse button. Using a Shortcut menu is often faster than using a menu or toolbar button.

Judith closes the Help window, opens the Vision database, and then displays a Shortcut menu.

To exit Help and open a database:
❶ Click the words **See Also** to close the jump window.
❷ Double-click the Microsoft Access Help **Control menu box** to close the Help window.
❸ Open the vision.mdb database.

Judith now opens the Shortcut menu for the table objects.

To display a Shortcut menu:
❶ Move the mouse pointer into the Database window and position it just below the last table listed.
❷ Click the right mouse button. Access displays the Shortcut menu. See Figure 1-35.

Figure 1-35
The Shortcut menu

If you select a Shortcut menu command, it applies to the highlighted table. Judith does not want to select a command, so she closes the Shortcut menu.

To close a Shortcut menu:
❶ Click the right mouse button again to close the Shortcut menu.

TROUBLE? If the Shortcut menu does not disappear, move the mouse pointer slightly outside the Shortcut menu and click the right mouse button again.

Judith experiments moving the toolbar to a different location on the screen.

Moving the Toolbar

The default location for the toolbar is just below the menu bar at the top of the screen. Most Windows software packages position the toolbar in the same location, so you do not usually want to move the toolbar to a different location on the screen. If you launch Access and find the toolbar in a location other than the default location, however, you should know how to move it back to its default location.

To move the toolbar to a different location:

❶ Click anywhere in the toolbar's background but not on a toolbar button.

❷ Click again in the toolbar's background and drag the toolbar to the bottom of the screen. As you drag the toolbar, the toolbar outline shows where the toolbar will be positioned if you release the mouse button. Release the mouse button when the toolbar is positioned as shown in Figure 1-36.

Figure 1-36
The toolbar
at the bottom
of the screen

Judith next moves the toolbar back to its default location. Although she could repeat the steps she previously used, Judith uses a command on the View menu instead.

To move the toolbar to its default location:

❶ Click **View** and then click **Toolbars...** to display the Toolbars dialog box. See Figure 1-37.

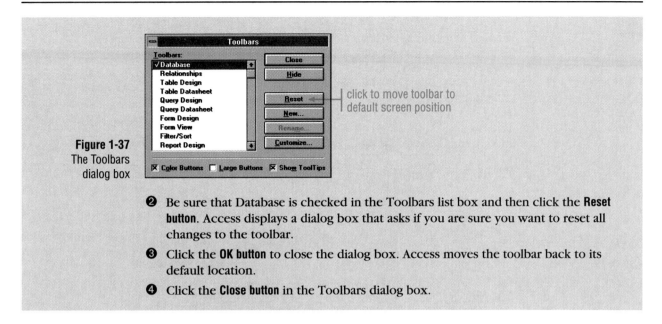

click to move toolbar to
default screen position

Figure 1-37
The Toolbars
dialog box

❷ Be sure that Database is checked in the Toolbars list box and then click the **Reset button**. Access displays a dialog box that asks if you are sure you want to reset all changes to the toolbar.

❸ Click the **OK button** to close the dialog box. Access moves the toolbar back to its default location.

❹ Click the **Close button** in the Toolbars dialog box.

Judith is done experimenting with Access and exits Access.

To exit Access:
❶ Double-click the Microsoft Access window **Control menu box** to exit Access. Double-click the Microsoft Office group window **Control menu box** to close it. You are returned to the Program Manager.

Judith has completed her initial assignment. In the next tutorial she will meet with Brian to give him her business article selections.

Questions

1. What three steps should you generally follow when you plan to create and store a new type of data?
2. What are fields and entities, and how are they related?
3. How do you form a relationship between two tables?
4. What are the differences between a primary key and a foreign key?
5. Describe what a DBMS is designed to do.
6. What is a ToolTip?
7. What are the six different objects you can create for an Access database?
8. What do the columns and rows of a datasheet represent?

9. To which record do you advance when you use each of the four navigation buttons?
10. Which open object, the table or form object, allows you to switch between datasheet view and form view?
11. Where in Access do you find jumps, and what purpose do they serve?
12. Explain the steps for using context-sensitive Help.

Use the data in Figure 1-38 to answer Questions 13 through 18.

CHECKING ACCOUNTS table

Account Number	Name	Balance
2173	Theodore Lamont	842.27
4519	Beatrice Whalley	2071.92
8005	Benjamin Hoskins	1132.00

CHECKS table

Account Number	Check Number	Date	Amount
4519	1371	10/22/95	45.00
4519	1372	10/23/95	115.00
2173	1370	10/24/95	50.00
4519	1377	10/27/95	60.00
2173	1371	10/29/95	20.00

Figure 1-38

13. How many fields are in the CHECKING ACCOUNTS table?
14. Name the fields in the CHECKS table.
15. How many records are in the CHECKS table?
16. What is the primary key of the CHECKING ACCOUNTS table?
E   17. What is the primary key of the CHECKS table?

E   18. Which table has a foreign key, and what is the field name of the foreign key?

Use the Access Help feature to answer Questions 19 through 21.

E   19. When you use the Close command on the File menu, do you need to save the changes to your data first?

E   20. You can use the navigation buttons to move from one record to another. How can you move to a specific record number in datasheet view or form view?

E   21. How can you print a Help topic?

Tutorial Assignments

Launch Access, open the Vision.mdb database on your Student Disk, and do the following:

1. Open the MAGAZINE ARTICLES table in the Datasheet View window.
2. Print preview the datasheet.
3. Print the last page of the datasheet.
4. Close the Datasheet View window.
5. Open the Magazine Articles form.
6. Print preview the form. What is the page number of the last page?
7. Print the last two pages of the form.
E   8. Use Access Help with the following active windows: the Database window, the Datasheet View window, and the Print Preview window. Describe the differences you see in each situation in the initial Microsoft Access Help window.

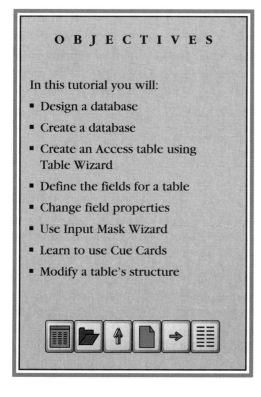

OBJECTIVES

In this tutorial you will:

- Design a database
- Create a database
- Create an Access table using Table Wizard
- Define the fields for a table
- Change field properties
- Use Input Mask Wizard
- Learn to use Cue Cards
- Modify a table's structure

Creating Access Tables

Creating the WRITERS Table at Vision Publishers

CASE

Vision Publishers   Brian Murphy, Judith Rossi, and Elena Sanchez meet to exchange ideas about the cover design and article layout for the 25th-anniversary issue of *Business Perspective*. Because Elena will coordinate all production phases of the special issue, she will be in contact with writers, editors, and marketing. First, she concentrates on creating a table of all the writers.

From Judith, Elena needs information about the articles from past issues, specifically, the article title, the issue of *Business Perspective* in which the article appeared, the length of the article, and the writer name. Because she will need to phone all the writers to tell them about their inclusion in the special issue, she also needs each writer's phone number.

Brian reminds Elena that only freelancers will need to be paid for reprints of their articles. In her database design, Elena will need to indicate if the writer is a freelancer and, if so, what the reprint payment amount is.

After scanning the articles, Elena remarks that the 25 articles were written by only 13 writers and Chong Kim wrote four of them. Brian points out that the writer of "Cola Advertising War" is a different Chong Kim, so Elena realizes that a writer name is not unique. She will need to identify the writer of each article with a unique writer ID. The data that Elena recorded during the meeting is shown in Figure 2-1.

Figure 2-1
Elena's data
requirements

article title	writer phone number
issue of Business Perspective	is the writer a freelancer?
length of article	freelancer reprint payment amount
writer name	writer ID

Elena knows from her previous work with databases that, before she can create her database tables on the computer, she must first design the database.

Database Design Guidelines

A database management system can be a useful tool, but only if you first carefully design your database to represent your data requirements accurately. In database design, you determine the fields, tables, and relationships needed to satisfy your data and processing requirements. Some database designs can be complicated because the underlying data requirements are complex. Most data requirements and their resulting database designs are much simpler, however, and these are the ones we will consider in the tutorials.

When you design a database, you should follow these guidelines:

- Identify all fields needed to produce the required information. For example, Elena needs information for contacting writers and for planning a magazine layout, so she listed the fields that would satisfy those informational requirements (Figure 2-1).
- Identify the entities involved in the data requirements. Recall that an entity is a person, place, object, event, or idea for which you want to store and process data. Elena's data requirements, for example, involve two entities, articles and writers. Entities usually become the names for the tables in a database.
- Group fields that describe each entity. Recall that fields are characteristics, or attributes, of entities, so it's logical to group together the characteristics of an entity. An entity and the fields that describe that entity represent a table in your database. Elena has articles and writers as entities, and she groups the fields for them under each entity name, as shown in Figure 2-2. So far, Elena's database design has an ARTICLES table and a WRITERS table.

Figure 2-2
Elena's fields describing
each entity

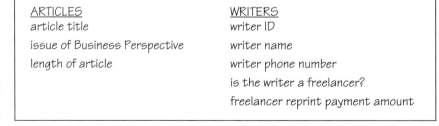

ARTICLES	WRITERS
article title	writer ID
issue of Business Perspective	writer name
length of article	writer phone number
	is the writer a freelancer?
	freelancer reprint payment amount

- Determine each table's primary key. Recall that a primary key uniquely identifies each record in a table. Although a primary key is not mandatory in Access, it's usually a good idea to have one for each table. Without a primary key, selecting the proper record can be a problem. For example, Elena has decided to include a writer ID to identify uniquely each writer because she needs to distinguish between the two writers named Chong Kim. At this point, however, Elena does not have a primary key for the ARTICLES table. No field in the table is guaranteed to have unique field values. Even a combination of these fields cannot be guaranteed to be unique. Elena delays a final decision on a primary key for the ARTICLES table until later in the database design process.
- Include a common field in related tables. You use the common field to link one table logically with another table. For example, in the ARTICLES table Elena includes writer ID, which is the primary key for the WRITERS table. When she views a record in the ARTICLES table, writer ID serves as a foreign key. She uses the foreign key value to find the one record in the WRITERS table having that field value as a primary key. This process allows Elena to know who wrote which article. She can also find all articles written by a writer; she uses the writer ID value for that writer and searches the ARTICLES table for all articles with that writer ID value.
- Avoid data redundancy. **Data redundancy** occurs when you store the same data in more than one place. With the exception of common fields to relate tables, you should avoid redundancy. Figure 2-3 shows a correct database design for an ARTICLES table and a WRITERS table with no redundancy. The Writer ID field serves as the common field to link the two tables.

ARTICLES table

Article Title	Issue of Business Perspective	Article Length	Writer ID
Trans-Alaskan Oil Pipeline Opening	1977 JUL	803	J525
Farm Aid Abuses	1978 APR	1866	J525
Herbert A. Simon Interview	1978 DEC	1811	C200
Alternative Energy Sources	1980 JUN	2085	S260
Windfall Tax on Oil Profits	1980 APR	1497	K500
Toyota and GM Joint Venture	1983 MAR	1682	S260

WRITERS table

Writer ID	Writer Name	Writer Phone Number	Freelancer?	Reprint Payment Amount
C200	Kelly Cox	(204)783-5415	Yes	$100
J525	Leroy W. Johnson	(209)895-2046	Yes	$125
K500	Chong Kim	(807)729-5364	No	$0
S260	Wilhelm Seeger	(306)423-0932	Yes	$250

Figure 2-3
Correct database design
with no redundancy

Data redundancy wastes storage space. Data redundancy can also cause inconsistencies, if, for instance, you type a field value one way in one table and a different way in the same table or in a second table. Figure 2-4 on the following page shows two examples of incorrect database design. Both designs illustrate data redundancy and the resulting waste of storage space and problem of inconsistent field values.

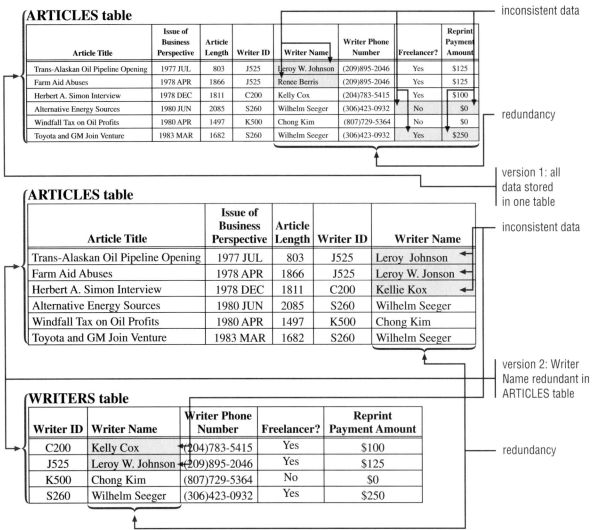

Figure 2-4
Incorrect database designs with redundancy

- Determine the properties of each field. You need to describe to the DBMS the **properties**, or characteristics, of each field, so that the DBMS knows how to store, display, and process the field. These properties include the field name, the field's maximum number of characters or digits, the field's description or explanation, and other field characteristics. For example, Elena notes that Length of Article is a field name, which has a maximum of four digits. You will learn more details about field properties later in this tutorial.

A diagram depicting the database design guidelines is shown in Figure 2-5.

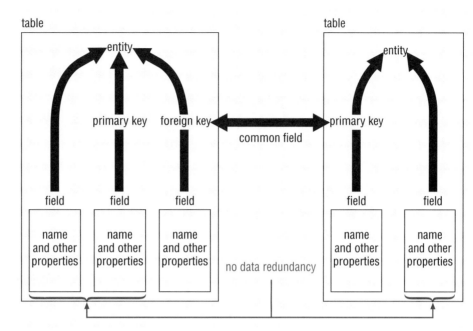

Figure 2-5
Database design
guidelines

Keeping the database design guidelines in mind, Elena develops her initial database design, as shown in Figure 2-6.

ARTICLES table	WRITERS table
Article Title	Writer ID—primary key
Issue of Business Perspective	Writer Name
Length of Article	Writer Phone Number
Writer ID—foreign key	Is the Writer a Freelancer?
	Freelancer Reprint Payment Amount

Figure 2-6
Elena's initial
database design

Guidelines for Creating an Access Table

In addition to following the database design guidelines, you must follow rules imposed by Access when you create a database. These rules apply to naming a database, naming fields and objects, and defining the properties of fields and objects. Rather than discuss all the property definition rules, let's initially consider the naming rules and three field-property rules.

Naming Databases

You must name each database you create. Access stores the database as a file on disk with the name you choose. You use that same name in the future when you open the database. When you select a database name, choose a descriptive name that will remind you of the database's purpose or contents. Vision Publishers' database is named Vision because it contains the company's data. Elena chooses for her new database the name Issue25, which is descriptive of the database's purpose.

In Access, the database name contains up to eight characters and must conform to standard DOS conventions for filenames. Access automatically adds the filename extension .mdb.

Naming Fields and Objects

You must name each field, table, and other object in a database. Access then stores these items in the database using the names you supply. Choose a field or object name that describes the purpose or contents of the field or object, so that later you can easily remember what the name represents. Elena names her two tables BUSINESS ARTICLES and WRITERS, because these names suggest their contents. Similarly, she chooses Writer ID, Writer Name, and Writer Phone Number as three of the field names in the WRITERS table. Although it is not one of the naming rules, Elena decides that identifying her critical tables might be easier if she uses a convention of all uppercase letters for table names and an appropriate mix of uppercase and lowercase for field names and the names of other database objects.

One set of rules applies to the naming of fields and objects:
- They can be up to 64 characters long.
- They can contain letters, numbers, spaces, and special characters except a period, exclamation mark, and square brackets.
- They must not start with a space.

Assigning Field Descriptions

When you define a field, you can assign an optional description for the field. If you choose a descriptive field name, you probably do not need to supply a description. Because, for example, Elena selected the descriptive field names Writer Name and Writer Phone Number, she does not plan to enter a description for these fields. For the Writer ID field in the BUSINESS ARTICLES table, however, Elena plans to assign the description "foreign key."

The field description can be up to 255 characters long. If you enter a description, choose one that explains the purpose or usage of the field.

Assigning Field Data Types

You must assign a data type for each field. The **data type** determines what field values you can enter for that field and what other properties the field will have. For example, Elena's Length of Article field is a number, so she tells Access that the field has the number data type. Access will allow Elena to enter only numbers as values for the field and will enable her to perform calculations on the field values.

In Access, you assign one of the following eight data types to each field:

- The **text data type** allows field values containing letters, digits, spaces, and special characters. Text fields can be up to 255 characters long. You should assign the text data type to fields in which you will store names, addresses, and descriptions, and to fields containing digits that are not used in calculations. Elena, for example, assigns the text data type to the Writer ID field; the Writer Name field; and the Writer Phone Number field, which contains digits not used in calculations.

- The **memo data type**, like the text data type, allows field values containing letters, digits, spaces, and special characters. Memo fields, however, can be up to 64,000 characters long and are used for long comments or explanations. Elena does not plan to assign the memo data type to any of her fields.

- The **number data type** limits field values to digits, an optional leading sign (+ or –), and an optional decimal point. Use the number data type for fields that you will use in calculations, except calculations involving money. Elena assigns the number data type to the Length of Article field in the BUSINESS ARTICLES table.

- The **date/time data type** allows field values containing valid dates and times only. Usually you enter dates in mm/dd/yy format, where mm is a two-digit month, dd is a two-digit day of the month, and yy are the last two digits of the year. This data type also permits other date formats and a variety of time formats. When using this data type, you can perform calculations on dates and times and you can sort them. The number of days between two dates, for example, can be determined. Elena does not assign the date/time data type to any of her fields.

- The **currency data type** allows field values similar to those for the number data type. Unlike calculations with number data type decimal values, calculations performed using the currency data type match to the penny exactly. Elena assigns the currency data type to the Freelancer Reprint Payment Amount field in the WRITERS table.

- The **counter data type** consists of integers that are values automatically controlled by Access. Access enters a value of 1 for the field in the first record of a table and adds 1 for each successive record's field value. This guarantees a unique field value, so that such a field can serve as a table's primary key. Elena does not assign the counter data type to any of her fields.

- The **yes/no data type** limits field values to yes and no entries. Use this data type for fields that indicate the presence or absence of a condition, such as whether an order has been filled, or if an employee is eligible for the company dental plan. Elena assigns the yes/no data type to the Is the Writer a Freelancer? field in the WRITERS table.

- The **OLE object data type** allows field values that are created in other software packages as objects, such as photographs, video images, graphics, drawings, sound recordings, voice-mail messages, spreadsheets, and word processing documents. **OLE** is an acronym for object linking and embedding. You can either import the object or link to the object, but you cannot modify it in Access. Elena does not assign the OLE object data type to any of her fields.

Assigning Field Sizes

The **field size** property defines a field value's maximum storage size for text and number fields only. The other data types have no field size property, because their storage size is either a fixed, predetermined amount or is variable, as shown in Figure 2-7 on the following page. You should still document every field's maximum size, however, so that you allow enough room for it on entry screens and on reports and other outputs, without wasting space.

Data Type	Storage Size
Text	1 to 255 bytes 50 bytes default
Memo	64,000 maximum exact size depends on field value
Number	1 to 8 bytes 8 bytes default
Date/Time	8 bytes
Currency	8 bytes
Counter	4 bytes
Yes/no	1 bit
OLE object	1 gigabyte maximum exact size depends on object size

Figure 2-7
Data type storage sizes

A text field has a default field size of 50 characters. You set its field size by entering a number in the range 1 to 255. You select the field size for a number field from the five choices of byte, integer, long integer, double, and single, as shown in Figure 2-8. Double is the default field size for a number field.

Field Size	Storage Size (Bytes)	Number Type	Field Values Allowed
Byte	1	Integer	0 to 255
Integer	2	Integer	–32,768 to 32,767
Long Integer	4	Integer	–2,147,483,648 to 2,147,483,647
Double	8	Decimal	15 significant digits
Single	4	Decimal	7 significant digits

Figure 2-8
Number data
type field size

Elena's Writer ID field is a text field that is always exactly four characters long, so she documents its field size as 4. Writer Name is also a text field, but each field value varies in size. After studying the different field values, she finds that a field size of 25 will accommodate the largest field value for the Writer Name field. In a similar fashion, Elena determines the field size for the other fields in her database.

Creating an Access Table

Before you create a database and its objects on the computer, you should spend time carefully documenting your data requirements. You must understand, and accurately represent, the structure of each table in the database.

Planning the Table Structure

Now that you have learned the guidelines for designing databases and creating Access tables, you are ready to work with Elena to create the Issue25 database. Elena first develops the structure of the WRITERS and BUSINESS ARTICLES tables. For each field, she documents the field name and its data type, input/display field size, and description (Figure 2-9).

	Data Type	Input/Display Field Size	Description
WRITERS table			
Writer ID	text	4	primary key
Writer Name	text	25	
Writer Phone Number	text	14	(999) 999-9999 format
Is the Writer a Freelancer?	yes/no	3	
Freelancer Reprint Payment Amount	currency	4	$250 maximum
BUSINESS ARTICLES table			
Article Title	text	44	
Issue of Business Perspective	text	8	
Length of Article	number	4	integer field size
Writer ID	text	4	foreign key

Figure 2-9
Elena's table structures for the WRITERS and BUSINESS ARTICLES tables

With the exception of some new information, the file structures for these two tables are consistent with the planning Elena has done so far. The five fields in the WRITERS table are Writer ID, Writer Name, Writer Phone Number, Is the Writer a Freelancer? and Freelancer Reprint Payment Amount. The four fields in the BUSINESS ARTICLES table are Article Title, Issue of Business Perspective, Length of Article, and Writer ID. Six of these nine fields are text fields, while Is the Writer a Freelancer? is a yes/no field, Freelancer Reprint Payment Amount is a currency field, and Length of Article is a number field.

Elena needs to choose field sizes only for text and number fields. However, she decides that documenting the maximum field sizes for all data types will help her plan how many positions each field requires for input and for screen and report display. For this purpose, she includes a column labeled Input/Display Field Size. Freelancers will receive $250 at most for their articles, so she plans a field size of four for the Freelancer Reprint Payment Amount currency field.

Finally, she adds descriptions for Length of Article to remind her of its field size, for Writer Phone Number to specify its format, and for Freelancer Reprint Payment Amount to document its format and size.

Creating a Database

Having completed the planning for her table structures, Elena creates the database named Issue25. When you create a database, you give it a unique eight-character name that conforms to standard DOS conventions for filenames. Access stores the database by that name as a file on disk with an .mdb extension. A new Access database uses 64KB of disk space. Most of this is used when you add your first fields, tables, and other objects. As your database grows in size and needs more disk storage, Access increases its size in 32KB increments.

REFERENCE WINDOW

Creating a Database

- Click the New Database button on the toolbar. The New Database dialog box appears.

- With the File Name text box highlighted, type the name of the database you want to create. Do not press [Enter] yet.

- Change the drive and directory information, if necessary.

- Click the OK button or press [Enter] to accept the changes in the New Database dialog box.

Let's create the Issue25 database. If you have not done so, launch Access before you follow the next set of steps.

To create a database:

❶ Click the **New Database button** 🗅 on the toolbar in the Microsoft Access window. Access displays the New Database dialog box. See Figure 2-10. The File Name text box highlights the default name, db1.mdb.

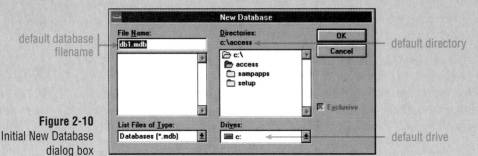

default database filename

default directory

Figure 2-10
Initial New Database dialog box

default drive

❷ Type **issue25** in the File Name text box. Click the **down arrow button** on the right side of the Drives box. A list of available drives drops down. Click the letter of the drive in which you put your Student Disk. See Figure 2-11. Your drive might be different.

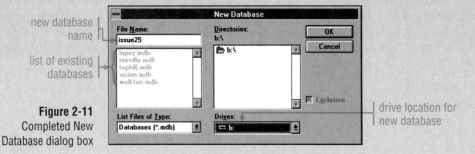

new database name

list of existing databases

Figure 2-11
Completed New Database dialog box

drive location for new database

TROUBLE? If the contents of the File Name text box do not show issue25, the text box might not have been highlighted when you began typing. If this is the case, highlight the contents of the text box and retype issue25.

❸ Click the **OK button** to let Access know you have completed the New Database dialog box. Access creates the Issue25 database, adding the extension .mdb, and opens the Database window. See Figure 2-12. Because this is a new database, no tables appear in the Tables list box.

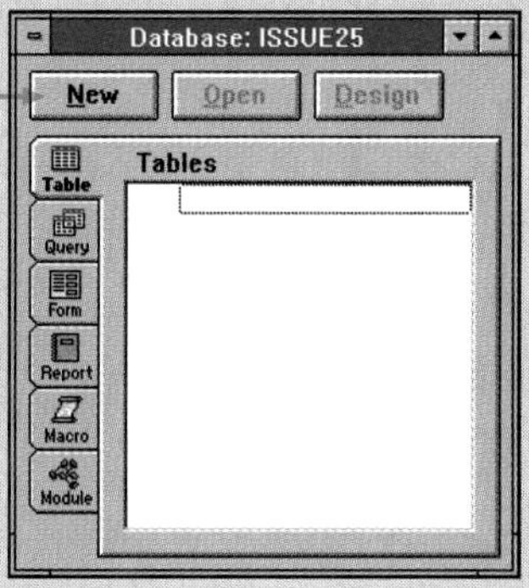

click to create a
new table

Figure 2-12
The Database
window for a
new database

Creating the Table Structure with Table Wizard

Having created her new database, Elena's next step is to create the WRITERS table structure. Creating a table structure consists of creating a table and defining the fields for the table. Therefore, Elena will create the WRITERS table and define its fields: Writer ID, Writer Name, Writer Phone Number, Is the Writer a Freelancer? and Freelancer Reprint Payment Amount.

In Access, you can keyboard the fields for a table or use Table Wizard to automate the table creation process. A **Wizard** is an Access tool that helps you create objects such as tables and reports by asking you a series of questions and then creating the objects based on your answers. **Table Wizard** asks you questions about your table and then creates the table based on your answers. Whether you use Table Wizard or keyboard the table fields, you can change a table's design after it is created.

Elena uses Table Wizard to create the WRITERS table.

To activate Table Wizard:

❶ Click the **New command button** in the Database window. Access displays the New Table dialog box. See Figure 2-13.

click to use
Table Wizard to
create a table

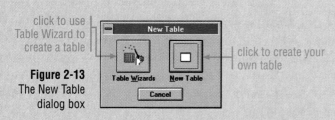

click to create your
own table

Figure 2-13
The New Table
dialog box

❷ Click the **Table Wizards button**. The first Table Wizard dialog box appears. See Figure 2-14 on the following page.

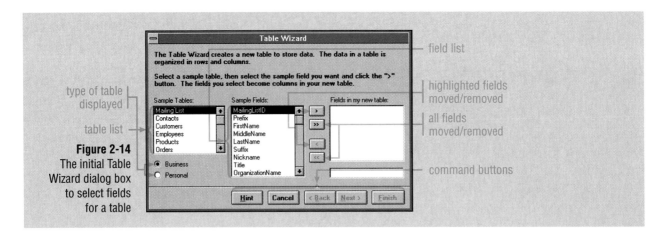

Figure 2-14
The initial Table
Wizard dialog box
to select fields
for a table

In the first Table Wizard dialog box, you select the fields for your table from sample fields in dozens of sample tables. The sample tables include those for business and personal use; simply click the Business or Personal radio button to display the corresponding list of sample tables. Scroll through the Sample Tables list until you find an appropriate table and then select fields to add to your table from the Sample Fields list. If necessary, you can select fields from more than one table. Do not be concerned about selecting field names that exactly match the ones you need because you can change the names later. Instead, select fields that seem like they have the general properties you need for your fields. If a field's properties do not exactly match, you can change the properties later.

You select fields in the order you want them to appear in your table. If you want to select fields one at a time, highlight a field by clicking it, and then click the > button. If you want to select all the fields, click the >> button. The fields appear in the list box on the right as you select them. If you make a mistake, click the << button to remove all the fields from the list box on the right or highlight a field and click the < button to remove fields one at a time.

At the bottom of each Table Wizard dialog box is a set of command buttons. These command buttons allow you to move quickly to other Table Wizard dialog boxes, to cancel the table creation process, and to display hints. You can display a hint for a Table Wizard dialog box by clicking the Hint command button. After reading the hint, click OK to remove the hint and continue with your work.

Elena selects fields from the Mailing List sample table to create the WRITERS table.

To select fields for a new table:
❶ If Mailing List is not highlighted in the Sample Tables list box, click it, so that it is highlighted. Click **MailingListID** in the Sample Fields list box and then click the **> button**. Access places MailingListID into the list box on the right as the first field in the new table.

❷ In order, select LastName, HomePhone, MembershipStatus, and DuesAmount for the WRITERS table by clicking the field name in the Sample Fields list box, scrolling as needed, and then clicking the **> button**.

Elena has selected all the fields she needs for her table, so she continues through the remaining Table Wizard dialog boxes to finish creating the WRITERS table.

To finish creating a table using Table Wizard:

❶ Click the **Next > button**. Access displays the second Table Wizard dialog box.

❷ Type **WRITERS** in the text box and then click the **radio button** beside "Set the primary key myself." See Figure 2-15.

primary key option

Figure 2-15
Choosing a table name and primary key option

table name

❸ Click the **Next > button**. Access displays the third Table Wizard dialog box.

❹ Let MailingListID remain in the text box at the top of the dialog box and click the **bottom radio button**, so that the primary key will contain "Numbers and/or letters I enter when I add new records." You have now selected MailingListID as the primary key for the table. See Figure 2-16.

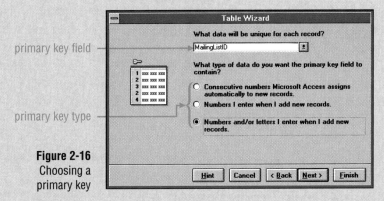

primary key field

primary key type

Figure 2-16
Choosing a primary key

❺ Click the **Next > button**. Access displays the final Table Wizard dialog box.

Elena needs to change the field names and other field properties for the sample fields inserted into the WRITERS table by Table Wizard, so that they agree with her table design. To make these changes she must modify the table design. First, she must exit Table Wizard.

To exit Table Wizard:

❶ Be sure that the "Modify the table design" radio button is on and that the Cue Cards box at the bottom is unchecked. See Figure 2-17 on the following page.

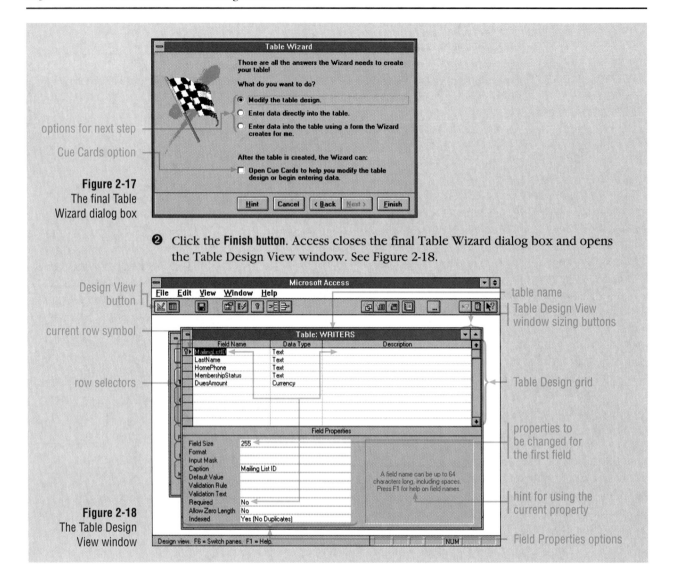

Figure 2-17
The final Table
Wizard dialog box

options for next step

Cue Cards option

❷ Click the **Finish button**. Access closes the final Table Wizard dialog box and opens
the Table Design View window. See Figure 2-18.

Design View
button

current row symbol

row selectors

Figure 2-18
The Table Design
View window

table name

Table Design View
window sizing buttons

Table Design grid

properties to
be changed for
the first field

hint for using the
current property

Field Properties options

Changing the Sample Field Properties

You use the Table Design View window to define or modify a table structure or the properties for the fields in a table. If you create a table without using Table Wizard, you enter
the fields and their properties for your table directly in this window.

Initially, the Design View button on the toolbar is selected, the table name appears in
the Table Design View window title bar, the first field name is highlighted, and the current
row symbol is positioned in the first row selector of the Table Design grid. When you click
a row selector, Access highlights the entire row and moves the current row symbol to that
row. If you click a field name, data type, or description for a different field, Access moves
the current row symbol to that row but does not highlight the entire row.

A hint for using the current property appears in the lower-right corner of the Table
Design View window. As you press [Tab] or click a different property, the hint changes
to define or explain the new property. If the hint does not answer your questions about
the property, press [F1] for a full explanation.

The field name, data type, and description field properties appear in the top half of the Table Design View window. In the Field Properties sheet, which appears in the lower-left corner of the window, you view and change other properties for the current field. For example, in the property sheet you can change the size of a text field or the number of decimal places for a number field. The Field Properties displayed are appropriate for the data type of the currently selected field.

For the first field, Elena changes the field name to Writer ID, the Field Size property to 4, the Required property to Yes, and adds "primary key" as a description.

To change the first field's properties:
❶ If MailingListID is not highlighted in the first row of the Field Name column, double-click it. Then type **Writer ID** to replace the highlighted MailingListID and press **[Tab]** twice to move the I to the Description box.

❷ Type **primary key** as the Description for the first field.

❸ Double-click **255** in the Field Size property box to highlight it and then type **4**.

❹ Click **Mailing List ID** in the Caption property box, press **[F2]** to highlight it, and then press **[Del]** to delete it.

❺ Click anywhere in the **Required property text box** and then click the **down arrow button** that appears in that box to display the Required list box. Click **Yes** in the Required list box to choose that as the property value.

Setting the **Required property** to Yes for a field means you must enter a value in the field for every record in the table. Every primary-key field should have the Required property set to Yes, so that each record has a unique value. Fields other than a primary key usually have the Required property set to No, which is the default value.

The Caption property allows you to use a **caption**, which is text that replaces the default field name in the datasheet column heading box and in the label on a form. Elena deletes all Caption property values because they do not represent the new field names she will use.

Elena next changes some of the properties for each of the remaining fields in the WRITERS table. If you make a mistake in typing a field name or description value, click that box, press [F2] to select the entire property value, and retype the value.

To change the properties of the remaining fields:
❶ Double-click **LastName** in the second row's Field Name text box and type **Writer Name**. Double-click **50** in the Field Size property box to highlight it and then type **25**. Finally, click **Last Name** in the Caption property box, press **[F2]** to highlight it, and then press **[Del]** to delete it.

❷ Double-click **HomePhone** in the third row's Field Name text box and type **Writer Phone Number**. Press **[Tab]** twice and type **(999) 999-9999 format** in the Description text box. Double-click **30** in the Field Size property box to highlight it and then type **14**. Finally, click **Home Phone** in the Caption property box, press **[F2]** to highlight it, and then press **[Del]** to delete it.

❸ Double-click **MembershipStatus** in the fourth row's Field Name text box and type **Is the Writer a Freelancer?** Press **[Tab]** and then click the **down arrow button** in the Data Type text box to display the Data Type list box. See Figure 2-19 on the following page.

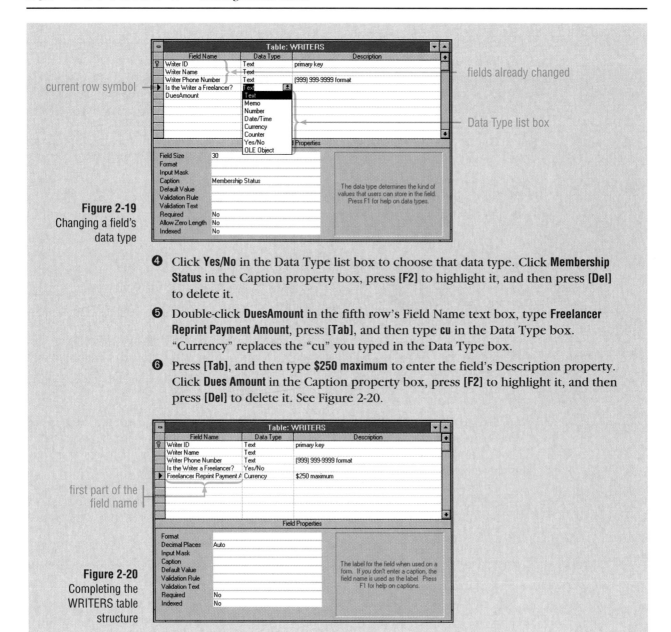

Figure 2-19
Changing a field's
data type

❹ Click **Yes/No** in the Data Type list box to choose that data type. Click **Membership Status** in the Caption property box, press **[F2]** to highlight it, and then press **[Del]** to delete it.

❺ Double-click **DuesAmount** in the fifth row's Field Name text box, type **Freelancer Reprint Payment Amount**, press **[Tab]**, and then type **cu** in the Data Type box. "Currency" replaces the "cu" you typed in the Data Type box.

❻ Press **[Tab]**, and then type **$250 maximum** to enter the field's Description property. Click **Dues Amount** in the Caption property box, press **[F2]** to highlight it, and then press **[Del]** to delete it. See Figure 2-20.

Figure 2-20
Completing the
WRITERS table
structure

Instead of selecting a field's data type by clicking one of the choices in the Data Type list box, you can type the entire data type in the field's Data Type box. Alternatively, type just the first character—or the first two characters for currency and counter—of the data type to select that data type.

Field names can be up to 64 characters long. However, the Field Name text box is not wide enough to show an entire long name. Freelancer Reprint Payment Amount is an example of a long field name.

Saving the Table Structure

Elena has finished defining and changing the WRITERS table structure, so she saves the table. When you first create a table, you save the table with its field definitions to add the table structure permanently to your database. If you use Table Wizard, Access saves your table before you switch to the Table Design View window. Elena saves the table, so that her field property changes are retained in the database.

To save a table:
❶ Click the **Save button** 🖫 on the toolbar. Access saves the WRITERS table on your Student Disk.

Switching to the Datasheet View Window

Once you have defined a table, you can view the table in either the Table Design View window or the Datasheet View window. Use the Table Design View window to view or change a table's fields, and use the Datasheet View window to view or change the field values and records stored in a table. Even though she has not yet entered field values and records in the WRITERS table, Elena displays the WRITERS table in the Datasheet View window. She wants to study the datasheet to determine if she needs to make further changes to the table structure.

To switch from the Table Design View window to the Datasheet View window:
❶ Click the **Datasheet View button** 🗊 on the toolbar. Access displays the Datasheet View window for the WRITERS table. See Figure 2-21.

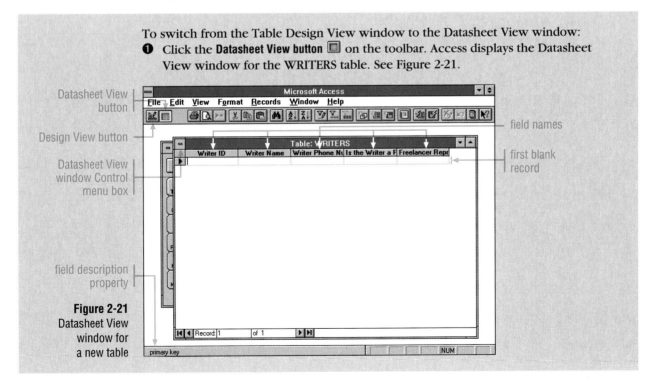

Figure 2-21
Datasheet View window for a new table

Elena notices that the description property for Writer ID appears in the status bar. Also, the first record has no field values. Thus, no records exist for the new WRITERS table. This is correct because Elena has not yet entered field values in the table.

Elena sees two problems in the Datasheet View window of the WRITERS table that she wants to correct. First, the field names Writer Phone Number, Is the Writer a Freelancer? and Freelancer Reprint Payment Amount are only partially displayed, and their field value boxes are wider than they need to be to accommodate the field values that will be entered. Second, the Writer Name field value box is too narrow to display the entire field value.

Printing a Datasheet

Before making any changes, Elena prints the datasheet for the WRITERS table, so that she can refer to it when she makes the field changes to correct the problems she discovered.

To print the datasheet:
❶ Click the **Print button** 🖨 on the toolbar to open the Print dialog box.
❷ Check the Printer section of the Print dialog box to make sure your computer's printer is selected. Click the **OK button** to initiate printing. After the message box disappears, Access returns you to the Datasheet View window.

Elena switches back to the Table Design View window to make her field property changes.

To switch from the Datasheet View window to the Table Design View window:
❶ Click the **Design View button** 📐 on the toolbar. Access again displays the Table Design View window for the WRITERS table.

If you want to take a break and resume the tutorial at a later time, you can exit Access by double-clicking the Microsoft Access window Control menu box. When you resume the tutorial, place your Student Disk in the appropriate drive, launch Access, open the Issue25 database on your Student Disk, and click the Design command button to open the Table Design View window for the WRITERS table.

Changing Field Properties

The first changes Elena makes are to shorten the field names for Writer Phone Number and Is the Writer a Freelancer? The field name for Freelancer Reprint Payment Amount is also too wide to fit in the datasheet column heading box. Rather than change the field name, however, Elena uses its Caption property to replace the default field name in the datasheet column heading box and in the label on a form. You use the Caption property to display a shorter version of a longer, more descriptive table field name.

Changing Field Names and Entering Captions

Let's change the names for the fields Writer Phone Number and Is the Writer a Freelancer?

To change a table field name in the Table Design View window:
❶ Double-click **Number** in the Field Name box for Writer Phone Number to highlight it. Press **[Backspace]** twice to leave Writer Phone as the new field name.
❷ Click anywhere in the Field Name box for Is the Writer a Freelancer? and then press **[F2]** to highlight the entire field name.
❸ Type **Freelancer** to make it the new field name.

Suppose you make a change that you immediately realize is a mistake. You can click the **Undo button** on the toolbar to cancel your change. Not all changes can be undone; the Undo button is dimmed in those cases.

Let's make a field name change to Writer Name that we will immediately undo.

To undo a change:
❶ Click anywhere in the Field Name box for Writer Name and then press **[F2]** to select the entire field name. Type **Amount**, which becomes the new field name.
❷ Click the **Undo button** ⬐. Access restores the previous field name, Writer Name.

Having completed her field name changes, Elena enters a caption for Freelancer Reprint Payment Amount.

To enter a caption:

❶ Click anywhere in the Field Name box for Freelancer Reprint Payment Amount. The current row symbol moves to the Freelancer Reprint Payment Amount row, and the Field Properties options apply to this current field. Click the **Caption text box** and then type **Amount**. See Figure 2-22.

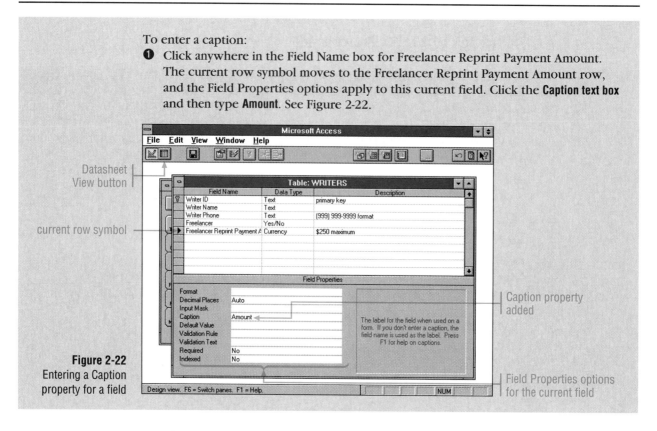

Datasheet
View button

current row symbol

Caption property
added

Figure 2-22
Entering a Caption
property for a field

Field Properties options
for the current field

Elena switches to the Datasheet View window to review the effects of the changes she's made so far.

To switch to the Datasheet View window:

❶ Click the **Datasheet View button** 📋 on the toolbar. Access displays the "Save now?" dialog box. See Figure 2-23.

Figure 2-23
The "Save now?"
dialog box

Access makes your table structure changes permanent only when you take action to save the changes or to close the Table Design View window. Switching to the Datasheet View window first involves closing the Table Design View window, so Access displays the dialog box to ask you about saving your table changes. If you want to keep the Table Design View window open and continue making table structure changes, click the **Cancel button**. If you would rather switch to the Datasheet View window, you need to save your changes first.

❷ Click the **OK button**. Access saves your table structure changes, closes the Table Design View window, and opens the Datasheet View window. See Figure 2-24.

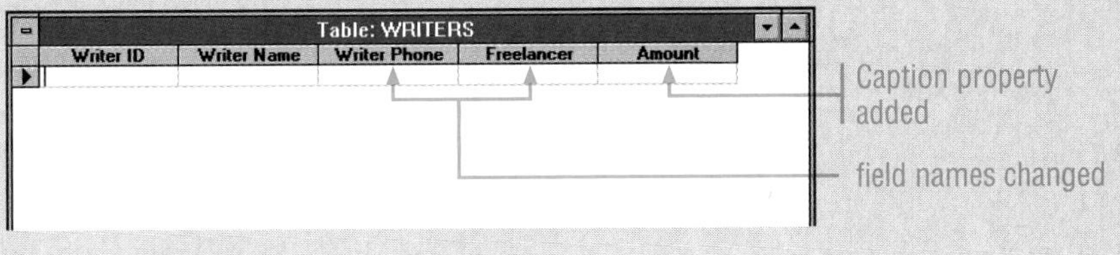

Figure 2-24
Reviewing file structure changes in the Datasheet View window

Table: WRITERS

Writer ID	Writer Name	Writer Phone	Freelancer	Amount

Caption property added

field names changed

Elena reviews the changes she has made to the WRITERS table structure. The two new field names, Writer Phone and Freelancer, appear; and the Amount caption replaces the Freelancer Reprint Payment Amount field name. Elena is still bothered by the column widths in some of the fields in the datasheet, so she changes them.

Resizing Columns in a Datasheet

There are often several ways to accomplish a task in Access. For example, you can close a database by double-clicking the Database window Control menu box; by clicking File and then clicking Close Database; or by pressing and holding [Alt] and then pressing [F], then releasing both keys, and then pressing [C]. Elena has been choosing the simplest and fastest method to accomplish her tasks and has not spent time experimenting with alternative methods. However, Elena has never resized datasheet columns before, so she wants to practice three different techniques.

Let's first resize a datasheet column using the Format menu.

To resize datasheet columns using the Format menu:
❶ Click anywhere in the **Writer ID column**, click **Format**, and then click **Column Width…**. Access opens the Column Width dialog box. See Figure 2-25. Access has automatically selected the default, standard column width of 18.8 positions and has checked the Standard Width check box.

Figure 2-25
The Column Width dialog box

default standard column width

❷ Type **11** and then click the **OK button**. The Column Width dialog box disappears, and Access resizes the Writer ID column from 18.8 to 11 positions.

Changing a datasheet column width does not change the field size for the table field. The standard column width of 18.8 positions is approximately 1" wide on the screen. The actual number of characters you can place in a column depends on the typeface and font size you are using. Elena chooses not to change the typeface and font size.

Elena resizes the Writer Name field with a second resizing method, which uses the mouse pointer to drag the column's right edge. To resize this way, you must first position the mouse pointer in the field's **column selector**, which is the gray box that contains the field name at the top of the column. A column selector is also called a **field selector**.

To resize datasheet columns using the mouse pointer to drag the column's right edge:

❶ Move the mouse pointer to the right edge of the Writer Name column selector until it changes to ✛. See Figure 2-26.

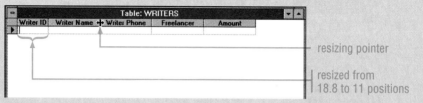

Figure 2-26
Resizing columns
using the
resizing pointer

resizing pointer

resized from
18.8 to 11 positions

❷ Click-and-drag the pointer to the right until the column width is approximately twice its original size.

❸ Release the mouse button to complete the resizing of the Writer Name field.

TROUBLE? Be sure that all five fields are still visible in the Datasheet View window. If not, you can repeat the previous steps to make the column narrower.

Elena tries a third technique—the best-fit column width method—to resize the Freelancer and Amount columns. When you use the **best-fit column width** method, Access automatically resizes the column to accommodate its largest value, including the field name at the top of the column. To use this method, you position the mouse pointer at the right edge of the column selector for the field and, when the mouse pointer changes to ✛, double-click the left mouse button. Access then automatically resizes the column. (A fourth method for resizing columns is to use the Best Fit button in the Column Width dialog box, but Elena does not experiment with this method.)

For both best-fit methods, you can resize two or more adjacent columns at the same time. Simply move the mouse pointer to the column selector of the leftmost of the fields. When the pointer changes to ↓, click-and-drag it to the column selector of the rightmost field and then release the mouse button. You then double-click the ✛ at the right edge of the column selector for the rightmost field.

To resize datasheet columns using the best-fit column width method:

❶ Move the mouse pointer to the Freelancer column selector. When it changes to ↓, click the left mouse button, drag the pointer to the right to the Amount column selector, and then release the mouse button. Both columns are now highlighted.

❷ Move the mouse pointer to the right edge of the Amount column selector. When it changes to ✛, double-click the left mouse button. Access automatically resizes both columns to their best fits. See Figure 2-27.

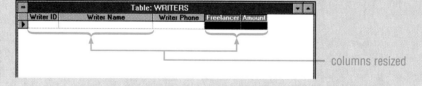

Figure 2-27
Four columns
resized

columns resized

For her final set of table structure changes, Elena assigns a default value to the Freelancer field, eliminates the decimal places in the Amount field, and adds an input mask to the Writer Phone field. These changes must be made in the Table Design View window, so Elena first switches from the Datasheet View window.

Assigning Default Values

With a few exceptions, Elena knows which writers are freelancers and which are staff writers. To be safe, Elena will assume that the exceptions are freelancers until she finds out for sure. She assigns the default value Yes to the Freelancer field, which means each writer will have the value Yes in the Freelancer field unless it is changed individually to No.

To assign a default value:

❶ Click the **Design View button** 📖 on the toolbar to switch to the Table Design View window.

❷ Click anywhere in the **Freelancer field row** to make it the current field, click the Field Properties **Default Value text box**, and then type **Yes**. See Figure 2-28.

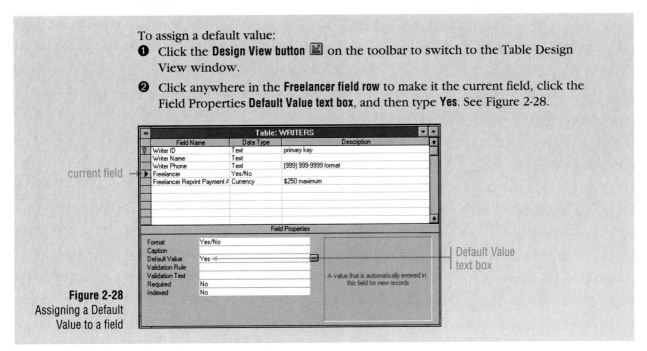

Figure 2-28
Assigning a Default Value to a field

Elena's next table structure change is to eliminate the decimal places in the Freelancer Reprint Payment Amount field.

Changing Decimal Places

Vision Publishers pays freelancers at most $250 for reprint rights to their articles. Some freelancers will be paid less, but in all cases, a whole dollar amount will be paid. Elena changes the Freelancer Reprint Payment Amount field to show only whole dollar amounts. To do this, she modifies the Decimal Places property for the field.

To change the number of decimal places displayed:

❶ Click anywhere in the **Freelancer Reprint Payment Amount field row** to make it the current field and to display its Field Properties options.

❷ Click the **Decimal Places text box**, and then click the **down arrow button** that appears in the box. Access displays the Decimal Places list box. See Figure 2-29.

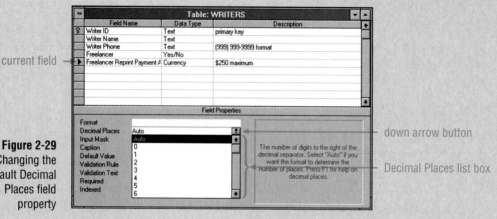

current field →

Figure 2-29
Changing the default Decimal Places field property

down arrow button

Decimal Places list box

❸ Click the **0** in the Decimal Places list box. The Decimal Places list box disappears, and 0 is now the value for the Decimal Places field property.

For the final table structure change, Elena uses Input Mask Wizard to create an input mask for the Writer Phone field.

Using Input Mask Wizard

One standard way to format a telephone number is with parentheses, a space, and a hyphen—as in (917) 729-5364. If you want these special formatting characters to appear whenever Writer Phone field values are entered, you need to create an input mask. An **input mask** is a predefined format you use to enter data in a field. An easy way to create an input mask is to use **Input Mask Wizard**, which is an Access tool that guides you in creating a predefined format for a field. To start Input Mask Wizard, click the text box for the Input Mask property and then click either the Build button that appears to the right of the text box or the Build button on the toolbar. You use the **Build button** to start a builder or wizard, which are Access tools to help you perform a task.

Let's use Input Mask Wizard to create an input mask for the Writer Phone field.

To start Input Mask Wizard:

❶ Click anywhere in the **Writer Phone field row** to make it the current field and to display its Field Properties options.

❷ Click the **Input Mask text box**. A Build button appears to the right of the Input Mask text box. See Figure 2-30.

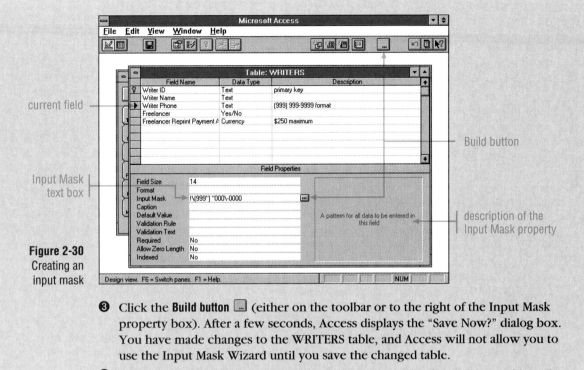

Figure 2-30
Creating an
input mask

❸ Click the **Build button** 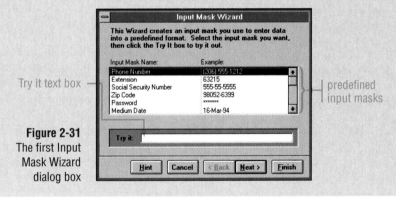 (either on the toolbar or to the right of the Input Mask property box). After a few seconds, Access displays the "Save Now?" dialog box. You have made changes to the WRITERS table, and Access will not allow you to use the Input Mask Wizard until you save the changed table.

❹ Click the **Yes button** to close the dialog box. Access saves the WRITERS table and, after a few seconds, displays the first Input Mask Wizard dialog box. See Figure 2-31.

Figure 2-31
The first Input
Mask Wizard
dialog box

You scroll through the Input Mask Name list box, select the input mask you want, and then enter representative values to experiment with the input mask. Elena selects the Phone Number input mask for the Writer Phone field.

To select an input mask:

❶ If necessary, click **Phone Number** in the Input Mask Name list box to highlight it.

❷ Click **Try it** and then type **9** in the Try it text box. Access displays (9__) ___-____ in the Try it text box. The underscores are placeholder characters that are replaced as you type.

❸ Type **876543210** to complete the sample entry.

❹ Click the **Next > button**. Access displays the second Input Mask Wizard dialog box. See Figure 2-32.

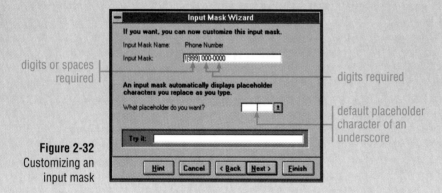

digits or spaces required

digits required

default placeholder character of an underscore

Figure 2-32
Customizing an
input mask

When you have more experience creating input masks, you can modify, or customize, the input mask. You can change the default underscore placeholder character, for example, to a space or one of the following special characters: #, @, !, $, %, or *. For now, Elena accepts the predefined input mask and continues through the remaining Input Mask Wizard dialog boxes.

To finish an input mask:

❶ Click the **Next > button**. Access displays the third Input Mask Wizard dialog box.

❷ Click the **top radio button**, so that you store the data "With the symbols in the mask, like this: (206) 555-1212." Then click the **Next > button**. Access displays the final Input Mask Wizard dialog box.

❸ Click the **Finish button**. Access ends Input Mask Wizard and displays the newly created input mask for Writer Phone.

Elena is done with her initial work on the WRITERS table structure, so she exits Access.

To exit Access after changing a table structure:

❶ Double-click the Microsoft Access window **Control menu box**. A dialog box asks, "Save changes to Table 'WRITERS'?"

❷ Click the **Yes button** to save your changes to the WRITERS table structure. Access saves the table structure changes, closes all windows, and then exits to Windows.

Selecting the Primary Key

As Elena thinks about her Issue25 database later that day, she can't remember if she made Writer ID the primary key of the WRITERS table. Although Access does not require that tables have a primary key, Elena knows that choosing a primary key has several advantages.

- Based on its definition, a primary key does serve to identify uniquely each record in a table. For example, Elena is using Writer ID to distinguish one writer from another when both have the same name.
- Access does not allow duplicate values in the primary key field. If Elena already has a record with N425 as the field value for Writer ID, Access prevents her from adding another record with this same field value in the Writer ID field. Preventing duplicate values ensures the uniqueness of the primary key field.
- Access enforces entity integrity on the primary key field. **Entity integrity** means that every record's primary key field must have a value. If you do not enter a value for a field, you have actually given the field what is known as a **null value**. You cannot give a null value to the primary key field; Access will not store the record for you unless you've entered a field value in the primary-key field.
- Access displays records in primary key sequence when you view a table in the Datasheet View window or the Form View window. If you enter records in no specific order, you are ensured that you will later be able to work with them in a more meaningful, primary key sequence.
- Access responds faster to your requests for specific records based on the primary key.

To verify that Writer ID is the primary key of the WRITERS table, Elena launches Access, opens the Issue25 database, and then opens the WRITERS table in the Table Design View window.

To open a table in the Table Design View window:

❶ Launch Access.

❷ Open the Issue25 database.

❸ WRITERS should be highlighted in the Tables list box, so click the **Design button**.
Access opens the Table Design View window for the WRITERS table. See Figure 2-33.

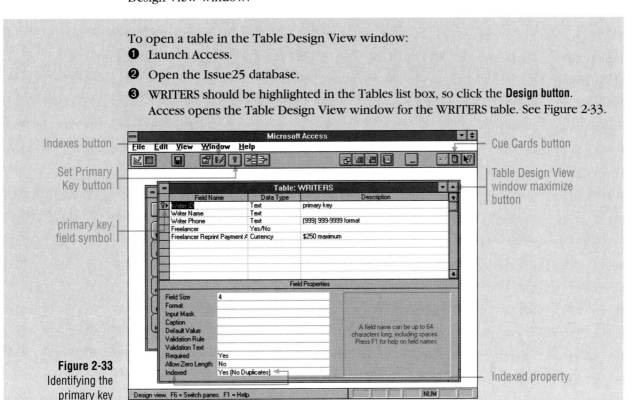

Figure 2-33
Identifying the primary key

Writer ID is highlighted and has the current row symbol in its row selector because Writer ID is the current field. Elena sees a key symbol to the left of the current row symbol. Access uses the key symbol as a **primary key field symbol** to identify the table's primary key. To change the primary key to another field, click the other field's row selector and then click the Set Primary Key button on the toolbar; Access will move the primary-key field symbol to that other field. If the primary key consists of two or more fields, hold down [Ctrl], click the row selector for each field, and then click the Set Primary Key button. Access will move the primary-key field symbol to all selected fields.

Elena sees the toolbar Indexes button to the left of the Set Primary Key button and the Indexed property as one of the Field Properties options. Elena uses Cue Cards to learn more about indexes.

Using Cue Cards and Creating Indexes

The Access Help system contains a Cue Cards feature. **Cue Cards** are interactive Access tutorials that remain visible to help you while you do the most common database tasks. They provide examples, guidance, and shortcuts to Access Help information.

REFERENCE WINDOW

Opening and Using Cue Cards

- Click the Cue Cards button on the toolbar. The Cue Cards window appears.

- Click the Cue Cards option you want to use.

- As each successive display appears, read the coaching information, and then click the option button of your choice. Continue until you have the information you need.

- When you finish using the Cue Cards, double-click the Cue Cards window Control menu box to close the Cue Cards window.

Let's use Cue Cards to learn about the Indexes property. First, maximize the Table Design View window so that the Cue Cards hide less of the window.

To maximize a window and open Cue Cards:
❶ Click the Table Design View window **maximize button**.
❷ Click the **Cue Cards button** 🔲 on the toolbar to open the Cue Cards window. See Figure 2-34 on the following page.

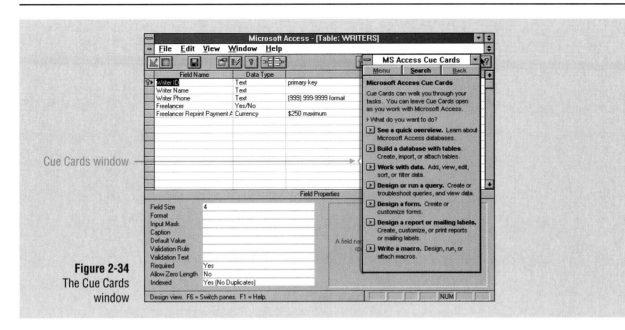

Figure 2-34
The Cue Cards
window

The Cue Cards window appears as an active window. Although normally only one window at a time is active, the Table Design View window is now also an active window. You can perform tasks in either window. If you switch from the Table Design View window to another Access window and from the current Cue Cards window to another Cue Cards window, both new windows will become active windows.

Review the displayed Cue Cards options. If you have time, you might want to investigate the Cue Cards topic called "See a quick overview." If you do, be sure to complete the topic so that you return to the Cue Cards window shown in Figure 2-34 before continuing with the tutorial.

Elena wants guidance working with table indexes, so she first chooses the Cue Cards topic "Build a database with tables" and then makes the appropriate choices on subsequent Cue Cards windows.

To open a Cue Cards topic:
❶ Click the **Build a database with tables button** to open the Cue Cards Build a Database with Tables window. See Figure 2-35.

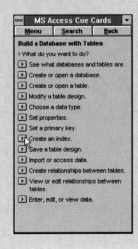

Figure 2-35
The Cue Cards
Build a Database
with Tables window

❷ Click the **Create an index button** to see the next Cue Cards window.

❸ Carefully read the contents of each Cue Cards window, then click the **Next button** in each Cue Cards window until you reach the last Cue Cards window in the sequence. See Figure 2-36.

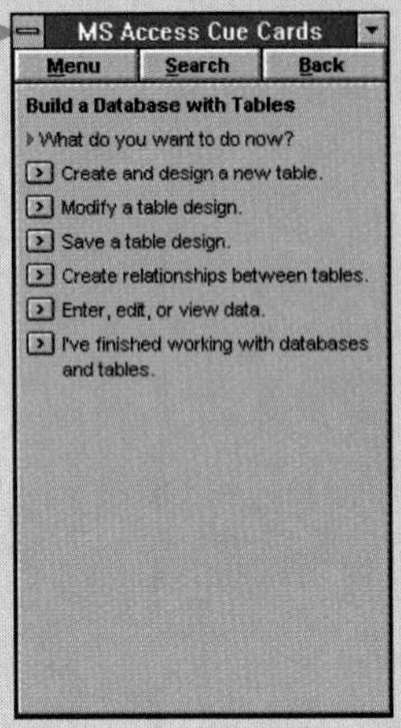

Cue Cards Control
menu box

Figure 2-36
The last Cue Cards
Build a Database
with Tables window

❹ Double-click the Cue Cards **Control menu box** to close the Cue Cards feature.

Elena has learned that Access automatically creates and maintains an index for the primary key field. An **index**, in this case, is a list of primary-key values and their corresponding record numbers. For a primary-key field, the index cannot have duplicate values. The index adds to the database disk storage requirements and takes time to maintain as you add and delete records. These are two disadvantages of having a primary key and its corresponding index for a table, but they are insignificant compared with the many advantages of an index. You cannot index fields that have the data types memo, yes/no, and OLE object, but this restriction should never be a problem.

You can also create indexes for other selected table fields. Do so to improve processing speed if you think you will often sort or find records based on data in those fields. However, each index requires extra disk space and additional processing time when records are added, changed, or deleted in the table.

Elena views the indexes that currently exist for the WRITERS table by using the Indexes button on the toolbar.

To display the indexes for a table:
❶ Click the **Indexes button** 🖽 on the toolbar. Access displays the Indexes window. See Figure 2-37.

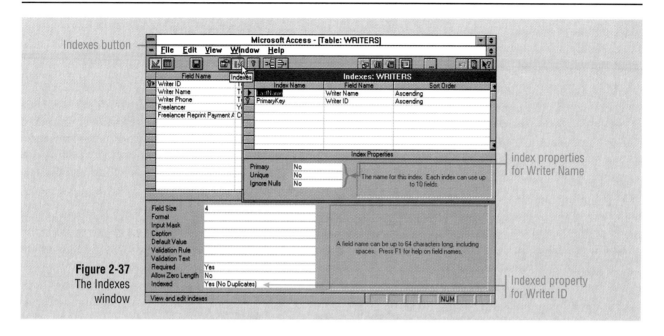

Figure 2-37
The Indexes
window

Two indexes appear in the Indexes window: one for the primary-key field of Writer ID and a second one for the Writer Name field. How was the second index created? Recall that you used Table Wizard to create the WRITERS table. When you select Table Wizard fields, you also select all their predefined properties. One of the fields you selected was LastName, which had "Yes (Duplicates OK)" as the value for its Indexed property. When you changed LastName to Writer Name, the field retained this Indexed property value.

Elena doesn't think she needs an index for Writer Name, so she deletes the index. If she ever needs an index for this field in the future, she can add it back by using the Indexes window or the Indexed property for Writer Name.

To delete an index:
❶ Position the mouse pointer in the first row of the Indexes window with the Index Name LastName and click the right mouse button. Access displays the Shortcut menu.
❷ Using the left mouse button, click **Delete Row**. Access deletes the index for Writer Name from the Indexes window.
❸ Click the **Indexes button** 🖼 on the toolbar to close the Indexes window.

If you want to take a break and resume the tutorial at a later time, you can exit Access by double-clicking the Microsoft Access window Control menu box and then clicking Yes in the dialog box that asks if you want to save your table changes. When you resume the tutorial, place your Student Disk in the appropriate drive, launch Access, open the Issue25 database on your Student Disk, and open the Table Design View window for the WRITERS table.

Modifying the Structure of an Access Table

Elena learns that Vision Publishers has a writer contact list containing each writer's name, phone number, and last contact date. Because Vision Publishers has not contacted some writers for many years, Elena decides that she should add a field named Last Contact Date to her WRITERS table. She will contact those writers who have a reasonably current date before she tries to track down those who wrote articles for the company many years ago.

When Elena shows Brian the WRITERS table she is developing, he realizes that he can use this information to contact writers and asks for a list of all the WRITERS table information arranged alphabetically by writer last name.

After the meeting, Elena realizes she has a problem with giving Brian this information. She had been planning to enter names in the Writer Name field in the regular order of first, middle, and last name. She needs to change her strategy for the Writer Name field. Her solution is to change the WRITERS table structure by deleting the Writer Name field and adding two fields that she names Last Name and First Name.

Deleting a Field

After meeting with Brian, Elena makes her table structure modifications to the WRITERS table. She first deletes the Writer Name field.

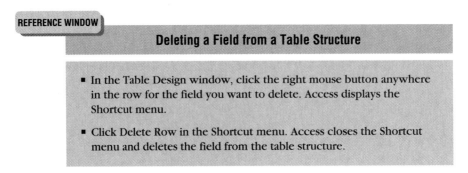

REFERENCE WINDOW

Deleting a Field from a Table Structure

- In the Table Design window, click the right mouse button anywhere in the row for the field you want to delete. Access displays the Shortcut menu.

- Click Delete Row in the Shortcut menu. Access closes the Shortcut menu and deletes the field from the table structure.

Let's delete the Writer Name field from the WRITERS table.

To delete a field from a table structure:
- ❶ Move the mouse pointer to the row for the Writer Name field and click the right mouse button. Access displays the Shortcut menu. See Figure 2-38.

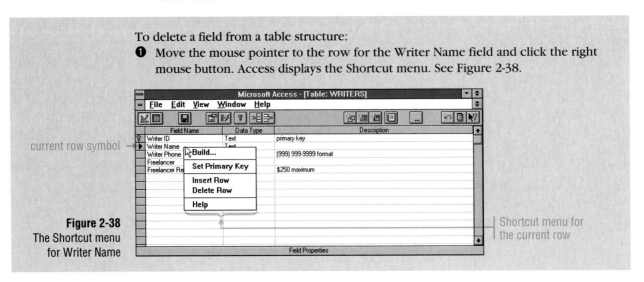

current row symbol →

Figure 2-38
The Shortcut menu
for Writer Name

Shortcut menu for
the current row

➋ Click **Delete Row** in the Shortcut menu. Access deletes the Writer Name field from the WRITERS table structure. The row where Writer Name had been positioned is also deleted.

TROUBLE? If you deleted the wrong field, immediately click the Undo button. The field you deleted reappears. You should repeat the deletion steps from the beginning for the correct field.

Adding a Field

The order of fields in the Table Design window determines the order of the fields in the Datasheet View window. Therefore, Elena decides that the two new fields, Last Name and First Name, should be positioned right after the Writer ID row. Then she will position the third new field, Last Contact Date, between the Writer Phone and Freelancer rows.

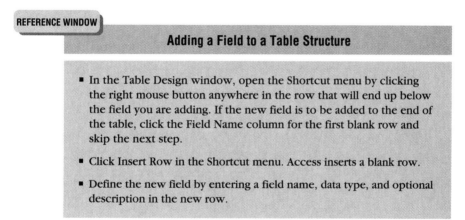

REFERENCE WINDOW

Adding a Field to a Table Structure

- In the Table Design window, open the Shortcut menu by clicking the right mouse button anywhere in the row that will end up below the field you are adding. If the new field is to be added to the end of the table, click the Field Name column for the first blank row and skip the next step.

- Click Insert Row in the Shortcut menu. Access inserts a blank row.

- Define the new field by entering a field name, data type, and optional description in the new row.

Let's add the three fields to the WRITERS table.

To add a field to a table structure:

➊ Click the right mouse button anywhere in the **Writer Phone row**. Above this row you want to insert two blank rows in preparation for adding two fields. Access displays the Shortcut menu.

➋ Click **Insert Row** in the Shortcut menu. Access adds a blank row between the Writer ID and Writer Phone rows and closes the Shortcut menu.

➌ Because you need to add two rows, click the right mouse button anywhere in the **Writer Phone row** and then click **Insert Row** in the Shortcut menu to insert the second blank row. See Figure 2-39.

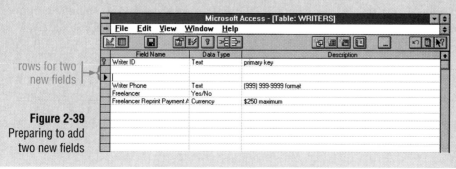

rows for two new fields

Figure 2-39
Preparing to add
two new fields

❹ Click the Field Name box for the first of the two new rows. To define the Last Name field, type **Last Name**, press **[Tab]**, and highlight the 50 in the Field Size box. Then type **15** and click the Field Name box for the second of the two new rows.

❺ To define the First Name field, type **First Name**, press **[Tab]**, highlight the 50 in the Field Size box, and then type **15**. See Figure 2-40.

new fields →

Figure 2-40
Completing the field
addition process

❻ After adding Last Name and First Name, Elena next adds Last Contact Date to the WRITERS table. Click the right mouse button anywhere in the Freelancer row and then click **Insert Row** in the Shortcut menu to insert a row between the Writer Phone and Freelancer rows. Access places the insertion point in the Field Name box of the new row.

❼ Type **Last Contact Date**, press **[Tab]**, type **d**, and then press **[Tab]**. See Figure 2-41. Last Contact Date is a date/time field.

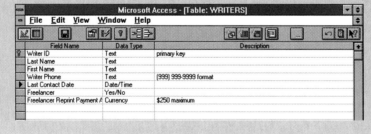

Figure 2-41
Last Contact Date
field added

Elena has now defined the WRITERS table structure. Once again, however, she wants to review, and possibly modify, the appearance of the WRITERS datasheet before exiting Access.

To review and modify a datasheet:

❶ Click the **Datasheet View button** ▣. The "Save now?" dialog box appears.

❷ Click the **OK button**. Access displays the Datasheet View window. The Last Name and First Name fields appear to the right of the Writer ID field, and Last Contact Date is to the right of Writer Phone. The one change you should make is to widen the column for Last Contact Date so the whole field name will be visible.

❸ Resize the column for Last Contact Date so that the entire field name appears in the heading box. See Figure 2-42.

Figure 2-42
The final Datasheet
View window for
the WRITERS table

❹ Double-click the Microsoft Access window **Control menu box**, and then click the **Yes button** in the "Save layout changes to table 'WRITERS'" dialog box to save your table changes and exit Access.

■   ■   ■

Elena has defined the WRITERS table structure and refined the table's datasheet. In the next tutorial, Elena will add data to the WRITERS table.

Questions

1. What two types of keys represent a common field when you form a relationship between tables?
2. What is data redundancy?
3. Which Access names must conform to standard DOS conventions for filenames?
4. Which Access field property can be up to 255 characters long?
5. What are the eight Access data types?
6. Which data type could automatically serve as a table's primary key because Access itself fills in each field value to guarantee uniqueness?
7. Which data types have the Field Size property?
8. What is a caption?
9. Describe three different ways to select a field's data type.
10. When is it appropriate to use the Undo button?
11. Describe three different ways to resize a datasheet column.
12. What is an input mask?
13. Explain entity integrity.
14. What are Cue Cards?
15. When is it possible to have two active windows?
E 16. Using Cue Cards for information on the technique, explain how to move a field in the Table Design View window.
E 17. Using Cue Cards for information, document for your instructor the tips for choosing a data type.
E 18. Use the "Work with data" Cue Cards to describe a method for rearranging columns in a datasheet while the Datasheet View window is active.

Tutorial Assignments

Elena creates the BUSINESS ARTICLES table structure, as shown in Figure 2-43.

BUSINESS ARTICLES table	Data Type	Input/Display Field Size	Description
Article Title	text	44	
Issue of Business Perspective	text	8	yyyy mmm format
Length of Article	number	4	Integer field size
Writer Name	text	25	

Figure 2-43

Launch Access, open the Issue25.mdb database on your Student Disk, and do the following:

1. Create a new table without using Table Wizard. Use Figure 2-43 to define these properties, as appropriate, for each of the four fields in the table: field name, data type, description, and field size. For the number data type field, use the Description column in Figure 2-43 to set its Field Size property.
2. Save the table with the name BUSINESS ARTICLES. Do not select a primary key.
3. Switch to the Datasheet View window and resize columns so that the entire field name can be read in the column heading for every field.
4. Print the datasheet for the table.
5. In the Table Design View window, change the field name Length of Article to Article Length. For the field Issue of Business Perspective, add the Caption property Issue. Resize the columns, if necessary, for these two fields in the Datasheet View window.
6. Print the datasheet for the table.
7. Delete the field Writer Name from the table structure.
8. Add a four-character text field named Writer ID to the end of the table. For a description, enter "foreign key."
9. Change the data type of the field Issue of Business Perspective to date/time.
10. Add a three-character text field named Type between the Article Length and Writer ID fields. For this new field, enter the description "article type" and the Default Value BUS, which represents a business article.
11. Resize columns, as necessary, in the Datasheet View window.
12. Print the datasheet for the table.
E 13. Switch the order of the Article Length and Type columns in the datasheet, using the "Work with data" Cue Cards for guidance. Do not switch their order in the table structure. Print the datasheet for the table.
E 14. Using Cue Cards for guidance, move the field named Type in the Table Design View window so that it follows the field named Article Title. Print the datasheet for the table and then close the Issue25 database.

Case Problems

1.   Walkton Daily Press Carriers

Grant Sherman, circulation manager of the Walkton Daily Press, wants a better way to keep track of the carriers who deliver the newspaper. Grant meets with Robin Witkop, one of the newspaper's computer experts, to discuss what can be done to improve his current tracking system.

Robin reviews Grant's informational needs and recommends that she design a database to keep track of carriers and their outstanding balances. Grant agrees and, after obtaining her manager's approval, Robin designs a database that has two tables: CARRIERS and BILLINGS. Robin first creates the CARRIERS table structure, as shown in Figure 2-44.

CARRIERS table

Field Name	Data Type	Input/Display Field Size	Description
Carrier ID	counter	3	primary key; unique carrier identification number
Carrier First Name	text	14	
Carrier Last Name	text	15	
Carrier Phone	number	8	Long Integer field size
Carrier Birthdate	date/time	8	

Figure 2-44

Launch Access and do the following:
1. Create a new database on your Student Disk with the name Press.
2. Create a new table without using Table Wizard. Use Figure 2-44 to define these properties, as appropriate, for each of the five fields in the table: field name, data type, and description. Define the Field Size property for only the text and number fields, using the Description column in Figure 2-44 to set the Field Size property for the number field.
3. Select Carrier ID as the table's primary key.
4. Save the table with the name CARRIERS.
5. Switch to the Datasheet View window and resize columns so that the entire field name can be read in the column heading for every field.
6. Print the datasheet for the table.
7. In the Table Design View window, change the field name Carrier Birthdate to Birthdate. Add the Caption property First Name for the field Carrier First Name. Add the Caption property Last Name for the field Carrier Last Name. Resize the columns, if necessary, for the fields in the Datasheet View window.
8. Print the datasheet for the table.
E 9. Using Cue Cards for guidance, move the field named Carrier Last Name in the Table Design View window so that it follows the field named Carrier ID. Print the datasheet for the table and then close the Datasheet View window.
Robin next creates the BILLINGS table structure, as shown in Figure 2-45.

BILLINGS table

Field Name	Data Type	Input/Display Field Size	Description
Route ID	text	4	primary key
Carrier ID	number	3	Integer field size; carrier assigned to the route; foreign key
Balance Amount	currency	5	outstanding balance due from the carrier

Figure 2-45

Launch Access, if necessary, and do the following:

10. Open the database named Press.mdb on your Student Disk.
11. Create a new table without using Table Wizard. Use Figure 2-45 to define these properties, as appropriate, for each of the three fields in the table: field name, data type, and description. Define the Field Size property for only the text and number fields, using the Description column in Figure 2-45 to set the Field Size property for the number field.
12. Select Route ID as the primary key and then save the table with the name BILLINGS.
13. Switch to the Datasheet View window and resize columns so that the entire field name can be read in the column heading for every field.
14. Print the datasheet for the table.
15. In the Table Design View window, add the Caption property Balance for the field Balance Amount, and change the Decimal Places property for the field Balance Amount from Auto to 2. Resize the columns, if necessary, for the fields in the Datasheet View window.
16. Print the datasheet for the table and then close the Press database.

2.   Lopez Used Cars

Maria and Hector Lopez own a chain of used-car lots throughout Texas. They have used a computer in their business for several years to handle their payroll and normal accounting functions. Their phenomenal expansion, both in the number of used-car locations and the number of used cars handled, forces them to develop a database to track their used-car inventory. They design a database that has two tables: USED CARS and LOCATIONS. They first create the USED CARS table structure, as shown in Figure 2-46.

USED CARS table

Field Name	Data Type	Input/Display Field Size	Description
Vehicle ID	text	5	primary key
Manufacturer	text	13	
Model	text	15	
Class Type	text	2	code for the type of sedan, van, truck, and so on; foreign key
Transmission Type	text	3	code for type of transmission; foreign key
Year	number	4	Integer field size
Cost	currency		
Selling Price	currency		
Location Code	text	2	lot location within the state; foreign key

Figure 2-46

Launch Access and do the following:

1. Create a new database on your Student Disk with the name Usedcars.
2. Create a new table without using Table Wizard. Use Figure 2-46 to define these properties, as appropriate, for each of the nine fields in the table: field name, data type, and description. Define the Field Size property for only the text and number fields, using the Description column in Figure 2-46 to set the Field Size property for the number field.

3. Select Vehicle ID as the table's primary key.
4. Save the table with the name USED CARS.
5. Switch to the Datasheet View window and resize columns so that the entire field name can be read in the column heading for every field. Maximize the Datasheet View window, and continue to resize columns until you can see all column headings on the screen at one time.
6. Print the datasheet for the table.
7. In the Table Design View window, change the field name Class Type to Class. Add the Caption property Transmission for the field Transmission Type and the Caption property Location for the field Location Code. Resize the columns, if necessary, for the fields in the Datasheet View window.
8. Print the datasheet for the table.

E

9. Using Cue Cards for guidance, move the field named Location Code in the Table Design View window so that it follows the field named Year. Print the datasheet for the table and then close the Datasheet View window.

Hector and Maria next create the LOCATIONS table structure, as shown in Figure 2-47.

LOCATIONS table

Field Name	Data Type	Input/Display Field Size	Description
Location Code	text	2	primary key
Location Name	text	15	
Manager Name	text	25	

Figure 2-47

Launch Access, if necessary, and do the following:
10. Open the database named Usedcars.mdb on your Student Disk.
11. Create a new table without using Table Wizard. Use Figure 2-47 to define these properties, as appropriate, for each of the three fields in the table: field name, data type, description, and field size.
12. Select Location Code as the primary key and then save the table with the name LOCATIONS.
13. Switch to the Datasheet View window and resize columns so that the entire field name can be read in the column heading for every field.
14. Print the datasheet for the table and then close the Usedcars database.

3. Tophill University Student Employment

Olivia Tyler is an administrative assistant in the Student Employment office of the Financial Aid department at Tophill University. She is responsible for tracking the companies that have announced part-time jobs for students. She keeps track of each available job and the person to contact at each company. Olivia had previously relied on student workers to do the paperwork, but reductions in the university budget have forced her department to reduce the number of part-time student workers. As a result, Olivia's backlog of work is increasing. After discussing the problem with her supervisor, Olivia meets with Lee Chang, a database analyst on the staff of the university computer center.

Lee questions Olivia in detail about her requirements and suggests that he could develop a database to reduce her workload. He designs a database that has two tables: JOBS and EMPLOYERS. He first creates the JOBS table structure, as shown in Figure 2-48 on the following page.

JOBS table

Field Name	Data Type	Input/Display Field Size	Description
Job Order	counter	5	primary key; unique number assigned to the job position
Employer ID	text	4	foreign key
Job Title	text	30	
Wage	currency	6	rate per hour
Hours	number	2	Integer field size; hours per week

Figure 2-48

Launch Access and do the following:

1. Create a new database on your Student Disk with the name Parttime.
2. Create a new table without using Table Wizard. Use Figure 2-48 to define these properties, as appropriate, for each of the five fields in the table: field name, data type, and description. Define the Field Size property for only the text and number fields, using the Description column in Figure 2-48 to set the Field Size property for the number field.
3. Select Job Order as the table's primary key.
4. Save the table with the name JOBS.
5. Switch to the Datasheet View window and resize columns so that the entire field name can be read in the column heading for every field.
6. Print the datasheet for the table.
7. In the Table Design View window, change the field name Hours to Hours/Week. Add the Caption property Job# for the field Job Order and the Caption property Wages for the field Wage. Resize the columns, if necessary, for the fields in the Datasheet View window.
8. Print the datasheet for the table.
E 9. Using Cue Cards for guidance, move the field named Hours/Week in the Table Design View window so that it follows the field named Job Order. Print the datasheet for the table and then close the Datasheet View window.

Lee next creates the EMPLOYERS table structure, as shown in Figure 2-49.

EMPLOYERS table

Field Name	Data Type	Input/Display Field Size	Description
Employer ID	text	4	primary key
Employer Name	text	40	
Contact Name	text	25	
Contact Phone	text	8	999-9999 format

Figure 2-49

Launch Access, if necessary, and do the following:

10. Open the database named Parttime.mdb on your Student Disk.
11. Create a new table without using Table Wizard. Use Figure 2-49 to define these properties, as appropriate, for each of the four fields in the table: field name, data type, description, and field size.
12. Select Employer ID as the primary key and then save the table with the name EMPLOYERS.
13. Switch to the Datasheet View window and resize columns so that the entire field name can be read in the column heading for every field.
14. Print the datasheet for the table and then close the Parttime database.

4.   **Rexville Business Licenses**

Chester Pearce works as a clerk in the town hall in Rexville, North Dakota. He has just been assigned responsibility for maintaining the licenses issued to businesses in the town. He learns that the town issues over 30 different types of licenses to over 1,500 businesses, and that most licenses must be renewed annually by March 1.

The clerk formerly responsible for the processing gives Chester the license information in two full boxes of file folders. Chester has been using a computer to help him with his other work, so he designs a database to keep track of the town's business licenses. When he completes his database design, he has two tables to create. One table, named LICENSES, contains data about the different types of business licenses the town issues. The second table, named BUSINESSES, contains data about all the businesses in town. Chester first creates the LICENSES table structure, as shown in Figure 2-50.

LICENSES table

Field Name	Data Type	Input/Display Field Size	Description
License Type	text	2	primary key
License Name	text	60	license description
Basic Cost	currency	4	cost of the license

Figure 2-50

Launch Access and do the following:
1. Create a new database on your Student Disk with the name Buslic.
2. Create a new table without using Table Wizard. Use Figure 2-50 to define these properties, as appropriate, for each of the three fields in the table: field name, data type, and description. Define the Field Size property for the text fields only.
3. Select License Type as the table's primary key.
4. Save the table with the name LICENSES.
5. Switch to the Datasheet View window and resize columns so that the entire field name can be read in the column heading for every field.
6. Print the datasheet for the table.
7. In the Table Design View window, change the field name License Name to License Description. Add the Caption property License Code for the field License Type. Change the Decimal Places property of the field Basic Cost from Auto to 0. Resize the columns, if necessary, for the fields in the Datasheet View window.
8. Print the datasheet for the table and then close the Datasheet View window.

Chester next creates the BUSINESSES table structure, as shown in Figure 2-51.

BUSINESSES table

Field Name	Data Type	Input/Display Field Size	Description
Business ID	counter	4	primary key; unique number assigned to a business
Business Name	text	35	official business name
Street Number	number	4	business street number; Integer field size
Street Name	text	25	
Proprietor	text	25	business owner name
Phone Number	text	8	999-9999 format

Figure 2-51

Launch Access, if necessary, and do the following:

9. Open the database named Buslic.mdb on your Student Disk.

10. Create a new table without using Table Wizard. Use Figure 2-51 to define these properties, as appropriate, for each of the six fields in the table: field name, data type, description, and field size. Define the Field Size property for only the text and number fields, using the Description column in Figure 2-51 to set the Field Size property for the number field.

11. Select Business ID as the primary key and then save the table with the name BUSINESSES.

12. Switch to the Datasheet View window and resize columns so that the entire field name can be read in the column heading for every field.

13. Print the datasheet for the table.

14. In the Table Design View window, add the Caption property Street# for the field Street Number. Resize the columns, if necessary, for the fields in the Datasheet View window.

15. Print the datasheet for the table.

E 16. Using Cue Cards for guidance, move the field named Phone Number in the Table Design View window so that it follows the field named Street Name. Print the datasheet for the table and then close the Buslic database.

Maintaining Database Tables

OBJECTIVES

In this tutorial you will:

- Add and change data in a table
- Move the insertion and selection points
- Change table structure and datasheet properties
- Delete records from a table
- Import data
- Delete and rename a table
- Find field values in a table
- Replace data in a table
- Sort records in a datasheet
- Print table documentation
- Back up and compact a database

Maintaining the WRITERS Table at Vision Publishers

Vision Publishers Special projects editor Elena Sanchez meets with the production staff of Vision Publishers to set the schedule for the special 25th-anniversary issue of *Business Perspective*. After the meeting, she plans the work she needs to do with the WRITERS table. Because Elena has already created the WRITERS table structure, she is ready to enter the writers' data.

Based on her prior experience working with databases, Elena decides to enter only three records into the WRITERS table. Then she will review the table structure and the datasheet. If she finds a difference between a field's values and its definition, she will change the table structure to correct the problem. For example, if Elena defined the field size for a text field as 25 characters and finds some field values as large as 30 characters, she can change the field size to 30. Elena might also need to change the table's datasheet. For example, if a field's column is too narrow to show the entire field value, she can resize the datasheet column to make it wider.

Elena plans to confirm her list of writers and articles for the special magazine issue with president Brian Murphy and managing editor Judith Rossi before entering the remaining records into the WRITERS table. Finally, Elena will examine the WRITERS table records and correct any errors she finds. Elena takes her written plan, as shown in Figure 3-1, to her computer and starts her work with the WRITERS table.

WRITERS table task list:
    Enter complete information for three writers
    Change the table structure, if necessary
    Change the table datasheet, if necessary
    Confirm the WRITERS table data
    Enter complete information for remaining
        writers
    Correct errors

Figure 3-1
Elena's task list for the
WRITERS table

Updating a Database

Elena built the table structure for the WRITERS table by defining the table's fields and their properties. Before the Issue25 database can provide useful and accurate information, however, Elena must update the database. **Updating a database**, or **maintaining a database**, is the process of adding, changing, and deleting records in database tables to keep them current and accurate.

Recall that the first step in creating a database is carefully planning the contents of the table structures. Similarly, the first step in updating a database is planning the field and record modifications that are needed. For example, preparing a task list of modifications was Elena's first step in updating the WRITERS table. In this tutorial, you will learn how to update the tables in a database.

Adding Records

When you initially create a database, adding records to the tables is the first step in updating a database. You also add records whenever you encounter new occurrences of the entities represented by the tables. At Vision Publishers, for example, an editorial assistant adds one record to the MAGAZINE ARTICLES table for each article in a new issue of one of its five magazines.

Using the Datasheet to Enter Data

In Tutorial 1 you used the Datasheet View window to view a table's records. You can also use a table's datasheet to update a table by adding, changing, and deleting its records. As her first step in updating the Issue25 database, for example, Elena adds to the WRITERS table the three records shown in Figure 3-2. She uses the WRITERS table datasheet to enter these records.

WRITERS table data

	Writer ID	Last Name	First Name	Writer Phone	Last Contact Date	Freelancer	Amount
Record 1:	N425	Nilsson	Tonya	(909) 702-4082	7/9/77	No	$0
Record 2:	S260	Seeger	Wilhelm	(706) 423-0932	12/24/93	Yes	$350
Record 3:	S365	Sterns	Steven B.	(710) 669-6518	12/13/84	No	$0

Figure 3-2
The first three
WRITERS table
records

Let's add the same three records to the WRITERS table. If you have not done so, place your Student Disk in the appropriate drive, launch Access, open the Issue25 database on your Student Disk, maximize the Database window, click the WRITERS table, and then click the Open command button. The Datasheet View window appears, and the insertion point is at the beginning of the Writer ID field for the first record.

To add records in a table's datasheet:

❶ Type **N425**, which is the first record's Writer ID field value, and press **[Tab]**. Each time you press **[Tab]**, the insertion point moves to the right to the next field in the record.

❷ Continue to enter the field values for all three records shown in Figure 3-2. For the Writer Phone field values, type the digits only. Access automatically supplies the parentheses, spaces, and hyphens from the field's input mask. If the value for the Freelancer field is the default value Yes, simply press **[Tab]** to accept the displayed value and move to the next field. Press **[Tab]** to move from the Amount field in the first two rows to the start of the next record, but do not press **[Tab]** after typing the Amount field for the third record. See Figure 3-3.

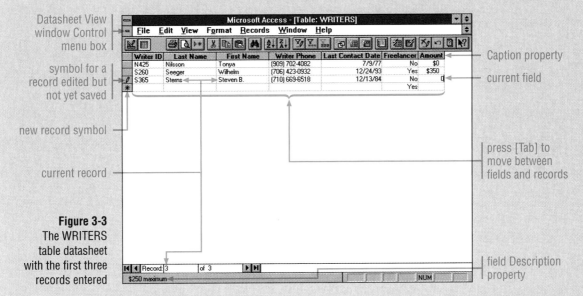

Datasheet View window Control menu box — symbol for a record edited but not yet saved — new record symbol — current record

Caption property — current field — press [Tab] to move between fields and records — field Description property

Figure 3-3
The WRITERS
table datasheet
with the first three
records entered

TROUBLE? If you enter any field value incorrectly, double-click the field value to highlight it and retype the field value correctly to replace it.

Two new symbols appear in the record selectors for rows three and four. The pencil symbol in the third row indicates that you have made changes to the current record and have not yet saved the changes. The asterisk symbol in the fourth row shows you the next row available for entering a new record.

TROUBLE? If the pencil symbol and the asterisk symbol do not appear exactly as shown in Figure 3-3, the insertion point might be in the fourth row. If the current record symbol (a black, right-facing triangle) appears in the record selector for row four, then just observe these two new symbols the next time you make a change. If the pencil symbol and asterisk symbol appear in the fourth and fifth rows, then you should double-click the Datasheet View window Control menu box and click the OK button two times to close the datasheet and return to the Database window. Then click the WRITERS table and click the Open command button to redisplay the datasheet.

Elena has completed her first task, so she continues with the next two tasks on her list.

Changing a Field's Properties

Elena's next two tasks are to change the WRITERS table structure and the table datasheet if changes are needed. Because all field values and field names fit in their datasheet boxes, Elena does not need to change the datasheet. If a datasheet column were too narrow to display the entire field name and all the field values, however, Elena could resize the column for that field to widen it.

The value $350 in the Amount field for the second record catches Elena's eye, because the field's description in the status bar reads "$250 maximum." Elena realizes that $250 is a maximum for each reprinted article and not a maximum value for the field. She changes the field description in the Table Design View window to "$250 maximum per article." Elena also reassesses the field name Freelancer Reprint Payment Amount and decides that Amount would be a shorter, acceptable table field name. This table structure change makes the field name and the field caption the same, so Elena deletes the Caption property for the field. All these changes are field definition changes that are made in the Table Design View window. You can add fields to a table and modify field properties even after you have added data to the table.

To change properties for a field:
❶ Click the **Design View button** to close the datasheet and open the Table Design View window.

❷ To change the description for the field, click the right end of the Description box for Freelancer Reprint Payment Amount, press **[Spacebar]**, and then type **per article**.

❸ To change the field's name, click anywhere in the Field Name box for Freelancer Reprint Payment Amount, press **[F2]** to highlight the entire field name, and then type **Amount**.

❹ To delete the field's Caption property, double-click **Amount** in the Caption text box, click the right mouse button in the same text box to open the Shortcut menu, and then click **Cut** in the Shortcut menu.

Now that she has changed field properties, Elena meets with Judith to discuss the list of articles for the special issue.

Changing Records

During the meeting with Judith, Elena notices some differences between the preliminary and final lists of writers for the special issue. First, Tonya Nilsson, who is one of the three writers she just added to the WRITERS table, is a freelancer and will be paid $450 for her two reprint articles. Elena entered Nilsson as a staff writer, so she needs to change both the Freelancer and Amount fields for Nilsson. Elena also added Steven B. Sterns to the WRITERS table, and he does not appear in the final list. Thus, Elena needs to delete his record from the table.

Changing Field Values

Elena's next task is to change the two field values for Tonya Nilsson in the WRITERS table datasheet. The field values for Freelancer and for Amount are to be Yes and $450, respectively. The Table Design View window for the WRITERS table should still be displayed on the screen, so Elena first opens the WRITERS table datasheet.

To change field values in a datasheet:
❶ Click the **Datasheet View button** 🔲 and then click the **OK button** in the "Save now?" dialog box.
❷ Double-click **No** in the Freelancer column for the first record, type **yes**, press **[Tab]**, and then type **450**. See Figure 3-4. Both field values in the first record are now correctly changed. Access changed the entered value "yes" to "Yes."

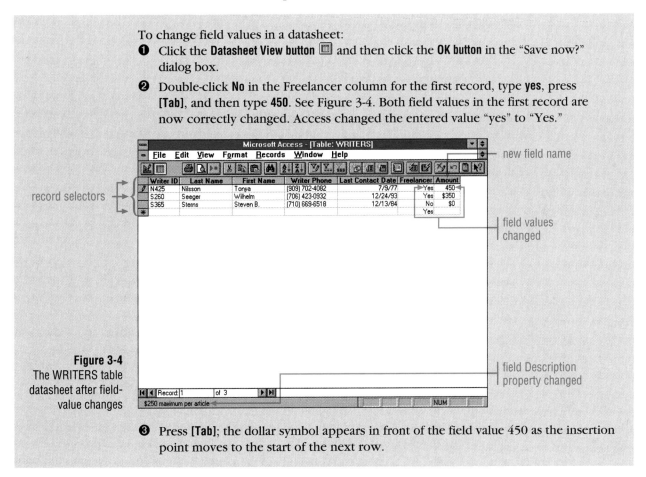

Figure 3-4
The WRITERS table
datasheet after field-
value changes

❸ Press **[Tab]**; the dollar symbol appears in front of the field value 450 as the insertion point moves to the start of the next row.

Access saves the changes you make to the current record whenever you move to a different record. Thus, your data is kept current as you make changes, and you do not need to worry about losing your changes if a hardware or software problem occurs.

Using the Mouse and Keyboard

You use the mouse to move through the fields and records in a datasheet or to make changes to field values. The mouse techniques you use include those for movement, selection, and placement. To move to a specific record in the Datasheet View window, for example, you click combinations of the scroll bars and arrows on the right and at the bottom, the navigation buttons on the lower-left, and the record selectors on the left. Also, clicking a record selector when the pointer appears as ➡ selects an entire row, and clicking a field name box when the pointer appears as ⬇ selects an entire column. You can also select entire field values by clicking the ⇗ that appears when you position the mouse pointer near the left side of a field-value box. Finally, when the pointer changes to I, clicking a field-value box makes that row the current record and places the insertion point at that field-value position.

Let's practice these mouse techniques on the WRITERS datasheet that you are now viewing.

To change the location of the selection and insertion points using a mouse:

❶ Click the **Last Record navigation button** 🔳 to highlight the Writer ID field value in the third, or last, record. The third row becomes the current record.

❷ Click the record selector for the first row when the pointer changes to ➡. Access highlights the entire first record.

❸ Click the **Writer Phone field-name box** when the pointer changes to ⬇. Access highlights the entire fourth column.

❹ Position the pointer on the left side of the field-value box for Wilhelm in the First Name column, and then click when it changes to ⇗. The entire field value is highlighted, and the second row becomes the current record.

❺ Position the I between the 1 and the 3 in the third record's Last Contact Date field value and click. The insertion point appears there, and the third row becomes the current record.

Most Access keyboard techniques are also compatible with those used in a Windows environment, but Access has some keyboard techniques that might be new to you. For example, Access handles navigation and selection through a combination of the usual cursor-movement keystrokes and the [F2] key.

The **[F2] key** is a toggle that you use to switch between navigation mode and editing mode.

- In **navigation mode**, Access highlights, or selects, an entire field value. If you type while you are in navigation mode, your typed entry replaces the highlighted field value. Using a cursor-movement key when you are in navigation mode results in the field value being highlighted in the new location.

- In **editing mode**, you can replace or insert characters in a field-value box based on the position of the insertion point. You press [Ins] to switch between replacement and insertion, which is the default. When you are replacing characters, the right side of the status bar at the bottom of the screen displays the letters OVR, which is an abbreviation for "overtype," and one character is highlighted. The character you type replaces the highlighted character. When you are inserting characters, the right side of the status bar displays spaces, and the insertion point blinks between characters. The character you type is inserted between the characters.

The navigation-mode and editing-mode keyboard movement techniques are shown in Figure 3-5. They allow numerous selection and insertion-point movement possibilities. You can perform moves that involve two keys by holding down the first key and pressing the second key. You will find, however, that using the mouse is faster than using the keyboard. Use Figure 3-5 for reference or if you want to practice some of the keyboard movement techniques.

Press	To Move the Selection Point in Navigation Mode	To Move the Insertion Point in Editing Mode
[Left Arrow]	Left one field value at a time	Left one character at a time
[Right Arrow] or [Tab] or [Enter]	Right one field value at a time	Right one character at a time
[Home]	Left to the first field value in the record	Before the first character in the field value
[End]	Right to the last field value in the record	After the last character in the field value
[Up Arrow] or [Down Arrow]	Up or down one record at a time	Up or down one record at a time and switch to navigation mode
[Pg Up]	To previous screen	To previous screen and switch to navigation mode
[Pg Dn]	To next screen	To next screen and switch to navigation mode
[Ctrl] [Left Arrow] or [Ctrl] [Right Arrow]	Left or right one field value at a time	Left or right one word at a time
[Ctrl] [Up Arrow] or [Ctrl] [Down Arrow]	To first or last record	Before the first character or after the last character in the field
[Ctrl] [PgUp]	Left to first field value in the record	Before the first character in the field value
[Ctrl] [PgDn]	Right to the last field value in the record	After the last character in the field value
[Ctrl] [Home]	To the first field value in the first record	Before the first character in the field value
[Ctrl] [End]	To the last field value in the last record	After the last character in the field value

Figure 3-5
Navigation-and editing-mode keyboard movement techniques

When you are in editing mode, Access supports the usual Windows keyboard deletion techniques, as shown in Figure 3-6 on the following page. If you are in navigation mode, however, using any of the deletion keystrokes causes Access to delete the entire selection.

Press	To Delete
[Del]	The character to the right of the insertion point
[Backspace]	The character to the left of the insertion point
[Ctrl] [Del]	Text from the insertion point to the end of the word
[Ctrl] [Backspace]	Text from the insertion point to the beginning of the word

Figure 3-6
Keyboard deletion techniques in editing mode

Let's practice these deletion techniques in editing mode.

To use the keyboard deletion techniques in editing mode:

❶ If you have moved the cursor, click between the 1 and the 3 in the third record's Last Contact Date field-value box to place the insertion point there and to switch to editing mode. Press **[Del]** to remove the 3 and then press **[Backspace]** to remove the 1.

❷ Press **[Ctrl][Backspace]** to remove the 12/ and then press **[Ctrl][Del]** to remove the /84. The field value should now be null.

❸ To restore the original field value, click the **Undo Current Field/Record button** 🔄 on the toolbar. Access highlights the entire field value and switches from editing mode to navigation mode.

Changing Datasheet Properties

Elena has completed her initial changes to the WRITERS table. Before continuing with her next task, however, Elena changes the datasheet font to a larger size. Because you can create tables with dozens of fields, Access uses the default font MS Sans Serif and the default font size 8 for screen display. The small font size allows Access to display more data on the screen than it could with a larger font size. If your table has few fields, you can make the data easier to read by choosing a larger font size.

REFERENCE WINDOW

Changing a Datasheet's Font Properties

- Open the Format menu.

- Click Font... to open the Font dialog box.

- Select the font from the Font list box.

- Select the font style from the Font Style list box.

- Select the font size from the Size list box.

- Click the Underline check box if you want to select this special effect.

- A sample of the font characteristics appears in the Sample box as options are chosen. Click the OK button to accept the changes in the Font dialog box.

Let's change the font size for the WRITERS datasheet.

To change the datasheet font size:

❶ Click **Format**, and then click **Font...** to display the Font dialog box. See Figure 3-7.

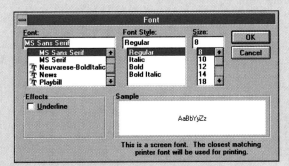

Figure 3-7
The Font
dialog box

❷ Click **10** in the Size list box. The Sample box changes to show the larger font size.

❸ Click the **OK button** to accept the font size change. The Font dialog box disappears, and the datasheet displays the selected font size in place of the original default size.

Access automatically increases the row height to accommodate the larger font size. You can change the row height using the Format menu, but it is usually better to let Access make row height adjustments automatically.

Now that Elena has changed the datasheet font size, she notices that several of the field name boxes no longer display the field names in their entirety. She resizes the datasheet column widths for all the datasheet fields.

To resize datasheet column widths:

❶ Use the Format menu, the mouse pointer, or the best-fit column width method to resize datasheet columns until each field-name box displays the entire field name. Fit the entire datasheet on the screen by narrowing some column widths, if necessary. See Figure 3-8.

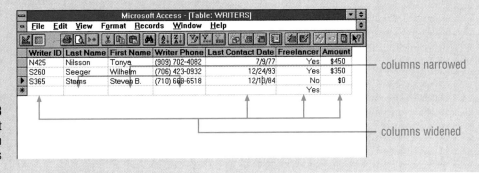

Figure 3-8
The datasheet
after column
width changes

Deleting Records

Elena needs to make one last update to the WRITERS table. Steven B. Sterns should not be included in the final list of writers for the special anniversary issue, so Elena deletes his record from the table.

REFERENCE WINDOW

Deleting Records from a Table

- Click the record selector of the record you want to delete. If you want to delete two or more consecutive records, click the record selector of the first record and hold the mouse button, while dragging the ➡ to the last record selector of the group, and then release.
- Click the right mouse button in the record selector to display the Shortcut menu.
- Click Cut in the Shortcut menu. The "Delete record" dialog box appears.
- Click the OK button to delete the record or records.

Let's delete the third record from the WRITERS datasheet and then close the datasheet.

To delete a datasheet record and close a datasheet:

❶ Click the record selector for the third record. Access highlights the entire third row.

❷ Click the right mouse button in the record selector for the third record. Access displays the Shortcut menu.

❸ Click **Cut** in the Shortcut menu. Access displays the "Delete record" dialog box. See Figure 3-9. The current record indicator is positioned in the third row's record selector, and all field values (except default values) in the third record have disappeared.

Datasheet View window Control menu box

current record to be deleted

Figure 3-9
The "Delete record" dialog box

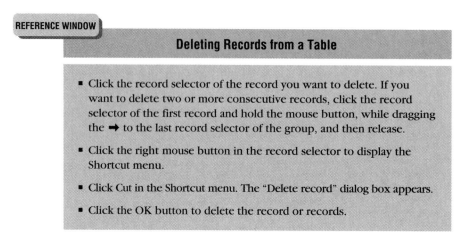

TROUBLE? If you selected the wrong record for deletion, click the Cancel button. Access ends the deletion process and redisplays the deleted record. Repeat Steps 1 and 2 for the third record.

❹ Click the **OK button**. Access deletes the third record from the WRITERS table.

❺ Double-click the Datasheet View window **Control menu box**. Access displays the message "Save layout changes to Table 'WRITERS'?"

❻ Click the **Yes button**. The dialog box disappears, and then the datasheet disappears. The Database window becomes the active window.

If you want to take a break and resume the tutorial at a later time, you can exit Access by double-clicking the Microsoft Access window Control menu box. When you resume the tutorial, place your Student Disk in the appropriate drive, launch Access, open the Issue25 database on your Student Disk, and maximize the Database window.

■   ■   ■

Importing Data

After Elena finishes deleting the table record, she asks Judith to help her add the remaining writers to the WRITERS table. While Judith and Brian were selecting the final articles for the special anniversary issue, Judith was also maintaining a database table containing data about the selected writers. If they use Access to transfer writers' data from Judith's database to Elena's database, Elena will save time and will be sure that the data is accurate.

Judith first verifies that she has all the fields Elena needs for the WRITERS table and finds that their table structures are compatible. Judith will show Elena how to import this special table from the Vision database to the Issue25 database.

Importing data involves copying data from a text file, spreadsheet, or database table into a new Access table. You can also import objects from another Access database into an open database. You can import data from Access tables; from spreadsheets, such as Excel and Lotus 1-2-3; from database management systems, such as Paradox, dBASE, and FoxPro; and from delimited text and fixed-width text files. Importing existing data, as shown in Figure 3-10, saves you time and eliminates potential data-entry errors.

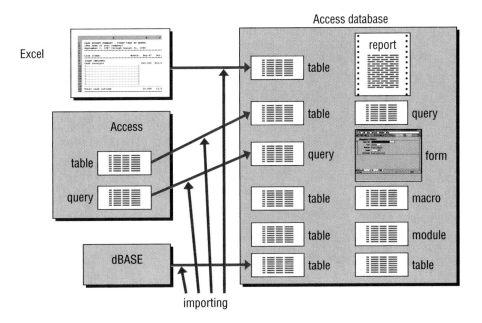

Figure 3-10
Importing data

Importing an Access Table

- Click the toolbar Import button (or click File, and then click Import...). The Import dialog box appears.

- Select Microsoft Access in the Data Source list box, and then click the OK button. The Import dialog box disappears, and the Select Microsoft Access Database dialog box appears.

- Select the drive and directory combination that has the database containing the table you want to import. From the File Name list box, select the database name.

- Click the OK button to accept your selections and close the dialog box. Access displays the Import Objects dialog box.

- Select Tables in the Object Type list box, select the desired table name from the Objects list box, click the Structure and Data option button, and then click the Import button to complete your selections. If you want to import only the table structure and not the table's records, click the Structure Only option button instead of the Structure and Data option button.

- Access imports the table and displays the "Successfully Imported" dialog box.

- Click the OK button in the dialog box, and then click Close in the Import Objects dialog box. Access adds the imported table name to the Tables list box in the Database window.

Let's import the table named "WRITERS tutorial 3 import" from the Vision database to your Issue25 database. Be sure that the Issue25 database is open and the active Database window is maximized.

To import an Access table:

❶ Click the **Import button** ⬛ on the toolbar. Access displays the Import dialog box. See Figure 3-11.

Figure 3-11
The Import
dialog box

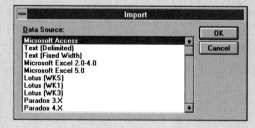

❷ If necessary, click **Microsoft Access** in the Data Source list box to highlight it; then click the **OK button**. The dialog box disappears, and Access displays the Select Microsoft Access Database dialog box.

❸ In the Drives drop-down list box, select the drive that contains your Student Disk. Next, scroll down the File Name list box and click **vision.mdb**. See Figure 3-12.

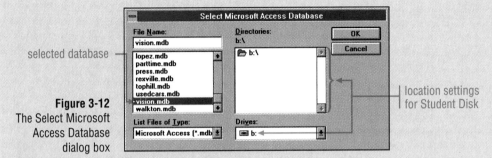

selected database

Figure 3-12
The Select Microsoft
Access Database
dialog box

location settings
for Student Disk

❹ Click the **OK button**. The dialog box disappears, and Access displays the Import Objects dialog box. See Figure 3-13.

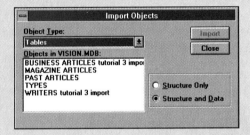

Figure 3-13
The Import Objects
dialog box

❺ The Tables selection should be highlighted in the Object Type list box. If not, then click **Tables** in the drop-down list box. Next, click **WRITERS tutorial 3 import** in the Objects in VISION.MDB list box, click the **Structure and Data button**, and then click the **Import button**. Access imports the table, and displays the "Successfully Imported" dialog box on top of the Import Objects dialog box.

❻ Click the **OK button** in the "Successfully Imported" dialog box to close the dialog box, and then click the **Close button** in the Import Objects dialog box. The dialog box disappears.

❼ The Database window now displays the new table in the Tables list box. If you want, you can open this new table to view its 14 records, but do not update any of the records. When you are done viewing the records, close the table by double-clicking the Datasheet View window Control menu box.

Deleting a Table

Because the "WRITERS tutorial 3 import" table contains the records she needs, Elena no longer needs the WRITERS table. She deletes this table.

Deleting a Table

- In the Database window, click the table that you want to delete.
- Click the right mouse button to open the Shortcut menu.
- Click Delete. The "Delete Table" dialog box appears.
- Click the OK button. The "Delete Table" dialog box disappears, and Access deletes the table. When the active Database window appears, it does not list the table you just deleted.

Let's delete the WRITERS table.

To delete a table:

❶ Click the **WRITERS** table and then click the **WRITERS** table again with the right mouse button. Access displays the Shortcut menu.

❷ Click **Delete**. The "Delete Table" dialog box appears. See Figure 3-14.

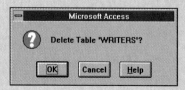

Figure 3-14
The "Delete Table"
dialog box

❸ Click the **OK button**. The dialog box disappears, and the WRITERS table no longer appears in the Tables list box.

Renaming a Table

Elena renames the "WRITERS tutorial 3 import" table to WRITERS.

To rename a table:

❶ Click **WRITERS tutorial 3 import** in the Tables list box and then click **WRITERS tutorial 3 import** again with the right mouse button. Access displays the Shortcut menu. See Figure 3-15.

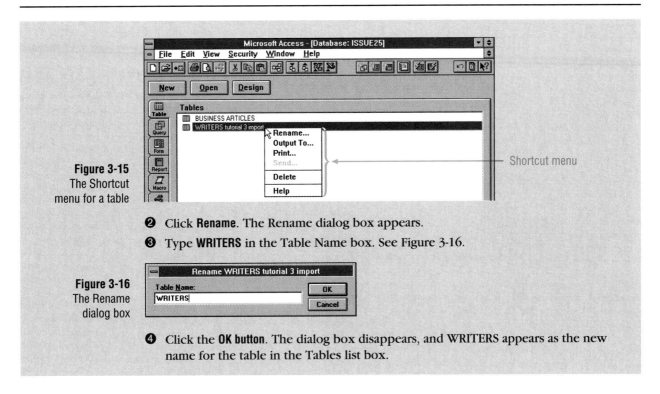

Figure 3-15
The Shortcut
menu for a table

Shortcut menu

❷ Click **Rename**. The Rename dialog box appears.

❸ Type **WRITERS** in the Table Name box. See Figure 3-16.

Figure 3-16
The Rename
dialog box

❹ Click the **OK button**. The dialog box disappears, and WRITERS appears as the new
name for the table in the Tables list box.

Elena next reviews the imported records in the WRITERS table by opening
the datasheet.

To open the WRITERS table datasheet:
❶ Double-click **WRITERS** in the Tables list box. The datasheet becomes the active
window, and the records appear arranged in order by Writer ID, which is the
primary key. See Figure 3-17.

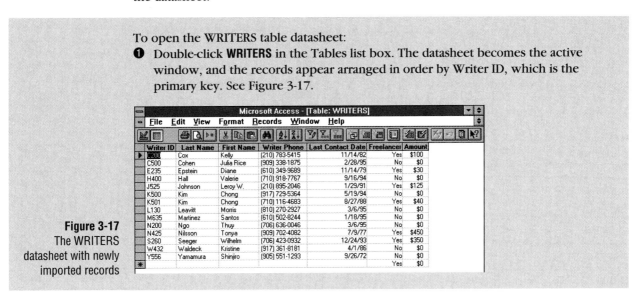

Figure 3-17
The WRITERS
datasheet with newly
imported records

To open a table's datasheet from the Database window, you click the table name and
then click the Open command button. You can also open a datasheet by double-clicking
the table name. Because the second method is faster, you will use it in future tutorials.

Finding and Replacing Data in a Datasheet

Even though records are physically stored on disk in the order in which you add them to a table, Access displays them in primary-key sequence in the datasheet. Finding a record in the WRITERS table based on a specific Writer ID value, therefore, is a simple process. Because of the small size of the WRITERS table, finding records based on a specific value for another field is also relatively simple.

Finding Data

Finding records based on a specific value for a field other than the primary key is not so simple when you are working with larger tables. You can spend considerable time trying to locate the records and can easily miss one or more of them in your visual search. For these situations, you can use the Find button on the toolbar to help your search.

REFERENCE WINDOW

Finding Data in a Table

- Click anywhere in the field column you want to search.
- Click the Find button on the toolbar.
- In the Find What box, type the field value you want to find.
- To find field values that entirely match a value, select Match Whole Field in the Where box.
- To find a match between a value and any part of a field's value, select Any Part of Field in the Where box.
- To find a match between a value and the start of a field's value, select Start of Field in the Where box.
- To search all fields for the search value, click the All Fields option button.
- To find matches with a certain pattern of lowercase and uppercase letters, click the Match Case option box.
- Click the Up option button if you want the search to go from the current record to earlier records in the table, rather than down, which is the default.
- Click the Find First button to have Access begin the search at the top of the table, or click the Find Next button to begin the search at the current record. If a match is found, Access scrolls the table and high-lights the field value.
- Click the Find Next button to continue the search for the next match. Access displays the "End of records" dialog box if the search began at a record other than the first and it reaches the last record without finding a match. Click the Yes button to continue searching from the first record.
- Click the Close button to stop the search operation.

Let's search the WRITERS table for phone numbers that have a 909 area code.

To find data in a table:

❶ Click the **Writer Phone box** for the fourth record.

❷ Click the **Find button** 🔍 on the toolbar. Access displays the Find dialog box. See Figure 3-18.

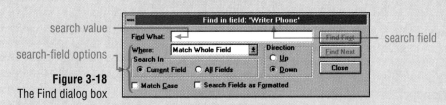

search value

search-field options

Figure 3-18
The Find dialog box

search field

❸ Type the search value **909** in the Find What text box. The left parenthesis, which is the first character of the Writer Phone field, is part of the input mask and not part of the field value. Therefore, searching for 909 at the start of the field is the same as searching for 909 area codes.

❹ Click the **down arrow button** in the Where drop-down list box, and then click **Start of Field** to restrict the search to the first three digits of the Writer Phone field. To start the search, click the **Find Next button**. Access finds a match in the 11th record. Record 11 is displayed as the current record number at the bottom of the screen between the navigation buttons, and the field value is hidden behind the dialog box. See Figure 3-19.

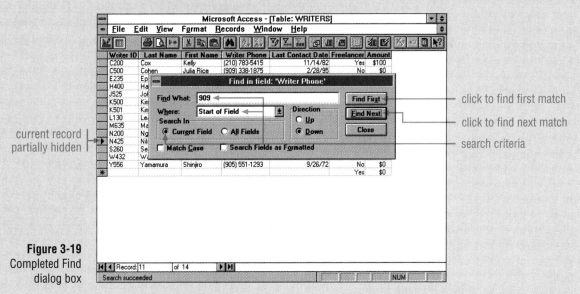

current record
partially hidden

click to find first match

click to find next match

search criteria

Figure 3-19
Completed Find
dialog box

TROUBLE? If the second record becomes the current record instead of the 11th record, you did not click the Writer Phone box for the fourth record in Step 1. Click the Close button in the Find dialog box and repeat your work starting with Step 1.

The Find dialog box remains open and hides a portion of the datasheet. You can move the dialog box so that it covers less critical parts of the datasheet.

To move a dialog box:

❶ Click the Find dialog box **title bar** and hold down the mouse button.

❷ Drag the dialog box outline to the lower-right corner of the screen and release the mouse button. See Figure 3-20.

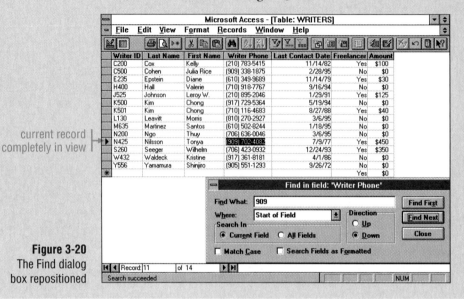

current record completely in view

Figure 3-20
The Find dialog box repositioned

You can now see the entire record found by the Find operation. To find other records that match the search criterion, you continue by again clicking the Find Next button.

To continue a Find operation:

❶ Click the **Find Next button**. Access reaches the end of the table without finding a match and displays the "End of records" dialog box.

❷ Click the **Yes button** to continue the search from the beginning of the table. Access finds a match in the second record and highlights the entire Writer Phone field value.

❸ Click the **Close button** in the Find dialog box. The Find dialog box disappears.

You can use the standard DOS wildcard characters in the Find What text box. Use an asterisk (*) to represent any sequence of characters, and use a question mark (?) to represent any single character. You can also use the number symbol (#) to represent any single digit.

Replacing Data

While verifying the WRITERS data, Judith and Elena notice that the digits 909 appear only in the area code portion of the Writer Phone field. If they need to search for records having a 909 area code again that day, they will not need to restrict the search to the start of the field. They also notice that the two records with 909 area codes should have 905 area codes instead. Elena corrects these values by using the Replace option on the Edit menu. You use the Replace option to find a specific value in your records and replace that value with another value.

REFERENCE WINDOW

Replacing Data in a Table

- Click anywhere in the field column in which you want to replace data.
- Click Edit and then click Replace....
- In the Find What box, type the field value you want to find.
- Type the replacement value in the Replace With box.
- To search all fields for the search value, click the All Fields option button.
- To find field values that entirely match a value, click the Match Whole Field option box.
- To find matches with a certain pattern of lowercase and uppercase letters, click the Match Case option box.
- Click the Find Next button to begin the search at the current record. If a match is found, Access scrolls the table and highlights the field value.
- Click the Replace button to substitute the replacement value for the search value, or click the Find Next button to leave the highlighted value unchanged and to continue the search for the next match.
- Access displays the "End of records" dialog box if the replacement began at a record other than the first and it reaches the last record without finding its next match. Click the Yes button to continue searching from the first record.
- Click the Replace All button to perform the search and replace without stopping for confirmation of each replacement.
- Click the Close button to stop the replacement operation.

Let's search the WRITERS table and replace the 909 phone number area codes with 905.

To replace data in a table:

❶ Click the **Writer Phone box** for the fifth record.

❷ Click **Edit**, and then click **Replace...**. Access displays the Replace dialog box. See Figure 3-21. Because you previously repositioned the Find dialog box, the Replace dialog box is similarly positioned. Your previous search value, 909, appears in the new Find What box.

search value
replacement value

Figure 3-21
The Replace
dialog box

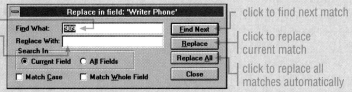

click to find next match

click to replace
current match

click to replace all
matches automatically

❸ Press **[Tab]** and then type **905** in the Replace With text box.

❹ To start the replacement process, click the **Replace All button**. Access finds all 909 area codes in the table and replaces them with 905 area codes.

❺ You might get one or more different "End of records" dialog boxes. For each one, click the **Yes button** or the **OK button**, as appropriate, to close the dialog box and continue the replace operation.

❻ Access displays a dialog box that states: "You won't be able to undo this replace operation. Choose OK to continue or Cancel to undo the change(s) you just made." Access displays this message when more than one replacement occurs, because it cannot undo all the replacements it makes. When this message box appears, click the **OK button** to complete the replacement operation.

❼ Click the **Close button** in the Replace dialog box.

TROUBLE? If no replacement occurred, try repeating the preceding steps starting with Step 2. Be sure the Match Whole Field option is not checked in the Replace dialog box before Step 4.

❽ Preview and print a copy of the datasheet, using the Print Preview button as you have done before.

TROUBLE? If, in the printed copy, a field, such as Writer Phone, contains only parts of the field values, return to the Datasheet View window, resize the column, and reprint the datasheet. Also, if the printed copy takes up two pages, return to the Datasheet View window, resize columns to make them narrower, without hiding any of the field names or field values, and reprint the datasheet.

You can use the standard DOS wildcard characters in the Find What text box, but not in the Replace With text box.

Sorting Records in a Datasheet

Elena will be contacting the writers who are listed in the WRITERS datasheet. She feels she will be more successful reaching those writers having a recent contact date, so she wants to view the datasheet records arranged by the Last Contact Date field. Because the datasheet displays records in Writer ID, or primary-key, sequence, Elena needs to sort the records in the datasheet.

Sorting is the process of rearranging records in a specified order or sequence. Most companies sort their data before they display or print it because staff use the information in different ways according to their job responsibilities. For example, Brian might want to review writer information arranged by the Amount field because he is interested in knowing what the writers will be paid. On the other hand, Elena wants her information arranged by date of last contact because she will be calling the writers.

When you sort records in a datasheet, Access does not change the sequence of records in the underlying table. Only the records in the datasheet are rearranged according to your specifications.

To sort a table's records, you select the **sort key**, which is the field used to determine the order of the records in the datasheet. For example, Elena wants to sort the WRITERS data by last contact date, so the Last Contact Date field will be the sort key. Sort keys can be text, number, date/time, currency, counter, or yes/no fields, but not memo or OLE object fields.

You sort records in either ascending (increasing) or descending (decreasing) order. Sorting the WRITERS data in descending order by last contact date means that the record with the most recent date will be the first record in the datasheet. The record with the earliest, or oldest, date will be the last record in the datasheet. If the sort key is a number, currency, or counter field, ascending order means from lowest to highest numeric value; descending means the reverse. If the sort key is a text field, ascending order means alphabetical order beginning with A. Descending order begins with Z. For yes/no fields, ascending order means yes values appear first; descending order means no values appear first.

Sort keys can be unique or nonunique. Sort keys are **unique** if the value of the sort-key field for each record is different. The Writer ID field in the WRITERS table is an example of a unique sort key, because each writer has a different value in the ID field. Sort keys are **nonunique** if more than one record can have the same value for the sort key field. The Freelancer field in the WRITERS table is a nonunique sort key because more than one record has the same value (either yes or no).

When the sort key is nonunique, records with the same sort-key value are grouped together, but they are not in a specific order within the group. To arrange these grouped records in a specific order, you can specify a **secondary sort key**, which is a second sort-key field. The first sort-key field is called the **primary sort key**. Note that the primary sort key is not the same as the table's primary-key field. A table has at most one primary key, which must be unique, whereas any field in a table can serve as a primary sort key.

Quick Sorting a Single Field

The **Sort Ascending** and the **Sort Descending buttons** on the toolbar are called quick-sort buttons. **Quick sort buttons** allow you to sort records immediately, based on the selected field. You first select the column on which you want to base the sort and then click the appropriate quick sort button on the toolbar to rearrange the records in either ascending or descending order.

Elena uses the Sort Descending button to rearrange the records in descending order by the Last Contact Date field.

To quick sort records in a datasheet:

❶ Click anywhere in the **Last Contact Date column** to establish that field as the current field.

❷ Click the **Sort Descending button** 🔽 on the toolbar. Access rearranges the records in descending order by last contact date. See Figure 3-22.

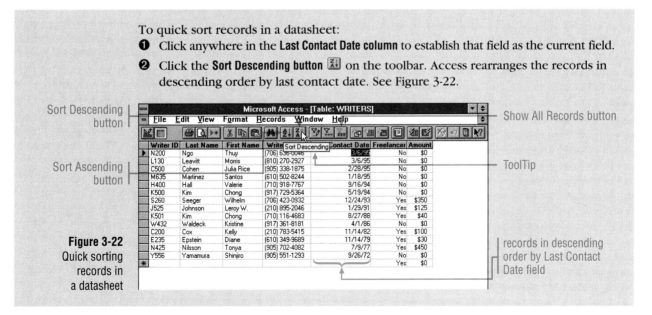

Sort Descending button

Sort Ascending button

Show All Records button

ToolTip

records in descending order by Last Contact Date field

Figure 3-22 Quick sorting records in a datasheet

You can restore the records to their original Writer ID order by clicking the Show All Records button on the toolbar.

To restore records to their original order:
❶ Click the **Show All Records button** 🖾 on the toolbar. Access rearranges the records in ascending Writer ID order.

Quick Sorting Multiple Fields

Access allows you to quick sort a datasheet using two or more sort keys. The sort-key fields must be in adjacent columns in the datasheet. You highlight the columns, and Access sorts first by the first column and then by each other highlighted column in order from left to right. Because you click either the Sort Ascending or the Sort Descending button to perform a quick sort, each of the multiple sort-key fields is in either ascending or descending sort order.

Elena selects the adjacent fields Freelancer and Amount and performs an ascending-order quick sort.

To use multiple sort keys to quick sort records in a datasheet:
❶ Click the **Freelancer field selector**, which is the gray box containing the field name at the top of the column, and, while holding down the mouse button, drag the ⬇ to the right until both the Freelancer and Amount columns are highlighted. Then release the mouse button.

❷ Click the **Sort Ascending button** 🔼 on the toolbar. Access rearranges the records to place them in ascending order by Freelancer and, when the Freelancer field values are the same, in ascending order by Amount. See Figure 3-23.

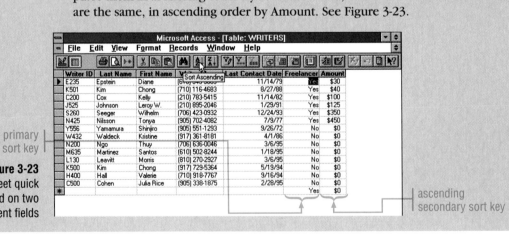

ascending primary
sort key

Figure 3-23
Datasheet quick
sorted on two
adjacent fields

ascending
secondary sort key

Elena does a final review of the data in the WRITERS table and determines that she is finished with her updates. She next uses the Access Database Documentor for the WRITERS table.

Printing Table Documentation

Access has a **Database Documentor**, which you use to print the characteristics of a database or of selected database objects. For a table, Access prints the table fields and their properties.

Let's print the Access documentation for the WRITERS table.

To start the Database Documentor:
❶ Double-click the Datasheet View window **Control menu box** to close the datasheet and activate the Database window.

❷ Be sure the WRITERS table is highlighted in the Tables list box. Click **File** and then click **Print Definition...** to open the Print Table Definition dialog box. See Figure 3-24.

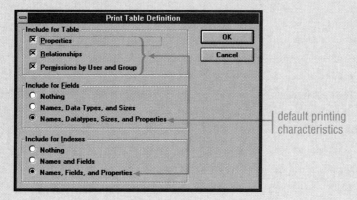

Figure 3-24
The Print Table
Definition dialog box

default printing
characteristics

The default characteristics for fields and indexes are fine. Because she has not yet defined any relationships or permissions for the WRITERS table, however, Elena turns off these check boxes.

To print table documentation:
❶ Click the **Relationships check box** and the **Permissions by User and Group check box** so that these table characteristics do not print.

TROUBLE? If your Print Table Definition dialog box looks different from Figure 3-24, just be sure that only the Properties box is checked and only the radio buttons shown are turned on.

❷ Click the **OK button** to close the dialog box. After a short wait, Access opens the Print Preview window and displays the top of the first page of the documentation. See Figure 3-25 on the following page.

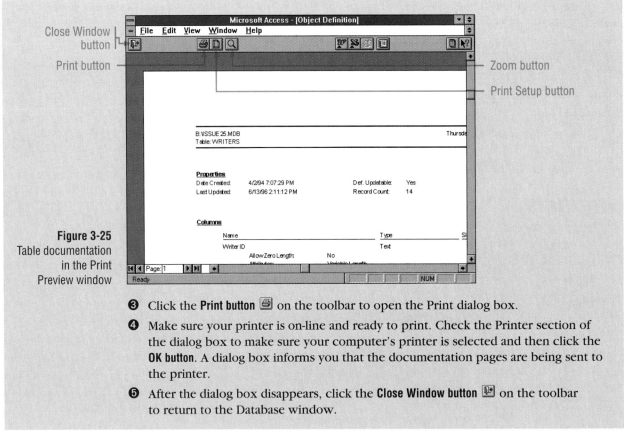

Figure 3-25
Table documentation
in the Print
Preview window

❸ Click the **Print button** 🖺 on the toolbar to open the Print dialog box.

❹ Make sure your printer is on-line and ready to print. Check the Printer section of the dialog box to make sure your computer's printer is selected and then click the **OK button**. A dialog box informs you that the documentation pages are being sent to the printer.

❺ After the dialog box disappears, click the **Close Window button** 🖳 on the toolbar to return to the Database window.

Backing Up a Database

Elena is done with her work on the WRITERS table. Before exiting Access, however, Elena backs up the Issue25 database. **Backing up** is the process of making a duplicate copy of a database on a different disk. Elena does this to protect against loss of or damage to the original database. If problems occur, she can simply use the backup database.

In Access, a database and all its objects are contained in a single file, so backing up an Access database consists of copying the database file from one disk to another disk. Before backing up a database file, however, you must close the database in Access.

Access does not have its own backup command, so you use the Windows File Manager to back up an Access database from one disk to another disk. If you have both a drive A and drive B, you copy the Issue25 database from the drive containing your Student Disk to the other drive. If you have a drive A but not a drive B, however, you copy the Issue25 database from your Student Disk in drive A to the hard disk. Next, you place a different disk, which serves as the backup disk, in drive A and move the database to it from the hard disk.

Let's back up the Issue25 database from your Student Disk to your backup disk.

To back up a database:

❶ Double-click the Database window **Control menu box** to close the Issue25 database.

❷ Switch to the Windows Program Manager without exiting Access using **[Alt] [Tab]**, and launch File Manager.

❸ Copy the issue25.mdb file from your Student Disk to a backup disk, using the procedure appropriate for your disk configuration.

❹ Exit File Manager.

❺ Be sure that your Student Disk is in the same drive you've been using for your Access work.

❻ Switch back to Access. The Access window is the active window.

Compacting a Database

Elena deleted a record from the WRITERS table during her updating work. She knows that, when records are deleted in Access, the space occupied by the deleted records does not become available for other records. The same is true if an object, such as a form or report, is deleted. To make the space available, you must compact the database. When you **compact a database**, Access removes deleted records and objects and creates a smaller version of the database. Unlike backing up a database, which you do to protect your database against loss or damage, you compact a database to make it smaller, thereby making more space available on your disk. Before compacting a database, you must close it.

REFERENCE WINDOW

Compacting a Database

- Close any database you are using, so that the Microsoft Access window is active.

- Click File, and then click Compact Database... to open the Database to Compact From dialog box.

- In the Drives list box and in the Directories list box, select the drive and directory that contain the database you want to compact.

- In the File Name list box, select the database you want to compact.

- Click the OK button. Access closes the Database to Compact From dialog box and opens the Database to Compact Into dialog box.

- In the Drives list box and in the Directories list box, select the drive and directory for the location of the compacted form of the database.

- Type the name you want to assign to the compacted form of the database.

- Click the OK button. The Database to Compact Into dialog box disappears, and Access starts compacting the database.

- If you use the same name for both the original and compacted database, Access displays the message "Replace existing file?" Click Yes to continue compacting the database.

- After the database compacting is complete, Access returns you to the Microsoft Access window.

Elena compacts the Issue25 database before exiting Access. Because she has just made a backup copy, she uses Issue25 as the compacted database name. You can use the same name, or a different name, for your original and compacted databases. If you use the same name, you should back up the original database first in case a hardware or software malfunction occurs in the middle of the compacting process.

Let's compact the Issue25 database and then exit Access.

To compact a database:

❶ Click **File**, and then click **Compact Database....** Access displays the Database to Compact From dialog box. See Figure 3-26.

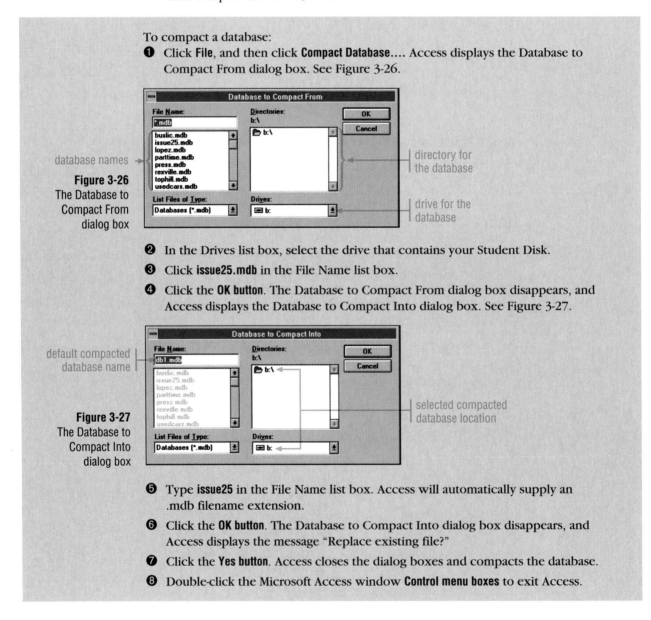

Figure 3-26
The Database to Compact From dialog box

database names →

directory for the database

drive for the database

❷ In the Drives list box, select the drive that contains your Student Disk.

❸ Click **issue25.mdb** in the File Name list box.

❹ Click the **OK button**. The Database to Compact From dialog box disappears, and Access displays the Database to Compact Into dialog box. See Figure 3-27.

default compacted database name

Figure 3-27
The Database to Compact Into dialog box

selected compacted database location

❺ Type **issue25** in the File Name list box. Access will automatically supply an .mdb filename extension.

❻ Click the **OK button**. The Database to Compact Into dialog box disappears, and Access displays the message "Replace existing file?"

❼ Click the **Yes button**. Access closes the dialog boxes and compacts the database.

❽ Double-click the Microsoft Access window **Control menu boxes** to exit Access.

Elena has finished updating the WRITERS table. In the next tutorial, she will use the Access query feature to answer questions about the data in the WRITERS table.

Questions

1. What operations are performed when you update a database?
2. What does a pencil symbol signify in a record selector? What does an asterisk symbol signify in a record selector?

E 3. You can use the Format menu to hide columns in a datasheet. Use the Access Help system to learn a reason for hiding columns in a datasheet.

4. When you make changes to a field value, what mode are you in when an entire field is highlighted? What mode do you change to if you then press [F2]?
5. When you change a datasheet's font size, what other datasheet property is automatically changed?

E 6. Use the Access Help system to document for your instructor the difference between exporting and importing.

7. In what sequence are records displayed in a datasheet?
8. When might you consider using a secondary sort key?
9. What is the Database Documentor?
10. How many different files do you copy when you back up one Access database?

E 11. Use Cue Cards to document for your instructor how to save changes to a record without moving to another record.

E 12. Use Cue Cards to find out which update operations you cannot undo.

13. What is the purpose of compacting a database?

Tutorial Assignments

Elena imports one of Judith's Vision database tables to replace her BUSINESS ARTICLES table in the Issue25 database. After importing the table, Elena adds, changes, and deletes date in the BUSINESS ARTICLES table.

Launch Access, open the Issue25 database on your Student Disk, maximize the Database window, and do the following:

1. Delete the BUSINESS ARTICLES table.
2. Import the "BUSINESS ARTICLES tutorial 3 import" table from the Vision database on your Student Disk.
3. Change the table name "BUSINESS ARTICLES tutorial 3 import" to BUSINESS ARTICLES.
4. Open the BUSINESS ARTICLES table. It should contain 23 records.
5. Print the BUSINESS ARTICLES datasheet.
6. Delete the third record, which is an article that appeared in a 1972 issue.
7. In the Type field, change the type of the 1988 article from LAW to POL.
8. Switch to the Table Design View window. Make the row for the Issue of Business Perspective field the current field, click in its Format property box, and start the Access Help system. Click Search..., type date/time, click the Show Topics button, click Format Property, and then click the Go To button. Next, click the Date/Time Data Types jump and read the explanation about the date/time format "yyyy mmm." Exit the Access Help system, switch back to the Datasheet View window, and observe the format of the field values in the Issue column.
9. Add the three new records shown in Figure 3-28 on the following page to the end of the BUSINESS ARTICLES table. Notice the format of the Issue field and enter the three new Issue field values in the exact same format.

```
BUSINESS ARTICLES table data

               Article Title                                Type   Issue      Article Length   Writer ID
Record 1:  The Economy Under Sub-Zero Population Growth     BUS    1972 Dec       1020           E235
Record 2:  New York City Fiscal Crisis                     POL    1975 Nov       1477           N425
Record 3:  Toyota and GM Joint Venture                     INT    1983 Mar       1682           S260
```

Figure 3-28

10. Resize the datasheet columns so that all field names and field values appear on the screen.
11. Print the datasheet.
12. Back up the Issue25 database from your Student Disk to your backup disk.
13. Compact the Issue25 database using Issue25 as the File Name in the Database to Compact Into dialog box.

Case Problems

1. Walkton Daily Press Carriers

Robin Witkop has created a database to help Grant Sherman track newspaper carriers and their outstanding balances. Grant starts his maintenance of the CARRIERS table. He imports data to his database and then adds, changes, and deletes data to update the CARRIERS table.

Launch Access and do the following:

1. Open the Press database on your Student Disk and maximize the Database window.
2. Delete the CARRIERS table.
3. Import the "CARRIERS starting data" table from the Walkton database on your Student Disk.
4. Change the table name "CARRIERS starting data" to CARRIERS.
5. Open the CARRIERS table, which should contain 19 records.
6. Print the CARRIERS datasheet.
7. Delete the record that has a value of 10 in the Carrier ID field. This is the record for Joe Carrasco.
8. In the Last Name field of the record having a Carrier ID value of 11, change Thompson to Thomson.
9. Make the following changes to the record that has a Carrier ID value of 17, which is the record for Bradley Slachter: change the First Name field to Sean; change the Birthdate field value 3/4/79 to 3/14/79.
10. Add the two new records shown in Figure 3-29 to the end of the CARRIERS table. Because Access automatically controls fields that are assigned a counter data type, press [Tab] instead of typing a field value in the Carrier ID field.

```
CARRIERS table data

            Carrier ID   Last Name   First Name   Carrier Phone   Birthdate
Record 1:      20        Rivera      Nelia        281-3787        6/3/80
Record 2:      21        Hansen      Gunnar       949-6745        4/30/81
```

Figure 3-29

11. Resize the datasheet columns, if necessary, so that all field names and field values appear on the screen.
12. Print the datasheet.
13. Back up the Press database from your Student Disk to your backup disk.
14. Compact the Press database using Press as the File Name in the Database to Compact Into dialog box.

2. Lopez Used Cars

Maria and Hector Lopez have created a database to track their used-car inventory in the lots they own throughout Texas. They start their maintenance of the USED CARS table. They import data and then add, change, and delete data to update the USED CARS table.

Launch Access and do the following:

1. Open the Usedcars database on your Student Disk and maximize the Database window.
2. Delete the USED CARS table.
3. Import the "USED CARS starting data" table from the Lopez database on your Student Disk.
4. Change the table name "USED CARS starting data" to USED CARS.
5. Open the USED CARS table. It should contain 25 records.
6. Print the USED CARS datasheet.
7. Delete the record that has the value JT4AA in the Vehicle ID field. The record is for a Cadillac Fleetwood.
8. In the Cost field of the record having the Vehicle ID QQRT6, which is a Nissan 240SX, change $6700 to $6200. You might need to resize the column to see the entire field value.
9. Make the following changes to the record that has the Vehicle ID value AB7J8, which is an Acura Legend: change the Model field from Legend to Integra; change the Cost field value from $300 to $4300.
10. Add the two new records shown in Figure 3-30 to the end of the USED CARS table.

USED CARS table data

	Vehicle ID	Manufacturer	Model	Class	Transmision Type	Year	Location Code	Cost	Selling Price
Record 1:	MX8M4	Ford	Taurus Wagon	WM	L4	1992	P1	5225	6600
Record 2:	BY7BZ	Subaru	Justy	S2	M5	1991	H1	1900	2700

Figure 3-30

11. Resize the datasheet columns so that all field names and field values appear on the screen.
12. Print the datasheet. If some columns are too narrow to print all field names and values, or if more than one page is needed to print the datasheet, resize the datasheet columns and reprint the datasheet.
13. Back up the Usedcars database from your Student Disk to your backup disk.
14. Compact the Usedcars database using Usedcars as the File Name in the Database to Compact Into dialog box.

3. Tophill University Student Employment

Lee Chang has created a database to help Olivia Tyler track employers and their advertised part-time jobs for students. Olivia starts her maintenance of the JOBS table. She imports data to her database and then adds, changes, and deletes data to update the JOBS table.

Launch Access and do the following:

1. Open the Parttime database on your Student Disk and maximize the Database window.
2. Delete the JOBS table.
3. Import the "JOBS starting data" table from the Tophill database on your Student Disk.
4. Change the table name "JOBS starting data" to JOBS.
5. Open the JOBS table. It should contain 17 records.

6. Print the JOBS datasheet.
7. Resize the datasheet columns so that all field names and field values appear on the screen.
8. Delete the record that has a value of 16 in the Job# field. This record describes a position for a night stock clerk.
9. In the Job Title field of the record having a Job# value of 3, change Computer Analyst to Computer Lab Associate.
10. Make the following changes to the record that has a Job# value of 13, which is the record describing a position for an actuarial aide: change the Employer ID field to BJ93; change the Wage field value $8.40 to $9.25.
11. Add the two new records shown in Figure 3-31 to the end of the JOBS table. Because Access automatically controls fields that are assigned a counter data type, press [Tab] instead of typing a field value in the Job# field.

Figure 3-31

JOBS table data					
	Job Order	Hours/Week	Employer ID	Job Title	Wage
Record 1:	18	21	ME86	Lab Technician	5.30
Record 2:	19	18	BJ92	Desktop Publishing Aide	5.80

12. Print the datasheet. If some columns are too narrow to print all field names and values, or if more than one page is needed to print the datasheet, resize the datasheet columns and reprint the datasheet.
13. Back up the Parttime database from your Student Disk to your backup disk.
14. Compact the Parttime database using Parttime as the File Name in the Database to Compact Into dialog box.

4. Rexville Business Licenses

Chester Pearce has created a database to help him track the licenses issued to businesses in the town of Rexville. Chester starts his maintenance of the BUSINESSES table. He imports data to his database and then adds, changes, and deletes data to update the BUSINESSES table.

Launch Access and do the following:

1. Open the Buslic database on your Student Disk and maximize the Database window.
2. Delete the BUSINESSES table.
3. Import the "BUSINESSES starting data" table from the Rexville database on your Student Disk.
4. Change the table name "BUSINESSES starting data" to BUSINESSES.
5. Open the BUSINESSES table. It should contain 12 records.
6. Print the BUSINESSES datasheet.
7. Change to the Table Design View window. Enter the Caption property value Bus ID for the Business ID field and the Caption property value Phone# for the Phone Number field.

8. Resize the datasheet columns so that all field names and field values appear on the screen.
9. Delete the record that has a value of 3 in the Business ID field. The content of the Business Name field for this record is Take a Chance.
10. In the Street Name field of the record having a Business ID value of 9, change West Emerald Street to East Emerald Street.
11. Make the following changes to the record that has a Business ID value of 8. The Business Name for this field reads Lakeview House. Change the Business Name field to Rexville Billiards; change the Street# field value 2425 to 4252.
12. Add the two new records shown in Figure 3-32 to the end of the BUSINESSES table. Because Access automatically controls fields that are assigned a counter data type, press [Tab] instead of typing a field value in the Business ID field.

BUSINESSES table data

	Business ID	Business Name	Street Number	Street Name	Phone Number	Proprietor
Record 1:	13	Kyle Manufacturing, Inc.	4818	West Paris Road	942-9239	Myron Kyle
Record 2:	14	Merlin Auto Body	2922	Riverview Drive	243-5525	Lester Tiahrt

Figure 3-32

13. Print the datasheet. If some columns are too narrow to print all field names and values, or if more than one page is needed to print the datasheet, resize the datasheet columns and reprint the datasheet.
14. Back up the Buslic database from your Student Disk to your backup disk.
15. Compact the Buslic database using Buslic as the File Name in the Database to Compact Into dialog box.

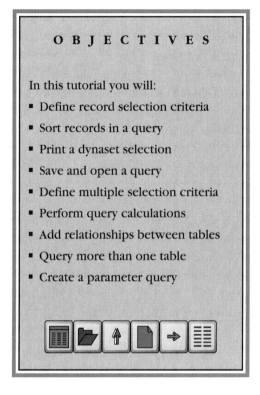

OBJECTIVES

In this tutorial you will:

- Define record selection criteria
- Sort records in a query
- Print a dynaset selection
- Save and open a query
- Define multiple selection criteria
- Perform query calculations
- Add relationships between tables
- Query more than one table
- Create a parameter query

Querying Database Tables

Querying the Issue25 Database at Vision Publishers

CASE

Vision Publishers   At the next progress meeting on the special 25th-anniversary issue of *Business Perspective*, Brian Murphy, Elena Sanchez, Judith Rossi, and Harold Larson discuss the information each needs to obtain from the database. Brian asks for a list of the freelancers, their phone numbers, and the amounts owed to them. He also wants to know the total amount owed to freelancers, the dollar impact of giving all writers an extra $50, and the dollar impact of giving the extra money to freelancers versus staff writers.

Judith and Elena decide to develop writer contact lists based on specific area codes and the last dates the writers were contacted. Because Elena is starting the magazine layout process, she wants to see the article titles and lengths.

Harold plans to highlight the diversity of articles in his marketing campaign, so he needs a list of writers, article titles, and article types arranged by article type. Harold also wants to feature one or two writers in the marketing campaign, and the group decides that Valerie Hall and Wilhelm Seeger should be the featured writers. Elena agrees to get Harold the contact information for these two writers.

After further discussion, the group agrees on a list of questions (Figure 4-1) that they want Elena to answer. Elena will use Access's query capability to obtain the answers.

Answer these questions:

1. What are the names, phone numbers, and amounts owed for all writers?

2. What is the complete information on Valerie Hall?

3. What are the names, phone numbers, last contact dates, and amounts owed for all freelancers?

4. What is the contact information for writers with 706 area codes, for Valerie Hall and Wilhelm Seger, and for writers last contacted prior to 1994?

5. Who are the staff writers and who are the freelancers, arranged in order by last contact date?

6. Who are the freelancers last contacted prior to 1990?

7. What is the phone contact information for freelancers with 210 or 706 area codes?

8. What is the impact of giving all writers an extra $50? What would be the total cost and average cost per writer with and without the extra $50? What would be the total cost and average cost for freelancers versus staff writers with and without the extra $50?

9. What are the article titles, types, and lengths for each writer in order by article type?

10. What are the article titles and lengths and the writer names for a specific article type in order by article title?

Figure 4-1
Elena's questions about the Issue25 database

Using a Query

A **query** is a question you ask about the data stored in a database. Elena's list of questions about the Issue25 database are examples of queries. When you create a query, you tell Access which fields you need and what criteria Access should use to select records for you. Access shows you just the information you want, so you don't need to scan through an entire database for that information.

Access has a powerful query capability that can:

- display selected fields and records from a table
- sort records
- perform calculations
- generate data for forms, reports, and other queries
- access data from two or more tables

The specific type of Access query Elena will use to answer her questions is called a select query. A **select query** asks a question about the data stored in a database and returns an answer in a format that is the same as the format of a datasheet. When you create a select query, you phrase the question with definitions of the fields and records you want Access to select for you.

Access has a set of **Query Wizards** that ask you questions about your queries and then create queries based on your answers. You use Query Wizards for specialized, complex queries such as finding duplicate records in a table and copying table records to a new table. For common queries such as select queries, however, you do not use Query Wizards.

You use Access's Query Design window to create a select query. In the Query Design window you specify the data you want to see by constructing a query by example. Using **query by example (QBE)**, you give Access an example of the information you are requesting. Access then retrieves the information that precisely matches your example.

Access also allows you to create queries using Structured Query Language (SQL). **SQL**, which can be pronounced either "sequel" or "ess cue ell," is a powerful computer language used in querying, updating, and managing relational databases. When you create a QBE query, Access automatically constructs the equivalent SQL statement. Although you will not use SQL in this tutorial, you can view the SQL statement by switching from the Query Design window to the SQL View window.

Access has a set of Cue Cards you can use while working with queries. Although we will not use these Cue Cards in this tutorial, you might find they enhance your understanding of queries. At any time during this tutorial, therefore, select Design a Query from the Cue Card menu window to launch the appropriate Cue Cards.

Creating a Query

Before Elena creates her first query, she compares the tables in the Issue25 database against those in the Vision database. She finds some differences and determines that the tables containing data about articles and article types are more complete and accurate in the Vision database. She imports these tables from the Vision database to the Issue25 database to make her data accurate.

Let's import the same two tables, named PAST ARTICLES and TYPES, to the Issue25 database. Doing so will ensure that your tables are consistent with the remaining tutorials even if you have not accurately completed previous Tutorial Assignments. If you have not done so, place your Student Disk in the appropriate drive, launch Access, and open the Issue25 database on your Student Disk.

To import tables:
❶ Import the PAST ARTICLES table from the Vision database on your Student Disk. Be sure that the Structure and Data option button in the Import Objects dialog box is selected.

❷ Click the **OK button** to close the "Successfully Imported" dialog box. The Import Objects dialog box becomes the active window. Do not close this window because you can import the next table from the same database by continuing in this active window.

❸ In the Import Objects dialog box, click **TYPES** in the Objects list box. Be sure that the Structure and Data option button is selected and click the **Import button**.

❹ Click the **OK button** to close the "Successfully Imported" dialog box and then click the **Close button** to close the Import Objects dialog box. The two new tables now appear in the Database window.

Elena has very little experience working with queries, so she practices with the first few questions on her list. She will not save any queries until she completes her practice. Elena creates her first query using the WRITERS table. She must first open the Query Design window.

REFERENCE WINDOW

Opening the Query Design Window for a Single Table

- In the Tables list box of the Database window, click the table name that you will use for the query.
- Click the New Query button. The New Query dialog box appears.
- Click the New Query button to open the Query Design window.

Let's open the Query Design window for the WRITERS table.

To open the Query Design window:

❶ Click **WRITERS** in the Tables list box. See Figure 4-2.

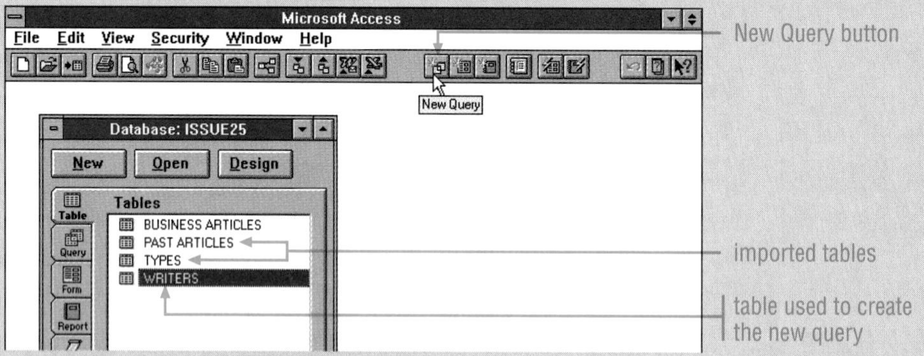

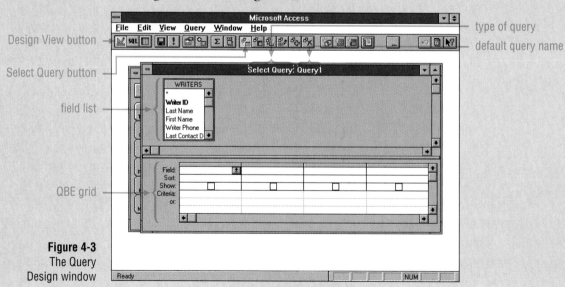

Figure 4-2
Database window
showing
imported tables
PAST ARTICLES
and TYPES

New Query button

imported tables

table used to create
the new query

❷ Click the toolbar **New Query button** 📷 to open the New Query dialog box.

❸ Click the **New Query button** in the New Query dialog box. Access opens the Query Design window. See Figure 4-3.

Design View button

Select Query button

field list

QBE grid

type of query

default query name

Figure 4-3
The Query
Design window

The Query Design Window

The Query Design window contains the standard title bar, menu bar, toolbar, and status bar. On the toolbar, both the Design View and Select Query buttons are automatically selected to identify that you are in the Query Design window designing a select query. The title bar displays the query type, Select Query, and the default query name, Query1. You change the default query name to a more meaningful one when you save the query.

In addition to the standard window components, the Query Design window contains a field list and the QBE grid. The **field list**, in the upper-left part of the window, contains the fields for the table you are querying. The table name appears at the top of the list box. The fields are listed in the order in which they appear in the Table Design window. If your query needs fields from two or more tables, each table's field list appears in this upper portion of the Query Design window. You choose a field for your query by dragging its name from the field list to the QBE grid in the lower portion of the window.

In the **QBE grid**, you include the fields and record selection criteria for the information you want to see. Each column in the QBE grid contains specifications about a field you will use in the query.

If Elena's query uses all fields from the WRITERS table, she can choose one of three methods to transfer all the fields from the field list to the QBE grid. You use the three methods as follows:

- In the first method, you click and drag each field individually from the field list to the QBE grid. Use this method if you want the fields in your query to appear in an order that is different from that in the field list.
- In the second method, you double-click the asterisk in the field list. Access places WRITERS.* in the QBE grid. This signifies that the order of the fields will be the same in the query as it is in the field list. Use this method if the query does not need to be sorted or to have conditions for the records you want to select. The advantage of using this method is that you do not need to change the query if you add or delete fields from the underlying table structure. They will all automatically appear in the query.
- In the third method, you double-click the field list title bar to highlight all the fields. Click and drag one of the highlighted fields to the QBE grid. Access places each field in a separate column and arranges the fields in the order in which they appear in the field list. Use this method rather than the previous one if your query needs to be sorted or to have record selection criteria.

To help you understand the purpose and relationship of the field list and QBE grid better, let's create a simple query.

Adding All Fields Using the Asterisk Method

Elena's first query is to find the names, phone numbers, and amounts owed for all writers. She decides to use all the fields from the WRITERS table in her query.

To use the asterisk method to add all fields to the QBE grid:

❶ The insertion point should be in the QBE grid's first column Field box; if it is not, click that box. Double-click the **asterisk** in the WRITERS field list. Access places WRITERS.* in the QBE grid's first column Field box. See Figure 4-4.

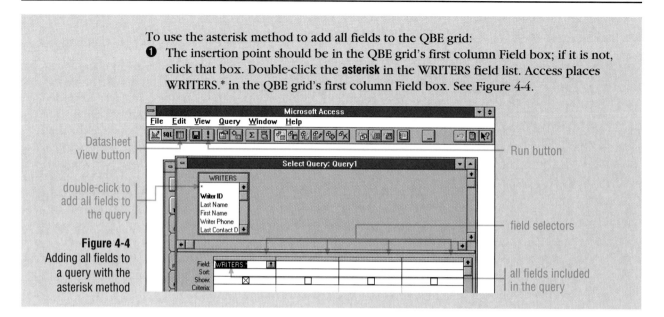

Figure 4-4
Adding all fields to
a query with the
asterisk method

While you are constructing a query, you can see the answer at any time by clicking the Run button or the Datasheet View button on the toolbar. In response, Access displays the **dynaset**, which is the set of fields and records that results from answering, or running, a query. Although a dynaset looks just like a table's datasheet and appears in the same Datasheet View window, the dynaset is temporary and its contents are based on the criteria you establish in the QBE grid. In contrast, the datasheet shows the permanent data in a table.

Elena views the dynaset for the query she just created.

To view a query's dynaset:

❶ Click the toolbar **Run button** 🔳. Access displays the dynaset for the query. See Figure 4-5.

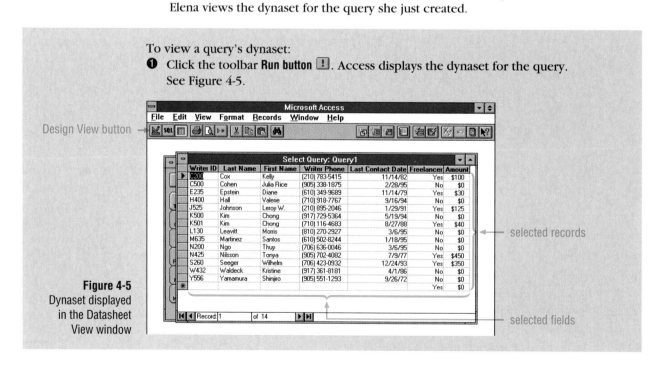

Figure 4-5
Dynaset displayed
in the Datasheet
View window

Viewing the WRITERS table datasheet would have produced the same results as shown in the dynaset because all the fields and records appear in the same order in both. Elena realizes that she did not ask the right question, which was to list just the writer names, phone numbers, and amounts. To change the query, Elena switches back to the Query Design window by clicking the Design View button.

Deleting a Field

You will rarely create a query to list all the fields from a table. More often, you will want to include some fields and exclude other fields. You might also want to rearrange the order of the included fields. Therefore, you seldom use the asterisk method to add all fields to a query. Let's remove WRITERS.* from the QBE grid in preparation for creating the correct first query.

To delete a field from the QBE grid:

❶ Click the toolbar **Design View button** 🖾 to switch to the Query Design window.

❷ The field selectors are the gray bars above the Field row in the QBE grid. Move the pointer to the field selector for the first column. When the pointer changes to ↓, click to highlight or select the entire column.

❸ Position the pointer again in the first column's field selector and click the right mouse button to display the Shortcut menu.

❹ Click **Cut** in the Shortcut menu. The Shortcut menu disappears and the contents of the first QBE grid column are deleted.

Adding All Fields by Dragging

Elena uses another method to add all the fields to the QBE grid. She then deletes those fields she does not need.

To add all fields to the QBE grid by dragging:

❶ Double-click the **title bar** of the WRITERS field list to highlight, or select, all the fields in the table. Notice that the asterisk in the first row of the field list is not highlighted.

❷ Click and hold the mouse button anywhere in the highlighted area of the WRITERS field list.

❸ Drag the pointer to the QBE grid's first column Field box. As you near the destination Field box, the pointer changes to 🖰. Release the mouse button in the Field box. Access adds each table field in a separate Field box, from left to right. See Figure 4-6 on the following page. You can use the QBE grid's horizontal scroll bars and arrows to see the fields that are off the screen.

field-list title bar

multiple-field pointer

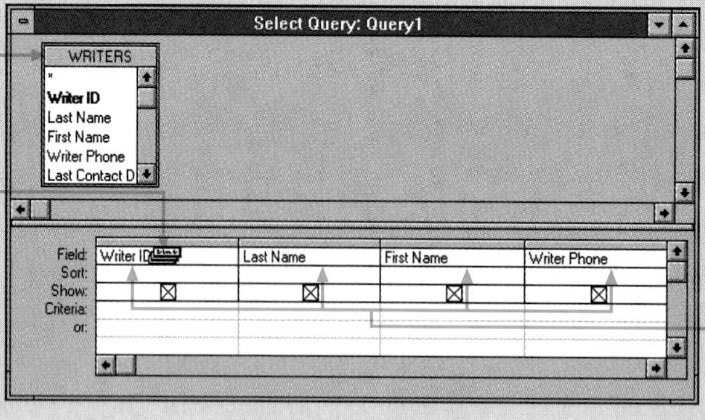

Figure 4-6
Adding all fields
to a query by the
dragging method

selected fields

Moving a Field

Elena does not need the Writer ID, Last Contact Date, and Freelancer fields for her first query. She also thinks viewing the dynaset would be easier for everyone if the First Name field preceded the Last Name field. Elena deletes the three unneeded fields and then moves the First Name field.

To delete multiple fields from the QBE grid:

❶ Move the pointer to the Writer ID field selector in the QBE grid. When the pointer changes to ↓, click to select the entire column. Position the pointer again in the Writer ID field selector and click the right mouse button to display the Shortcut menu.

❷ Click **Cut** in the Shortcut menu. The Shortcut menu disappears, and Access deletes the Writer ID column. The remaining fields shift one column to the left.

❸ If necessary, click the horizontal scroll bar's **right arrow button** once so that the Last Contact Date and Freelancer fields are visible in the QBE grid.

❹ Move the pointer to the Last Contact Date field selector. When the pointer changes to ↓, click to select the entire column and, while holding the mouse button, drag the pointer to the right until the Freelancer field is also highlighted. Release the mouse button and click the right mouse button in either field selector to display the Shortcut menu.

❺ Click **Cut** in the Shortcut menu. The Shortcut menu disappears, and Access deletes the Last Contact Date and Freelancer columns. Access moves the Freelancer Reprint Payment Amount field to the column next to the Writer Phone field.

Elena next moves the First Name field to the left of the Last Name field.

To move a field in the QBE grid:

❶ If necessary, click the horizontal scroll bar's **left arrow button** once so that the Last Name field is visible in the QBE grid.

❷ Click the **First Name field selector** to highlight the entire column. Click the **First Name field selector** again and drag the pointer, which appears as ⬚, to the left. When the pointer is anywhere in the Last Name column, release the mouse button. Access moves the First Name field to the left of the Last Name field. See Figure 4-7.

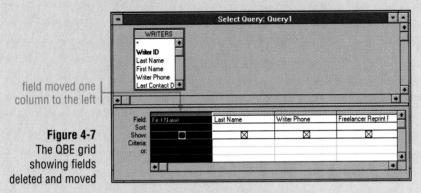

Figure 4-7
The QBE grid
showing fields
deleted and moved

field moved one
column to the left

TROUBLE? If the field does not move, you probably did not drag it far enough to the left. Repeat the move process to correct the problem.

Elena now views the dynaset for this query.

To view a dynaset for a query that uses a subset of the fields from a table:

❶ Click the toolbar **Run button** 🔳. Access displays the dynaset for the query. See Figure 4-8. The First Name field appears to the left of the Last Name field, and the three deleted fields do not appear in the dynaset.

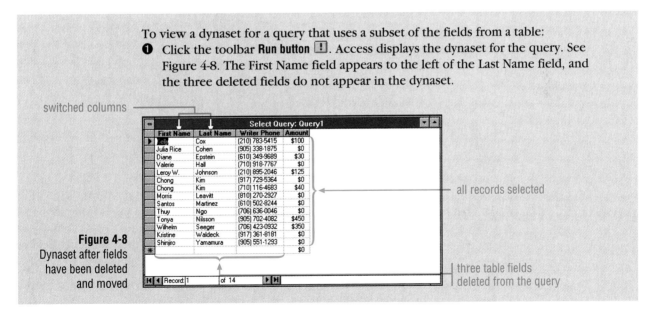

switched columns

Figure 4-8
Dynaset after fields
have been deleted
and moved

all records selected

three table fields
deleted from the query

Deleting and moving fields in the query and resulting dynaset has no effect on the underlying WRITERS table. All fields remain in the table in the order you specified in the table structure design. With queries, you can view information any way you want without being restricted by the table structure.

Inserting a Field

Elena does not need to see the Freelancer field in this first query, but she realizes that others might want the field to appear in the dynaset. She adds the Freelancer field to the QBE grid between the Writer Phone and Freelancer Reprint Payment Amount fields.

To insert a field in the QBE grid:

❶ Click the toolbar **Design View button** 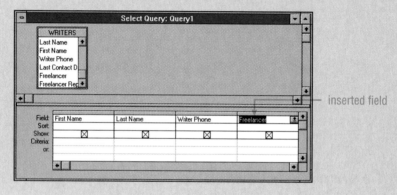 to switch to the Query Design window.

❷ Scroll the WRITERS field list and click **Freelancer**. The Freelancer field becomes the only highlighted field in the WRITERS field list.

❸ Drag Freelancer from the field list to the Freelancer Reprint Payment Amount column in the QBE grid, where the cursor changes to 〈2-int〉, and then release. See Figure 4-9. The Freelancer field is positioned between the Writer Phone and Freelancer Reprint Payment Amount columns. You might need to scroll to the right to see the Freelancer Reprint Payment Amount column.

Figure 4-9
Inserting a field in the QBE grid

Excluding a Field from a Dynaset

When others at Vision Publishers use this query, they will simply run it. When Elena runs the query, however, she does not need the Freelancer field to appear in the dynaset. She knows the writers who are freelancers because they have values greater than zero in their Amount fields. Before she runs the query, she can click the Freelancer Show box in the QBE grid. This removes the ✕ from the Show box and prevents the field from appearing in the dynaset. Clicking the Show box again puts the ✕ back in the Show box and includes the field in the dynaset.

Let's use the Freelancer Show box to exclude and then include the Freelancer field in the dynaset.

To exclude and include a field in a dynaset:

❶ Click the **Freelancer Show box** to remove the ✕. Access will no longer show the Freelancer field in the dynaset.

❷ Click the toolbar **Run button** 〔!〕 to display the dynaset. The Freelancer field does not appear in the dynaset.

❸ Click the toolbar **Design View button** 〔⊠〕 to display the Query Design window.

❹ Click the **Freelancer Show box** to place the × back in the box. Access will now display the Freelancer field in the dynaset.

❺ Click the ▣ to display the dynaset. The Freelancer field now appears in the dynaset.

❻ Click the ▣ to return to the Query Design window.

Renaming Fields in a Query

Elena thinks that Phone Number would look better than Writer Phone as the dynaset column heading for this query. She could change the field name in the table structure. Instead, she renames the field in the Query Design window. You change a field name in the table structure when you want the change to be permanent and reflected throughout the database. Rename the field in the Query Design window when the name change is intended only for that query.

To rename a field in the Query Design window:

❶ Move the pointer to the beginning of the Field box in the QBE grid for Writer Phone. When the I appears on the left side of the W, click to position the insertion point there.

❷ Type **Phone Number:** to insert it before Writer Phone. See Figure 4-10. This name will now appear (without the colon) in the dynaset in place of the field name.

Figure 4-10
Renaming a
field in a query

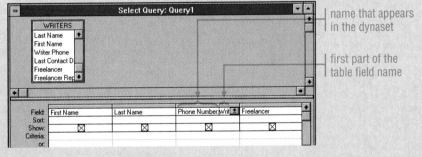

❸ Click the toolbar **Run button** ▣. Access displays the dynaset and shows Phone Number instead of Writer Phone.

TROUBLE? If you omit the colon, Access displays the Syntax error dialog box when you run the query. Click the OK button, insert the colon, and repeat step three.

❹ Click the toolbar **Design View button** ▣ to switch back to the Query Design window.

After practicing with this query, Elena refers to her list of questions for her next task. She needs the Last Contact Date field for the next query, so she adds it to the QBE grid between the Phone Number and Freelancer fields.

To add a field to the QBE grid:

❶ Click **Last Contact Date** in the WRITERS field list.

❷ Drag Last Contact Date from the WRITERS field list to the Freelancer column in the QBE grid and then release the mouse button. The Last Contact Date field is now positioned between the Phone Number and the Freelancer columns.

Defining Record Selection Criteria

Elena's next few questions include showing the complete information on Valerie Hall, listing information on freelancers only, locating writers who have specific area codes, and finding which writers were last contacted prior to 1994. Unlike her first query, which selected some fields but all records from the WRITERS table, these questions ask Access to select specific records based on a condition.

A **condition** is a criterion, or rule, that determines which records are selected. For example, Elena wants records selected if they meet the condition that a writer is a freelancer. To define a condition for a field, you place in the QBE grid Criteria text box the condition for the field against which you want Access to match. To select only records for those writers who are freelancers, Elena can enter =Yes for the Freelancer field in the Criteria row of the QBE grid.

When you select records based on one condition, for a single field, you are using a **simple condition**. To form a simple condition, you enter a comparison operator and a value. A **comparison operator** asks Access to compare the relationship of two values and to select the record if the relationship is true. For example, the simple condition =Yes for the Freelancer field selects all records having Freelancer field values equal to Yes. The Access comparison operators are shown in Figure 4-11.

Operator	Meaning	Example
=	Equal to (optional, default operator)	="Hall"
<	Less than	<#1/1/94#
<=	Less than or equal to	<=100
>	Greater than	>"C400"
>=	Greater than or equal to	>=18.75
<>	Not equal to	<>"Hall"
Between...And	Between two values (inclusive)	Between 50 And 325
In ( )	In a list of values	In ("Hall", "Seeger")
Like	Matches a pattern that includes wildcards	Like "706*"

Figure 4-11
Access comparison operators

Simple conditions fit into the following categories. Do not be concerned about the details of the simple condition examples—they will be covered more thoroughly in the following sections.

- **Exact match**—selects records that have a value for the selected field exactly matching the simple condition value. To find information on freelancers, Elena will enter =Yes as the simple condition value.
- **Pattern match**—selects records that have a value for the selected field matching the pattern of the simple condition value. To find information on writers with 706 area codes, Elena will enter Like "706*" as the simple condition value.

- **List-of-values match**—selects records that have a value for the selected field matching one of two or more simple condition values. If Elena wants to obtain contact information for Valerie Hall and Wilhelm Seeger, she will enter In ("Hall","Seeger") as the simple condition value.
- **Non-matching value**—selects records that have a value for the selected field that does not match the simple condition value. To list contact information on writers having an area code other than 706, Elena will enter Not Like "706*" as the simple condition value.
- **Range-of-values match**—selects records that have a value for the selected field within a range specified in the simple condition. To find writers last contacted prior to 1994, Elena will enter <#1/1/94# as the simple condition value.

Using an Exact Match

Elena creates a query to select the complete information on Valerie Hall. She enters the simple condition ="Hall" in the Criteria text box for the Last Name field. When Elena runs the query, Access selects records that have the exact value Hall in the Last Name field. For text fields only, you need to use quotation marks around the condition value if the value contains spaces or punctuation. For text-field condition values without spaces or punctuation, the quotation marks are optional; Access inserts them automatically for you. Elena consistently uses the quotation marks for text-field condition values so that she will not accidentally omit them when they are required.

To select records that match a specific value:

❶ Click the **Criteria text box** in the QBE grid for the Last Name field and then type ="Hall". See Figure 4-12. Access will select a record only if the Last Name field value matches Hall exactly. You can omit the equals symbol, because it is the default comparison operator automatically inserted by Access.

Figure 4-12
Record selection
based on an
exact match

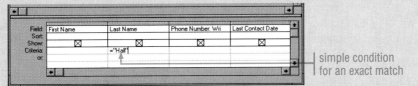

❷ Click the toolbar **Run button** 🔘. The dynaset appears, showing only the record for Valerie Hall.

❸ Click the toolbar **Design View button** 🔲 to switch back to the Query Design window.

Elena's third task is to create a query to show the names, phone numbers, last contact dates, and amounts owed for all freelancers. Before she continues her practice and enters the new condition in the QBE grid, she removes the previous condition.

To remove a previous condition from the QBE grid:

❶ Click the **Criteria text box** for the Last Name field and press [F2] to highlight the entire condition.

❷ Press [Del] and Access removes the previous condition.

Elena now enters the simple condition =Yes in the QBE grid for the Freelancer field. When she runs the query, Access selects records that have the value Yes for the Freelancer field.

To select records that match a specific value of a field with a yes/no data type:

❶ If necessary, scroll to the right in the QBE grid to display the Freelancer column.

❷ Click the **Criteria text box** in the QBE grid for the Freelancer field, and then type **=Yes** (note that you do not use quotation marks in a criterion for a yes/no data type).

❸ Click the toolbar **Run button** ⏺. The dynaset appears and displays only records having the Freelancer field value Yes. See Figure 4-13.

First Name	Last Name	Phone Number	Last Contact Date	Freelancer	Amount
Kelly	Cox	(210) 783-5415	11/14/82	Yes	$100
Leroy W.	Johnson	(210) 895-2046	1/29/91	Yes	$125
Chong	Kim	(710) 116-4683	8/27/88	Yes	$40
Diane	Epstein	(610) 349-9689	11/14/79	Yes	$30
Tonya	Nilsson	(905) 702-4082	7/9/77	Yes	$450
Wilhelm	Seeger	(706) 423-0932	12/24/93	Yes	$350
				Yes	$0

Figure 4-13
Dynaset showing records with Yes in the Freelancer field

❹ Click the toolbar **Design View button** 🖾 to switch back to the Query Design window.

Using a Pattern Match

The fourth question on Elena's list is to find the contact information for writers with 706 area codes. She can do this using the Like comparison operator. The **Like comparison operator** selects records by matching field values to a specific pattern that includes one or more wildcard characters—asterisk (*), question mark (?), and number symbol (#).

Elena enters the simple condition Like "706*" for the Phone Number field. Access will select records that have a Phone Number field value containing 706 in positions one through three. Any characters can appear in the last seven positions of the field value. Because the Phone Number field has an input mask, the displayed placeholder characters are not part of the field value.

To select records that match a specific pattern:

❶ Click the **Criteria text box** for the Freelancer field, press **[F2]** to highlight the entire condition, and then press **[Del]** to remove the previous condition.

❷ Click the **Criteria text box** in the QBE grid for the Phone Number field and then type **Like "706*"**. See Figure 4-14. Note that Access will automatically add Like and the quotation marks to the simple condition if you omit them.

Figure 4-14
Record selection based on matching a specific pattern

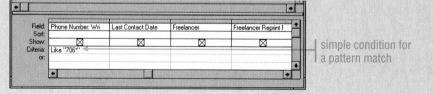

simple condition for a pattern match

❸ Click the toolbar **Run button** 🔲. The dynaset appears and displays the two records having the area code 706.

❹ Click the toolbar **Design View button** 📖 to switch back to the Query Design window.

Using a List-of-Values Match

Elena's next task is to find the contact information for Valerie Hall and Wilhelm Seeger. She uses the In comparison operator to create the condition. The **In comparison operator** allows you to define a condition with two or more values. If a record's field value matches one value from the list of values, Access selects that record.

Elena wants records selected if the Last Name field value is equal to Hall or to Seeger. These are the values she will use with the In comparison operator. The simple condition she enters is: In ("hall","Seeger"). Because matching is not case-sensitive, Hall and HALL and other variations will also match. Notice that when you make a list of values, you place them inside parentheses.

To select records having a field value that matches a value in a list of values:

❶ Click the **Criteria text box** for the Phone Number field, press [F2] to highlight the entire condition, and then press [Del] to remove the previous condition.

❷ Scroll left in the QBE grid if necessary to display the Last Name column. Click the **Criteria text box** for the Last Name field and then type **In ("hall","Seeger")**. See Figure 4-15.

Figure 4-15
Record selection based on matching field values to a list of values

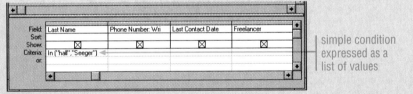

simple condition expressed as a list of values

❸ Click the toolbar **Run button** 🔲. The dynaset appears and displays the two records having hall or Seeger in the Last Name field.

❹ Click the toolbar **Design View button** 📖 to switch back to the Query Design window.

Using a Non-Matching Value

Elena now needs to find all writers who do not have 706 area codes. She uses a combination of the Like comparison operator and the Not logical operator. The **Not logical operator** allows you to find records that do not match a value. If Elena wants to find all records that do not have Hall in the Last Name field, for example, her condition is Not ="Hall".

Elena enters the simple condition Not Like "706*" in the Phone Number field to select writers who do not have 706 area codes.

To select records having a field value that does not match a specific pattern:

❶ Click the **Criteria text box** for the Last Name field, press **[F2]** to highlight the entire condition, and then press **[Del]** to remove the previous condition.

❷ Click the **Criteria text box** for the Phone Number field and then type **Not Like "706*"**. See Figure 4-16. Access will select a record only if the Phone Number field value does not have a 706 area code.

Figure 4-16
Record selection based on not matching a specific pattern

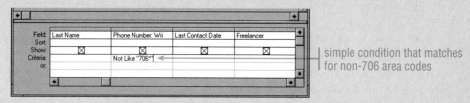

simple condition that matches for non-706 area codes

❸ Click the toolbar **Datasheet View button** 🔲. The dynaset appears and displays only those records having a Phone Number field value that does not have a 706 area code.

❹ Click the toolbar **Design View button** 🔲 to switch back to the Query Design window.

Matching a Range of Values

Elena next finds all writers who were last contacted prior to 1994. She uses the less than (<) comparison operator with a date value of 1/1/94 and enters <#1/1/94# as the simple condition. Access will select records that have, in the Last Contact Date field, a date anywhere in the range of dates prior to January 1, 1994. You place date and time values inside number symbols (#). If you omit the number symbols, however, Access will automatically include them.

To select records having a field value in a range of values:

❶ Click the **Criteria text box** for the Phone Number field, press **[F2]** to highlight the entire condition, and then press **[Del]** to remove the previous condition.

❷ Click the **Criteria text box** for the Last Contact Date field and then type **<#1/1/94#**. See Figure 4-17. Access will select a record only if the Last Contact Date field value is in the range of dates prior to January 1, 1994.

Figure 4-17
Record selection based on matching a value to a range of values

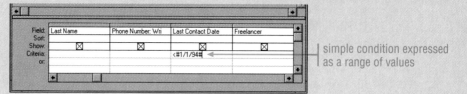

simple condition expressed as a range of values

❸ Click the toolbar **Datasheet View button** 🖳. The dynaset appears and displays only those records having a Last Contact Date field value prior to 1994. See Figure 4-18.

Figure 4-18
Selected records
for writers last
contacted prior
to 1994

First Name	Last Name	Phone Number	Last Contact Date	Freelancer	Amount
Kelly	Cox	(210) 783-5415	11/14/82	Yes	$100
Leroy W.	Johnson	(210) 895-2046	1/29/91	Yes	$125
Chong	Kim	(710) 116-4683	8/27/88	Yes	$40
Kristine	Waldeck	(917) 361-8181	4/1/86	No	$0
Shinjiro	Yamamura	(905) 551-1293	9/26/72	No	$0
Diane	Epstein	(610) 349-9689	11/14/79	Yes	$30
Tonya	Nilsson	(905) 702-4082	7/9/77	Yes	$450
Wilhelm	Seeger	(706) 423-0932	12/24/93	Yes	$350
				Yes	$0

❹ Click the toolbar **Design View button** 📝 to switch back to the Query Design window.

As Elena finishes her query, Harold stops by to remind her of a meeting with the marketing staff. Elena quickly closes the Query Design window without saving the query.

To close the Query Design window without saving the query:

❶ Double-click the Query Design window **Control menu box**. The "Save changes to Query 'Query1'?" dialog box appears. See Figure 4-19.

Figure 4-19
The "Save changes
to Query
'Query1'?"
dialog box

Microsoft Access

❓ **Save changes to Query 'Query1'?**

[Yes]   [No]   [Cancel]   [Help]

❷ Click the **No button**. Access closes the Query Design window without saving the query.

If you want to take a break and resume the tutorial at a later time, you can exit Access by double-clicking the Microsoft Access window Control menu box. When you resume the tutorial, place your Student Disk in the appropriate drive, launch Access, open the Issue25 database on your Student Disk, and click the WRITERS table.

Sorting Data

After the meeting, Elena resumes work on the Issue25 database queries. The next item on her list of questions asks for staff writers and freelancers in order by last contact date. Because the WRITERS table displays records in WRITER ID, or primary-key, sequence, Elena will need to sort records from the table to produce the requested information.

When you sort records from a table, Access does not change the sequence of records in the underlying table. Only the records in the dynaset are rearranged according to your specifications.

Sorting a Single Field

You sort records in an Access query by selecting one or more fields to be sort keys in the QBE grid. Elena chooses the Last Contact Date field to be the sort key for her next query. Because her last Access task was to return to the Database window, she first opens the Query Design window. Elena then adds all the fields from the WRITERS table to the QBE grid.

To start a new query for a single table:

❶ Click the toolbar **New Query button** 🔲 to open the New Query dialog box.

❷ Click the **New Query button** in the New Query dialog box. Access opens the Query Design window.

❸ Double-click the **title bar** of the WRITERS field list to highlight all the fields in the table.

❹ Click and hold the mouse button anywhere in the highlighted area of the WRITERS field list.

❺ Drag the pointer to the QBE grid's first column Field text box and release the mouse button when the pointer changes to 🖳. Access adds all the fields from the WRITERS table to separate boxes in the QBE grid.

Elena now selects the Last Contact Date field to be the sort key.

REFERENCE WINDOW

Selecting a Sort Key in the Query Window

- Click the Sort text box for the field designated as the sort key.

- Click the down arrow button on the right side of the Sort text box to display the Sort list.

- Click Ascending or Descending from the Sort list. The Sort list disappears, and Access displays the selected sort order in the Sort text box.

Elena decides a descending sort order for the Last Contact Date will be the best way to display the query results, and she now selects the sort key and its sort order. She does this by clicking the Sort text box for the last Contact Date column in the QBE grid. Access then displays a down arrow button on the right side of the text box. The text box has changed into a drop-down list box. Clicking the down arrow button displays the contents of the drop-down list box.

In most cases, you can use a quicker method to display the contents of the drop-down list box. If you click the text box near the right side, Access displays both the down arrow button and the contents of the drop-down list box.

To select a sort key and view a sorted dynaset:

❶ If necessary, scroll right in the QBE grid to display the Last Contact Date column. Click the **Sort text box** in the QBE grid for the Last Contact Date field to position the insertion point there. A down arrow button appears on the right side of the Sort text box.

❷ Click the **down arrow button** in the Sort text box. Access displays the Sort list. See Figure 4-20.

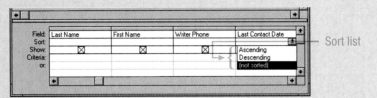

Figure 4-20
Specifying the sort order for the Last Contact Date field

❸ Click **Descending** in the Sort list. The Sort list disappears, and Descending appears in the Sort text box as the selected sort order.

❹ Click the toolbar **Run button** 🔳. The dynaset appears and displays all the fields of the WRITERS table and all its records in descending order by last contact date. See Figure 4-21. Notice that Writer Phone appears in the column heading box instead of Phone Number. Recall that Writer Phone is the table field name that appears in a dynaset unless you rename the field in the Query window.

Figure 4-21
Records sorted in descending order based on last contact date

Writer ID	Last Name	First Name	Writer Phone	Last Contact Date	Freelancer	Amount
N200	Ngo	Thuy	(706) 636-0046	3/6/95	No	$0
L130	Leavitt	Morris	(810) 270-2927	3/6/95	No	$0
C500	Cohen	Julia Rice	(905) 338-1875	2/28/95	No	$0
M635	Martinez	Santos	(610) 502-8244	1/18/95	No	$0
H400	Hall	Valerie	(710) 918-7767	9/16/94	No	$0
K500	Kim	Chong	(917) 729-5364	5/19/94	No	$0
S260	Seeger	Wilhelm	(706) 423-0932	12/24/93	Yes	$350
J525	Johnson	Leroy W.	(210) 895-2046	1/29/91	Yes	$125
K501	Kim	Chong	(710) 116-4683	8/27/88	Yes	$40
W432	Waldeck	Kristine	(917) 361-8181	4/1/86	No	$0
C200	Cox	Kelly	(210) 783-5415	11/14/82	Yes	$100
E235	Epstein	Diane	(610) 349-9689	11/14/79	Yes	$30
N425	Nilsson	Tonya	(905) 702-4082	7/9/77	Yes	$450
Y556	Yamamura	Shinjiro	(905) 551-1293	9/26/72	No	$0
					Yes	$0

Elena studies the dynaset, rereads the question that the new query is supposed to answer, and realizes that her sort is incorrect. The question (Who are the staff writers and who are the freelancers, arranged in order by last contact date?) requires two sort keys. Elena needs to select Freelancer as the primary sort key and Last Contact Date as the secondary sort key.

Sorting Multiple Fields

Access allows you to select up to 10 different sort keys. When you have two or more sort keys, Access first uses the sort key that is leftmost in the QBE grid. Therefore, you must arrange the fields you want to sort from left to right in the QBE grid with the primary sort key being the leftmost sort-key field.

The Freelancer field appears to the right of the Last Contact Date field in the QBE grid. Because the Freelancer field is the primary sort key, Elena must move it to the left of the Last Contact Date field.

To move a field in the QBE grid:

❶ If necessary, click the toolbar **Design View button** 🔲 to switch back to the Query Design window.

❷ Click the QBE grid horizontal scroll bar **right arrow button** until the Last Contact Date and Freelancer fields are visible.

❸ Click the **Freelancer field selector** to highlight the entire column.

❹ Click the **Freelancer field selector** again and drag the pointer, which appears as ▨, to the left. When the pointer is anywhere in the Last Contact Date column, release the mouse button. Access moves the Freelancer field one column to the left.

Elena previously selected the Last Contact Date field to be a sort key and it is still in effect. She now chooses the appropriate sort order for the Freelancer field. Elena wants staff writers to appear first in the query, and they are identified in the Freelancer field by a value of No. Thus, Elena uses descending sort order for the Freelancer field so that all No values appear first. The Freelancer field will serve as the primary sort key because it is to the left of the Last Contact Date field, which will be the secondary sort key.

To select a sort key:

❶ Click the **Sort text box** in the QBE grid for the Freelancer field to position the insertion point there. A down arrow button appears on the right side of the Sort text box.

❷ Click the **down arrow button** in the Sort text box. Access displays the Sort list.

❸ Click **Descending** in the Sort list. The Sort list disappears, and Descending appears in the Sort text box as the selected sort order. See Figure 4-22.

Figure 4-22
Sort orders specified for two fields

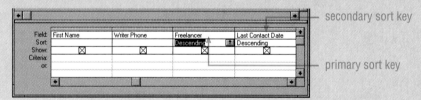

❹ Click the toolbar **Run button** ⊞. The dynaset appears and displays all the fields of the WRITERS table and all its records, in descending order, based on the Freelancer field. Within the two groups of records that have the same Freelancer field value (No and Yes), the records are in descending order by last contact date. See Figure 4-23.

Figure 4-23
Dynaset sorted on two fields

Writer ID	Last Name	First Name	Writer Phone	Freelancer	Last Contact Date	Amount
N200	Ngo	Thuy	(706) 636-0046	No	3/6/95	$0
L130	Leavitt	Morris	(810) 270-2927	No	3/6/95	$0
C500	Cohen	Julia Rice	(905) 338-1875	No	2/28/95	$0
M635	Martinez	Santos	(610) 502-8244	No	1/18/95	$0
H400	Hall	Valerie	(710) 918-7767	No	9/16/94	$0
K500	Kim	Chong	(917) 729-5364	No	5/19/94	$0
W432	Waldeck	Kristine	(917) 361-8181	No	4/1/86	$0
Y556	Yamamura	Shinjiro	(905) 551-1293	No	9/26/72	$0
S260	Seeger	Wilhelm	(706) 423-0932	Yes	12/24/93	$350
J525	Johnson	Leroy W.	(210) 895-2046	Yes	1/29/91	$125
K501	Kim	Chong	(710) 116-4683	Yes	8/27/88	$40
C200	Cox	Kelly	(210) 783-5415	Yes	11/14/82	$100
E235	Epstein	Diane	(610) 349-9689	Yes	11/14/79	$30
N425	Nilsson	Tonya	(905) 702-4082	Yes	7/9/77	$450
				Yes		$0

secondary sort key

primary sort key

Printing a Dynaset Selection

Next, Elena prints the dynaset. Rather than print the staff writers and freelancers together, however, she prints just the staff writers and then just the freelancers. Elena could change the query to select one group, run the query, print the dynaset, and then repeat the process for the other group. Instead, she selects one group in the dynaset, prints the dynaset selection, and then does the same for the other group. She uses this method because it is faster than changing the query.

To print a dynaset selection:

❶ Click the record selector for the first dynaset record and, while holding the mouse button, drag the pointer to the record selector of the last record that has a No value in the Freelancer field. Release the button. The group of records with Freelancer field values of No is highlighted. See Figure 4-24.

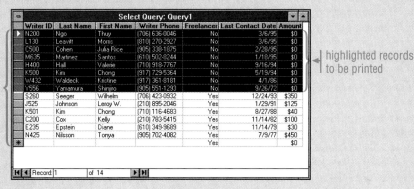

record selectors

highlighted records
to be printed

Figure 4-24
Dynaset records
selected for printing

❷ Click the toolbar **Print button** 🖨 to open the Print dialog box.

❸ Make sure your printer is on-line and ready to print.

❹ Check the Printer section of the Print dialog box to make sure that your computer's printer is selected.

❺ Click the **Selection radio button** to print just those records that are highlighted in the dynaset. See Figure 4-25.

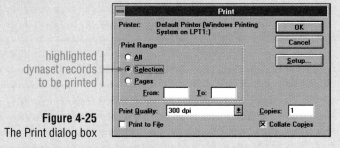

highlighted
dynaset records
to be printed

Figure 4-25
The Print dialog box

❻ Click the **OK button** to initiate printing. After the printing dialog box disappears, you are returned to the dynaset.

Saving a Query

Elena saves the query, so that she and others can open and run it again in the future.

Saving a New Query from the Dynaset Window

- Click File, and then click Save Query (or Save Query As...). The Save As dialog box appears.

- Type the new query name in the Query Name text box.

- Click the OK button or press [Enter]. Access saves the query and closes the dialog box.

Elena saves the query using the name "WRITERS sorted by Freelancer, Last Contact Date."

To save a new query:

❶ Click **File**, and then click **Save Query**. The Save As dialog box appears.

TROUBLE? If the options in the File menu are Save and Save As..., then you are saving from the Query Design window. Click Save and continue with the next step.

❷ Type **WRITERS sorted by Freelancer, Last Contact Date**.

❸ Press **[Enter]**. The Save As dialog box disappears, and Access saves the query for later use.

❹ Double-click the dynaset **Control menu box**. The dynaset disappears, and the Database window becomes the active window.

❺ Click the **Query object button** and then click the **Database window maximize button**. Access displays the newly saved query in the Queries list box. See Figure 4-26.

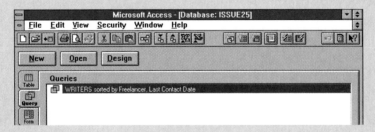

Figure 4-26
Query listed in the Database window

You can use a similar procedure to save a query from the Query Design window. In the Query Design window, the options on the File menu are Save and Save As.... If you try to close either the Query Design window or the dynaset without saving the query, Access displays a dialog box asking if you want to save the query. If you click Yes, Access displays the Save As dialog box.

If you want to take a break and resume the tutorial at a later time, you can exit Access by double-clicking the Microsoft Access window Control menu box. When you resume the tutorial, place your Student Disk in the appropriate drive, launch Access, open the Issue25 database on your Student Disk, maximize the Database window, and click the Query object button.

Opening a Query

Elena decides to use her saved query as a starting point for the next question on her list. She opens the saved query and then changes its design for the next query.

REFERENCE WINDOW

Opening a Saved Query

- Click the Query object button to display the Queries list box in the Database window.

- To view the query dynaset, either click the query name and then click the Open command button or double-click the left mouse button on the query name.

- Click the query name and then click the Design command button to open the Query Design window. You can change the query design in this window.

Let's open the Query Design window for the query saved with the name "WRITERS sorted by Freelancer, Last Contact Date."

To open a saved query to change its design:
❶ If the Query object button is not selected, click it to display the Queries list box. The most recently saved query is highlighted in the Queries list box. In this case, there is only one saved query.
❷ Click the **Design command button**. The Query Design window appears with the saved query on the screen.

Defining Multiple Selection Criteria

Elena's next task is to find all freelancers who were last contacted prior to 1990. This query involves two conditions.

Multiple conditions require you to use **logical operators** to combine two or more simple conditions. When you want a record selected only if two or more conditions are met, then you need to use the **And logical operator**. For an Access query, you use the And logical operator when you place two or more simple conditions in the same Criteria row of the QBE grid. If a record meets every one of the conditions in the Criteria row, then Access selects the record.

If you place multiple conditions in different Criteria rows, Access selects a record if at least one of the conditions is satisfied. If none of the conditions is satisfied, then Access does not select the record. This is known as the **Or logical operator**. The difference between the two logical operators is illustrated in Figure 4-27.

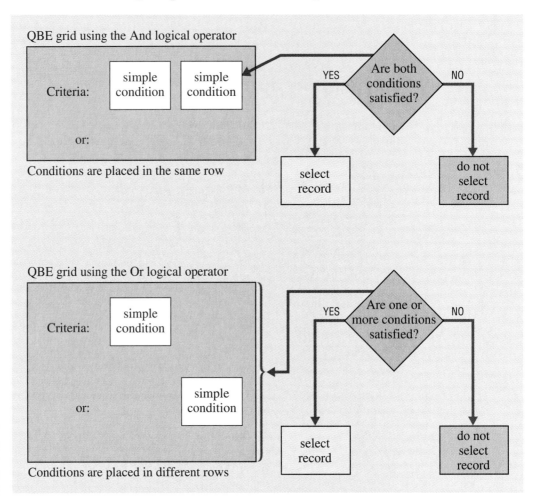

Figure 4-27
Logical operators
And and Or
for multiple
selection criteria

The use of the word "and" in a question is usually a clue that you should use the And logical operator. The word "or" in a question usually means that you should use the Or logical operator.

The And Logical Operator

Elena will use the And logical operator and enter conditions for the Freelancer field and the Last Contact Date field in the same Criteria row. She will enter =Yes as the condition for the Freelancer field and <#1/1/90# as the condition for the Last Contact Date field. Because the conditions appear in the same Criteria row, Access selects records only if both conditions are met.

Elena's new query does not need sort keys, so Elena removes the sort keys for the Freelancer and Last Contact Date fields.

To remove sort keys from the QBE grid:

❶ Click the **Sort text box** in the Freelancer column and then click the **down arrow button**. Access displays the Sort list.

❷ Click **(not sorted)** in the Sort list. The Sort list disappears, and Access removes the sort order from the Sort text box.

❸ If necessary, scroll to the right in the QBE grid until the Last Contact Date column appears. Click the **Sort text box** in the Last Contact Date column and then click the **down arrow button**. Access displays the Sort list.

❹ Click **(not sorted)** in the Sort list. The Sort list disappears, and Access clears the sort order from the Sort text box.

Elena now enters the two conditions.

To select records using the And logical operator:

❶ Click the **Freelancer Criteria text box** and then type **=Yes**.

❷ Click the **Last Contact Date Criteria text box** and then type **<#1/1/90#**. See Figure 4-28. Access will select a record only if both conditions are met.

Figure 4-28
Criteria to find
freelancers last
contacted prior
to 1990

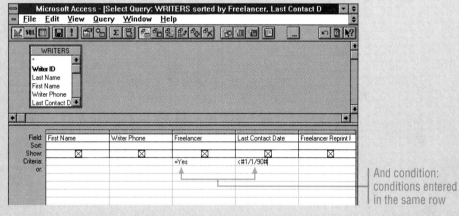

❸ Click the toolbar **Run button** ⬚. The dynaset appears and displays only records for freelancers last contacted prior to 1990.

❹ Click the toolbar **Design View button** ⬚ to switch back to the Query Design window.

The Or Logical Operator

Elena's next query asks for those writers who have 210 or 706 area codes. For this query, Elena uses the Or logical operator and enters conditions for the Writer Phone field in two different Criteria rows. She will enter Like "210*" in one row and Like "706*" in another row. Because the conditions appear in different Criteria rows, Access selects records if either condition is satisfied. The Or logical operator used in one field is similar to the In comparison operator.

To select records using the Or logical operator:

❶ Move the pointer to the left side of the Criteria text box for the first column and click when the pointer changes to **➡**. Access highlights the entire Criteria row.

❷ Click the right mouse button in the first column's Criteria text box to display the Shortcut menu. Click **Cut** to remove the previous conditions from the QBE grid.

TROUBLE? If the Shortcut menu does not appear, you clicked too far from the point where you originally clicked in Step 1. Repeat Step 1 and, without moving the mouse pointer, click the right mouse button once again.

❸ Click the **Criteria text box** in the Writer Phone column and then type **Like "210*"**.

❹ Click the **Criteria text box** below the one you just used and type **Like "706*"**. See Figure 4-29. Access will select a record if either condition is met.

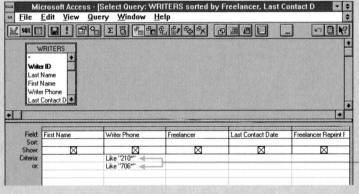

Figure 4-29
Criteria to find
writers with 210
or 706 area codes

Or condition:
conditions entered in
different rows

❺ Click the toolbar **Run button** 🔘. The dynaset appears and displays just those records for writers with 210 or 706 area codes.

❻ Click the toolbar **Design View button** 🔲 to switch back to the Query Design window.

Using And with Or

To make sure that she created the right query, Elena rechecks the question on her list and discovers she misread it. She really should be selecting records for freelancers who have 210 or 706 area codes. In other words, she really wants writers who are freelancers and have 210 area codes, or who are freelancers and have 706 area codes. To form this query, she needs to add the =Yes condition for the Freelancer field to both rows that already contain the Writer Phone conditions. Access will select a record if either And condition is met. Only freelancers will be selected, but only if their area codes are 210 or 706.

Elena adds the Freelancer conditions to the QBE grid to complete her new query.

To select records using the And logical operator with the Or logical operator:

❶ Click the **Criteria text box** in the Freelancer column and then type **=Yes**.

❷ Press **[Down Arrow]** and then type **=Yes**. See Figure 4-30. Access will select a record if either And condition is met.

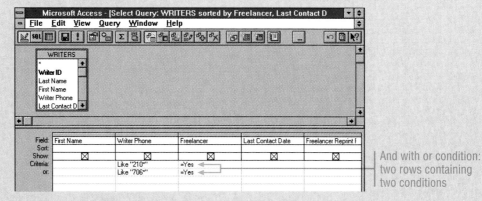

Figure 4-30
Criteria to find freelancers who have 210 or 706 area codes

And with or condition:
two rows containing
two conditions

❸ Click the toolbar **Run button** ⯐. The dynaset appears and displays only records for freelancers with 210 or 706 area codes. See Figure 4-31.

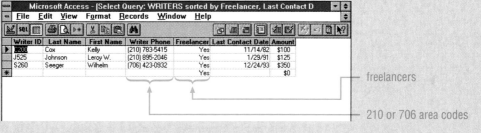

Figure 4-31
Results of a query to find freelancers who have 210 or 706 area codes

freelancers

210 or 706 area codes

❹ Click the toolbar **Design View button** ⯐ to switch back to the Query Design window.

Performing Calculations

Elena's next task is to find the impact of giving all writers an extra $50. This query requires the addition of a calculated field in the QBE grid.

A **calculated field** is a new field that exists in a dynaset but does not exist in a database. The value of a calculated field is determined from fields that are in a database. You can define a calculated field in a query. When you run the query, Access determines the value for the calculated field. You perform your calculations using number, currency, or date/time fields from your database. Among the arithmetic operators you can use are those for addition (+), subtraction (–), multiplication (*), and division (/).

Using Calculated Fields

Elena creates a calculated field that adds 50 to the amount stored in the Freelancer Reprint Payment Amount field. Whenever a calculation includes a field name, you place brackets around the name to tell Access that the name is from your database. Elena's calculation, for example, will be expressed as [Freelancer Reprint Payment Amount]+50. Access supplies the default name Expr1 for your first calculated field, but you can change the name at any time. Elena uses Add50 as the name for the calculated field. Because the Field text box is too small to show the entire calculated field, Elena uses the Zoom box while she enters the calculated field. The **Zoom box** is a large text box for entering text or other values. You open the zoom box either by pressing [Shift][F2] or by using the Shortcut menu.

The new query will select all records in the WRITERS table, so Elena first removes the conditions in the two Criteria rows. At the same time, she decides to simplify the query by deleting three fields: Writer ID, Writer Phone, and Last Contact Date.

To remove conditions and delete fields from the QBE grid:

❶ Move the pointer to the left side of the Criteria text box for the first column. The pointer changes to ➡. Click and, while holding the mouse button, drag the pointer down to the next row before releasing the mouse button. The two rows are highlighted. Click the right mouse button in either highlighted row to display the Shortcut menu and click **Cut** to remove the previous conditions from the QBE grid.

❷ Scroll to make the Writer ID column visible. Move the pointer to the Writer ID field selector and then click it to highlight the entire column. Click the right mouse button in the Writer ID field selector to display the Shortcut menu and click **Cut** to delete the column.

❸ In a similar manner, delete the Writer Phone and Last Contact Date columns in the QBE grid.

The QBE grid now contains four fields: Last Name, First Name, Freelancer, and Freelancer Reprint Payment Amount. Elena next adds the calculated field.

To add a calculated field to the QBE grid and run the query:

❶ Click the right mouse button in the Field text box for the first unused column to open the Shortcut menu.

❷ Click **Zoom...** to open the Zoom box.

❸ Type **Add50:[Freelancer Reprint Payment Amount]+50**. See Figure 4-32.

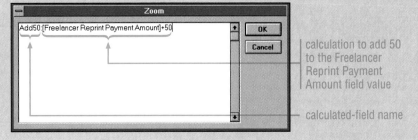

Figure 4-32
The Zoom box
for entering
long calculations

calculation to add 50 to the Freelancer Reprint Payment Amount field value

calculated-field name

❹ Click the **OK button**. The Zoom box disappears.

❺ Click the toolbar **Run button** 🔲. The dynaset displays all records in the WRITERS table and includes the new calculated field. See Figure 4-33.

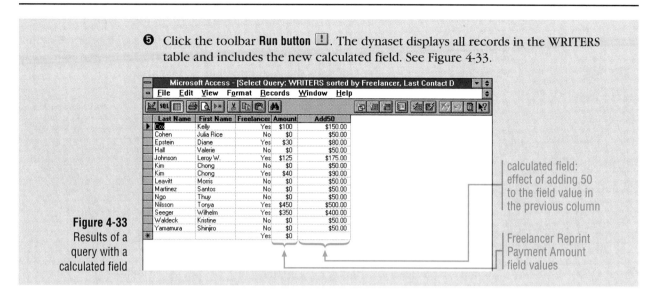

Figure 4-33
Results of a
query with a
calculated field

calculated field:
effect of adding 50
to the field value in
the previous column

Freelancer Reprint
Payment Amount
field values

The calculated field values in the new Add50 column are $50 more than those in the Amount column, which is the Caption property name for the Freelancer Reprint Payment Amount field.

Using Record Calculations

Elena must now find both the total cost and the average cost per writer, with and without the extra $50. For this query, she uses aggregate functions. **Aggregate functions** perform arithmetic operations on the records in a database. The most frequently used aggregate functions are shown in Figure 4-34. Aggregate functions operate upon the records that meet a query's selection criteria. You specify an aggregate function for a specific field, and the appropriate operation applies to that field's values for the selected records.

Function	Meaning
Avg	Average of the field values for the selected records
Count	Number of records selected
Min	Lowest field value for the selected records
Max	Highest field value for the selected records
Sum	Total of the field values for the selected records

Figure 4-34
Frequently used
aggregate functions

Elena uses the Sum and Avg aggregate functions for both the Freelancer Reprint Payment Amount field and for the calculated field she just created in her previous query. The Sum aggregate function gives the total of the field values, and the Avg aggregate function gives the average of the field values. Elena's query result will be a dynaset with one record displaying the four requested aggregate function values.

To use aggregate functions in the Query Design window, you click the toolbar Totals button. Access inserts a Total row between the Field and Sort rows in the QBE grid. You specify the aggregate functions you want to use in the Total row. When you run the query, one record appears in the dynaset with your selected aggregate function values. The individual table records themselves do not appear.

Elena does not need any fields other than the Freelancer Reprint Payment Amount field and the calculated field, so she deletes the Last Name, First Name, and Freelancer fields. She then restores the Query Design window to its smaller size.

To delete fields from the QBE grid:

❶ Click the toolbar **Design View button** 🖹 to switch back to the Query Design window.

❷ If necessary, scroll to make the Last Name, First Name, and Freelancer fields visible. Move the pointer to the Last Name field selector. Then click to highlight the entire column, hold the mouse button, drag the pointer to the right until the First Name and Freelancer fields are also highlighted, and release the mouse button. Click the right mouse button in the field selector for one of these three fields to display the Shortcut menu, and click **Cut** to delete the three columns.

TROUBLE? If the fields are not side by side, delete one column and then the others in separate steps.

❸ Click the Query Design window **restore button**, which is on the right side of the menu bar.

Elena now has two fields left in the QBE grid: the Freelancer Reprint Payment Amount field and the Add50 calculated field. She needs two columns for each of these: one for a Sum aggregate function, and the other for an Avg aggregate function. The four columns will allow her to find the total cost and average cost per writer with and without the extra $50. She inserts a second copy of the Freelancer Reprint Payment Amount field in the QBE grid. She then renames the first Freelancer Reprint Payment Amount field AmountSum and the second AmountAvg. She likewise makes a second copy of the Add50 calculated field and renames the first one Add50Sum and the second Add50Avg.

First Elena adds the copy of the Freelancer Reprint Payment Amount field to the QBE grid and renames all three fields.

To add and rename fields in the QBE grid:

❶ If necessary, scroll to the left to make both fields visible in the QBE grid. Click **Freelancer Reprint Payment Amount** in the WRITERS field list, drag it to the Add50 calculated field column in the QBE grid, and then release the mouse button. The three fields in the QBE grid, from left to right, are Freelancer Reprint Payment Amount, Freelancer Reprint Payment Amount, and Add50.

❷ Click the beginning of the Field box for the first Freelancer Reprint Payment Amount field and type **AmountSum:**.

❸ Click the beginning of the Field box for the second Freelancer Reprint Payment Amount field and type **AmountAvg:**.

❹ Click just before the colon in the Field box for the Add50 calculated field and type **Sum**. The name of the calculated field is now Add50Sum.

Elena next selects aggregate functions for these three fields.

To select aggregate functions:

❶ Click the **Totals button** ∑ on the toolbar. The Total row appears in the QBE grid.

❷ Click the **Total text box** for the AmountSum field and then click the **down arrow button** that appears. Click **Sum** in the Total list box.

❸ Click the **Total text box** for the AmountAvg field and then click the **down arrow button** that appears. Click **Avg** in the Total list box.

❹ Click the **Total text box** for the Add50Sum field and then click the **down arrow button** that appears. See Figure 4-35.

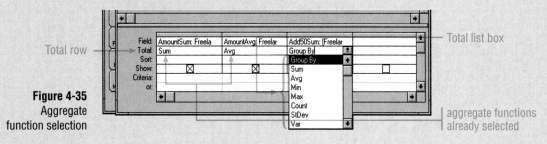

Figure 4-35
Aggregate
function selection

❺ Click **Sum** in the Total list box.

Elena's last steps are to copy the calculated field, paste it to the fourth column, rename the new field Add50Avg, and change its Total text box to Avg.

To copy and paste a new calculated field with an aggregate function:

❶ Click the **Add50Sum field selector** to highlight the entire column.

❷ Click the right mouse button in the Add50Sum field selector to display the Shortcut menu and then click **Copy** to copy the column to the Clipboard.

❸ Click the **field selector** for the fourth column to highlight the entire column. Click the right mouse button in the fourth column's field selector to display the Shortcut menu and then click **Paste**. A copy of the third column appears in the fourth column.

❹ Highlight **Sum** in the Field text box for the fourth column and type **Avg**. The renamed field name is now Add50Avg.

❺ Click the **Total text box** for the Add50Avg column and then click the **down arrow button** that appears. Click **Avg** in the Total list box. See Figure 4-36.

Figure 4-36
Calculating total
cost and average
cost per writer
with and without
an extra $50

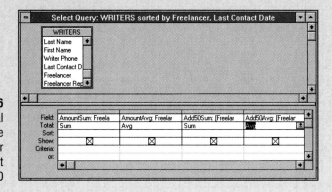

As her final step, Elena views the query's dynaset.

To view a query dynaset:

❶ Click the toolbar **Run button** ⏺. The dynaset appears and displays one record containing the four aggregate function values. See Figure 4-37.

Figure 4-37
Results of a
query using
aggregate
functions

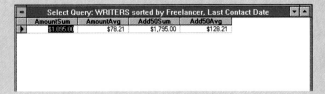

Using Record Group Calculations

Elena has one more query to create requiring the use of aggregate functions. Brian wants to know the total cost and average cost for freelancers versus staff writers with and without the extra $50. This query is exactly like her previous query, except Elena needs to add the Freelancer field and assign the Group By operator to it.

The **Group By operator** combines records with identical field values into a single record. The Group By operator used with the Freelancer field results in two records: one record for the Yes field values, and the other for the No field values. Subtotals for each of the two records are created if you use aggregate functions.

Elena adds the Freelancer field to the QBE grid in the first column, assigns it the Group By operator, and views the dynaset for the revised query.

To add a field with the Group By operator and view the dynaset:

❶ Click the toolbar **Design View button** ▦ to switch back to the Query Design window.

❷ Click **Freelancer** in the WRITERS field list and drag it to the first QBE grid column. The Total text box for the field shows the Group By operator by default. See Figure 4-38.

Figure 4-38
Query using
aggregate
functions on
groups of records

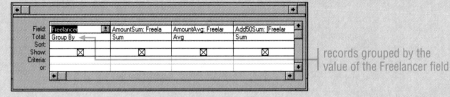

records grouped by the
value of the Freelancer field

❸ Click the toolbar **Run button** ⏺. The dynaset appears and displays two records, each containing the four aggregate function values. See Figure 4-39.

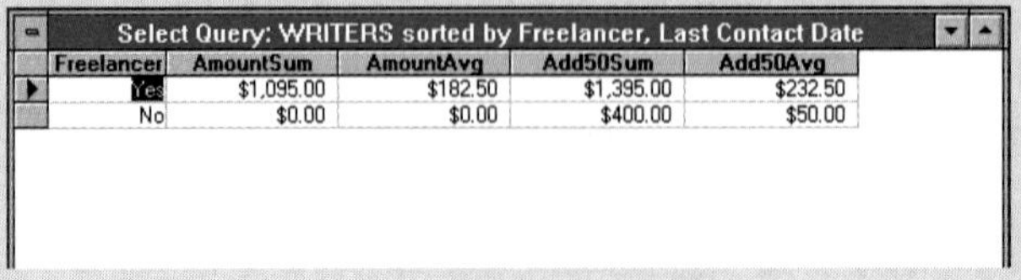

Figure 4-39
Results of a query
using aggregate
functions on
groups of records

Elena has some phone calls to make, so she closes the dynaset without saving her latest queries.

> To close a dynaset without saving the query:
> ❶ Double-click the Datasheet View window **Control menu box**. The "Save changes to Query" dialog box appears.
> ❷ Click the **No button**. Access closes the dialog box and then closes the dynaset without saving the query.

If you want to take a break and resume the tutorial at a later time, you can exit Access by double-clicking the Microsoft Access window Control menu box. When you resume the tutorial, place your Student Disk in the appropriate drive, launch Access, open the Issue25 database on your Student Disk, and click the Query object button.

■   ■   ■

Establishing Table Relationships

One of the most powerful features of a database management system is its ability to establish relationships between tables. You use a common field to relate, or link, one table with another table. The process of linking tables is often called performing a **join**. When you link tables with a common field, you can extract data from them as if they were one larger table. For example, Elena links the WRITERS and PAST ARTICLES tables by using the Writer ID field in both tables as the common field. She can then use a query to extract all the article data for each writer, even though the fields are contained in two separate tables. The WRITERS and PAST ARTICLES tables have a type of relationship called a one-to-many relationship. The other two types of relationships are the one-to-one relationship and the many-to-many relationship.

Types of Relationships

A **one-to-one relationship** exists between two tables when each record in one table has exactly one matching record in the other table. For example, suppose Elena splits the WRITERS table into two tables, as shown in Figure 4-40. These two tables have a one-to-one relationship. Both the WRITERS CONTACT table and the WRITERS PAYMENT table have Writer ID as the primary key. Writer ID is also the common field between the two tables. Each record in the WRITERS CONTACT table matches one record in the WRITERS PAYMENT table through the common field. The reverse is also true that each record in the WRITERS PAYMENT table matches one record in the WRITERS CONTACT table through the common field. You can query the data from the two tables as if they were one table by linking, or joining, the two tables on the common field. Unless you set criteria to limit the dynaset to specific records, the resulting dynaset contains the same number of records each table has and fields from both tables—but only the fields you need.

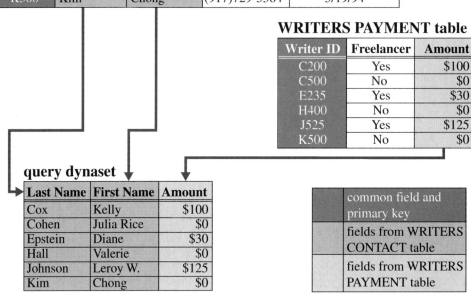

WRITERS CONTACT table

Writer ID	Last Name	First Name	Writer Phone	Last Contact Date
C200	Cox	Kelly	(210)783-5415	11/14/82
C500	Cohen	Julia Rice	(905)338-1875	2/28/95
E235	Epstein	Diane	(610)349-9689	11/14/79
H400	Hall	Valerie	(710)918-7767	9/16/94
J525	Johnson	Leroy W.	(210)895-2046	1/29/91
K500	Kim	Chong	(917)729-5364	5/19/94

WRITERS PAYMENT table

Writer ID	Freelancer	Amount
C200	Yes	$100
C500	No	$0
E235	Yes	$30
H400	No	$0
J525	Yes	$125
K500	No	$0

query dynaset

Last Name	First Name	Amount
Cox	Kelly	$100
Cohen	Julia Rice	$0
Epstein	Diane	$30
Hall	Valerie	$0
Johnson	Leroy W.	$125
Kim	Chong	$0

	common field and primary key
	fields from WRITERS CONTACT table
	fields from WRITERS PAYMENT table

Figure 4-40
One-to-one relationship

A **one-to-many relationship** exists between two tables when one record in the first table matches many records in the second table, but one record in the second table matches only one record in the first table. The relationship between the WRITERS CONTACT table and the PAST ARTICLES table, as shown in Figure 4-41 on the following page, is an example of a one-to-many relationship. Each record in the WRITERS CONTACT table matches many records in the PAST ARTICLES table. Valerie Hall's record in the WRITERS CONTACT table with a Writer ID of H400, for example, links to three records in the PAST ARTICLES table: "25% Tax Cut Bill Approved," "The BCCI Scandal Revealed," and "Computers in the Future." Many can also mean zero records or one record. There is no article listed for Leroy W. Johnson, for example. There is one article for Kelly Cox. Conversely, each record in the PAST ARTICLES table links to a single record in the WRITERS CONTACT table, with Writer ID used as the common field.

PAST ARTICLES table

Article Title	Type	Issue	Article Length	Writer ID
The Economy Under Sub-Zero Population Growth	BUS	1972 Dec	1020	E235
Milton Friedman Interview	ITV	1976 Dec	1994	C200
Chrysler Asks U.S. For $1 Billion	POL	1979 Aug	975	K500
25% Tax Cut Bill Approved	LAW	1981 Aug	2371	H400
AT&T Antitrust Settlement	BUS	1982 Feb	1600	K500
Building Trade Outlook	BUS	1984 Apr	1437	K500
Reagan's $1.09 Trillion Budget	POL	1988 Mar	1798	C500
The BCCI Scandal Revealed	EXP	1991 Jul	2461	H400
Computers in the Future	TEC	1994 Jan	2222	H400

common field as a foreign key

WRITERS CONTACT table

common field as a primary key

Writer ID	Last Name	First Name	Writer Phone	Last Contact Date
C200	Cox	Kelly	(210)783-5415	11/14/82
C500	Cohen	Julia Rice	(905)338-1875	2/28/95
E235	Epstein	Diane	(610)349-9689	11/14/79
H400	Hall	Valerie	(710)918-7767	9/16/94
J525	Johnson	Leroy W.	(210)895-2046	1/29/91
K500	Kim	Chong	(917)729-5364	5/19/94

query dynaset

Article Title	Issue	Last Name	First Name
The Economy Under Sub-Zero Population Growth	1972 Dec	Epstein	Diane
Milton Friedman Interwiew	1976 Dec	Cox	Kelly
Chrysler Asks U.S. For $1 Billion	1979 Aug	Kim	Chong
25% Tax Cut Bill Approved	1981 Aug	Hall	Valerie
AT&T Antitrust Settlement	1982 Feb	Kim	Chong
Building Trade Outlook	1984 Apr	Kim	Chong
Reagan's $1.09 Trillion Budget	1988 Mar	Cohen	Julia Rice
The BCCI Scandal Revealed	1991 Jul	Hall	Valerie
Computers in the Future	1994 Jan	Hall	Valerie

	common field
	fields from WRITERS CONTACT table
	fields from PAST ARTICLES table

Figure 4-41
One-to-many relationship

For a one-to-many relationship, like a one-to-one relationship, you can query the data from the two tables as if they were one table by linking the two tables on the common field. The resulting dynaset can contain the same number of records as does the table that has the foreign key; this table is the table on the "many" side of the one-to-many relationship.

A **many-to-many relationship** exists between two tables when one record in the first table matches many records in the second table and one record in the second table matches many records in the first table. For example, suppose that an article was written by cowriters. The relationship between the WRITERS CONTACT and PAST ARTICLES tables would then be a many-to-many relationship, as shown in Figure 4-42. To handle this type of relationship, you first make sure that each table has a primary key. A counter field named Article ID needs to be added as a primary key to the PAST ARTICLES table, which did not have a primary key. Then you create a new table that has a primary key combining the primary keys of the other two tables. The WRITERS AND PAST ARTICLES table is created. Its primary key is Article ID *and* Writer ID. Each record in this new table represents one article and one of the article's writers. Even though an article ID and writer ID can appear more than once, each combination of article ID and writer ID is unique.

WRITERS CONTACT table

Writer ID	Last Name	First Name	Writer Phone	Last Contact Date
C200	Cox	Kelly	(210)783-5415	11/14/82
C500	Cohen	Julia Rice	(905)338-1875	2/28/95
E235	Epstein	Diane	(610)349-9689	11/14/79
H400	Hall	Valerie	(710)918-7767	9/16/94
J525	Johnson	Leroy W.	(210)895-2046	1/29/91
K500	Kim	Chong	(917)729-5364	5/19/94

WRITERS AND PAST ARTICLES table

Article ID	Writer ID
1	E235
2	C200
3	K500
3	E235
4	H400
5	K500
6	K500
7	C500
8	H400
8	C200
9	H400

new table handling the many-to-many relationship between the other two tables

common field

PAST ARTICLES table

Article ID	Article Title	Type	Issue	Article Length
1	The Economy Under Sub-Zero Population Growth	BUS	1972 Dec	1020
2	Milton Friedman Interview	ITV	1976 Dec	1994
3	Chrysler Asks U.S. For $1 Billion	POL	1979 Aug	975
4	25% Tax Cut Bill Approved	LAW	1981 Aug	2371
5	AT&T Antitrust Settlement	BUS	1982 Feb	1600
6	Building Trade Outlook	BUS	1984 Apr	1437
7	Reagan's $1.09 Trillion Budget	POL	1988 Mar	1798
8	The BCCI Scandal Revealed	EXP	1991 Jul	2461
9	Computers in the Future	TEC	1994 Jan	2222

query dynaset

Article Title	Last Name	First Name
The Economy Under Sub-Zero Population Growth	Epstein	Diane
Milton Friedman Interview	Cox	Kelly
Chrysler Asks U.S. For $1 Billion	Kim	Chong
Chrysler Asks U.S. For $1 Billion	Epstein	Diane
25% Tax Cut Bill Approved	Hall	Valerie
AT&T Antitrust Settlement	Kim	Chong
Building Trade Outlook	Kim	Chong
Reagan's $1.09 Trillion Budget	Cohen	Julia Rice
The BCCI Scandal Revealed	Hall	Valerie
The BCCI Scandal Revealed	Cox	Kelly
Computers in the Future	Hall	Valerie

	primary key
	fields from WRITERS CONTACT table
	fields from PAST ARTICLES table

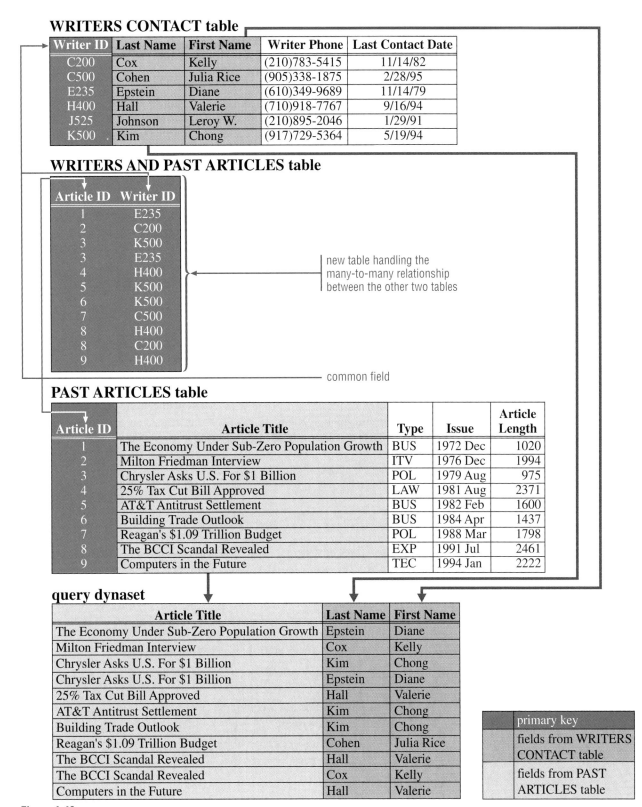

Figure 4-42
Many-to-many relationship

The many-to-many relationship between the WRITERS CONTACT and PAST ARTICLES tables has been changed into two one-to-many relationships. The WRITERS CONTACT table has a one-to-many relationship with the WRITERS AND PAST ARTICLES table, and the PAST ARTICLES table has a one-to-many relationship with the WRITERS AND PAST ARTICLES table.

For a many-to-many relationship, you can query the data from the tables as if they were one table by linking the tables on their common fields. For example, you link the WRITERS CONTACT and the WRITERS AND PAST ARTICLES tables on their common field, Writer ID, and you link the PAST ARTICLES and the WRITERS AND PAST ARTICLES tables on their common field, Article ID. The resulting dynaset can contain the same number of records as does the new table that you created—in this case, the WRITERS AND PAST ARTICLES table.

Access refers to the two tables that form a relationship as the primary table and the related table. The **primary table** is the one table in a one-to-many relationship, and the **related table** is the many table. In a one-to-one relationship, you can choose either table as the primary table and the other table as the related table.

When two tables are related, you can choose to enforce referential integrity rules. The **referential integrity** rules are:

- When you add a record to a related table, a matching record must already exist in the primary table.
- You cannot delete a record from a primary table if matching records exist in the related table, unless you choose to cascade deletes.

When you delete a record with a particular primary-key value from the primary table and choose to **cascade deletes**, Access automatically deletes from related tables all records having foreign-key values equal to that primary-key value. You can also choose to cascade updates. When you change a table's primary-key value and choose to **cascade updates**, Access automatically changes all related tables' foreign-key values that equal that primary-key value.

Let's see how to define relationships and choose referential integrity and cascade options in Access.

Adding a Relationship between Two Tables

When two tables have a common field, you can define the relationship between them in the Relationships window. The **Relationships window** illustrates the one-to-one and one-to-many relationships among a database's tables. In this window you can view or change existing relationships, define new relationships between tables, and rearrange the layout of the tables.

Elena defines the one-to-many relationship between the WRITERS and PAST ARTICLES tables. First, she opens the Relationships window.

To open the Relationships window:

❶ Click the toolbar **Relationships button** ⬚. Access displays the Add Table dialog box on top of the Relationships window.

❷ In the Add Table dialog box, double-click **WRITERS** and then double-click **PAST ARTICLES** in the Table/Query list box. Access adds both tables to the Relationships window.

❸ Click the **Close button** in the Add Table dialog box. Access closes the Add Table dialog box and reveals the entire Relationships window. See Figure 4-43.

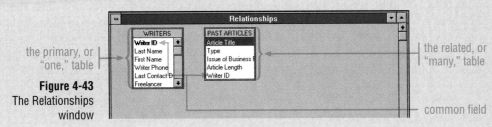

the primary, or "one," table

the related, or "many," table

common field

Figure 4-43
The Relationships window

To form a relationship between the two tables, you drag the common field from one table to the other table. Specifically, you click the primary-key field in the primary table and drag it to the foreign-key field in the related table. Access then displays the Relationships dialog box, in which you select the relationship options for the two tables.

Elena drags Writer ID from the WRITERS table to the PAST ARTICLES table and then selects the relationship options in the Relationships dialog box.

To define a relationship between two tables:

❶ Click **Writer ID** in the WRITERS table list and drag it to Writer ID in the PAST ARTICLES table list. When you release the mouse button, Access displays the Relationships dialog box.

❷ Click the **Enforce Referential Integrity check box** to turn this option on. Access turns on the Many radio button in the One To list.

❸ Click the **Cascade Update Related Fields check box** to turn this option on. See Figure 4-44. Do not turn on the Cascade Delete Related Records option.

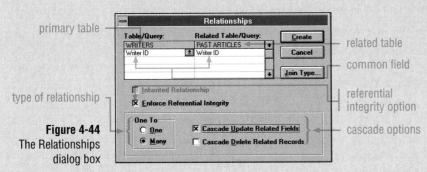

primary table

type of relationship

related table

common field

referential integrity option

cascade options

Figure 4-44
The Relationships dialog box

❹ Click the **Create button**. Access saves the defined relationship between the two tables, closes the Relationships dialog box, and reveals the entire Relationships window. See Figure 4-45.

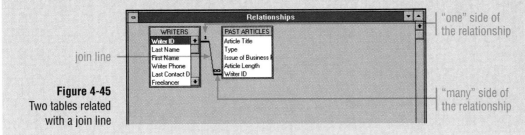

join line

"one" side of the relationship

"many" side of the relationship

Figure 4-45
Two tables related with a join line

Notice the join line that connects the Writer ID fields common to the two tables. The **join line** shows you the common field between two fields. The common fields link (or join) the two tables, which have either a one-to-one or one-to-many relationship. The join line is bold at both ends; this signifies that you have chosen the option to enforce referential integrity. If you do not select this option, the join line is thin at both ends. The "one" side of the relationship has the digit 1 at its end, and the "many" side of the relationship has the infinity symbol (∞) at its end. Although the two tables are still separate tables, you have now defined the one-to-many relationship between them.

Now that she has defined the relationship between the WRITERS and PAST ARTICLES tables, Elena closes the Relationships window.

To close the Relationships window:
❶ Double-click the Relationships window **Control menu box**. Access displays the "Save layout changes to 'Relationships'?" dialog box.
❷ Click the **Yes button** to save the layout. Access closes the dialog box and the Relationships window and returns you to the Database window.

Elena can now build her next query, which requires data from both the WRITERS and PAST ARTICLES tables.

Querying More Than One Table

Elena's next query seeks the article titles, types, and lengths for each writer ordered by article type. This query involves fields from both the WRITERS and PAST ARTICLES tables and requires a sort.

Elena first opens the Query Design window and selects the two needed tables.

To start a query using two tables:
❶ Be sure that the Query object button is selected in the Database window and then click the **New command button**. The New Query dialog box appears.
❷ Click the **New Query button** in the dialog box. The Add Table dialog box appears on top of the Query Design window.
❸ Double-click **WRITERS** and then double-click **PAST ARTICLES** in the Table/Query list box. Access displays the WRITERS and PAST ARTICLES field lists in the upper portion of the Query Design window.

❹ Click the **Close button**. The Add Table dialog box disappears. See Figure 4-46.

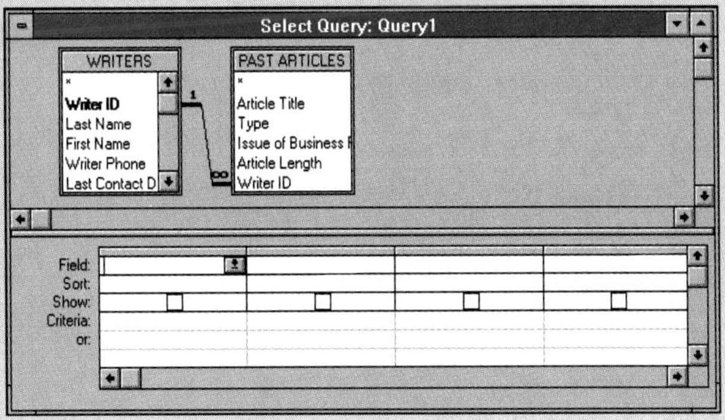

Figure 4-46
Two tables related
with a join line in
the Query Design
window

Elena now defines the query. In the QBE grid she inserts the Article Title, Type, and Article Length fields from the PAST ARTICLES table. She inserts the Last Name and First Name fields from the WRITERS table. She then chooses ascending sort order for the Type field.

To define a query using two tables:
❶ Double-click **Article Title** in the PAST ARTICLES field list. Access places this field in the first column's Field text box.
❷ Double-click **Type** in the PAST ARTICLES field list. Access places this field in the second column's Field text box.
❸ Double-click **Article Length** in the PAST ARTICLES field list. Access places this field in the third column's Field text box.
❹ Double-click **Last Name** in the WRITERS field list. Access places this field in the fourth column's Field text box.
❺ Double-click **First Name** in the WRITERS field list. Access places this field in the fifth column's Field text box.
❻ Click the **Sort text box** for the Type field, and then click the **down arrow button** in the Sort text box. Access displays the Sort list.
❼ Click **Ascending** in the Sort list. The Sort list disappears, and Ascending appears in the Sort text box as the selected sort order.

Elena switches to the dynaset to verify her query.

To view a query dynaset:

❶ Click the toolbar **Run button** ⚠. The dynaset appears and displays the fields from the two tables.

❷ Click the dynaset's **maximize button** to see all the fields and records. See Figure 4-47.

fields from the
PAST ARTICLES
table

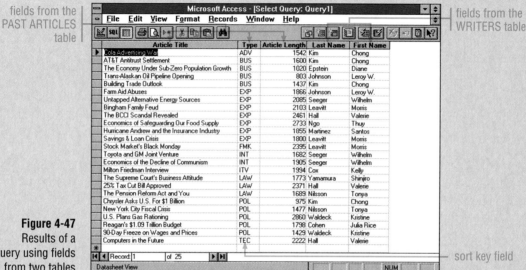

fields from the
WRITERS table

sort key field

Figure 4-47
Results of a
query using fields
from two tables

TROUBLE? You should see 25 records in the dynaset. If you see none, then you probably did not import the PAST ARTICLES table correctly with the Data and Structure option. Save the query with the name Article Type Query. Delete the table and import it again. Then try running the query. If you see more than 25 records, then you created the relationship between the two tables incorrectly. Save the query with the name Article Type Query, repeat the steps for adding the relationship between the two tables, and then try running the query again.

Elena next saves this query and then closes the dynaset.

To save a new query:

❶ Click **File**, and then click **Save Query As...** The Save As dialog box appears.

❷ Type **Article Type Query**.

❸ Click the **OK button**. The Save As dialog box disappears, and Access saves the query for later use.

❹ Double-click the Datasheet View window **Control menu box**. The dynaset disappears, and the Database window becomes the active window and lists all saved queries alphabetically. See Figure 4-48.

Figure 4-48
List of saved
queries

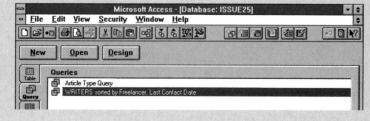

Creating a Parameter Query

Elena's last query asks for the article titles and lengths and the writer names for a specific article type arranged by article title. She will use the WRITERS table for the Article Title, Article Length, and Type fields and the PAST ARTICLES table for the Last Name and First Name fields. Article Title will be the sort key and will have an ascending sort order. Because this query is similar to her last saved query, Elena will open the Article Type Query in the Query Design window and modify its design.

ADV for advertising, BUS for business, EXP for exposé, and POL for political are examples of specific article types. Elena can create a simple condition using an exact match for the Type field that she can change in the Query Design window every time she runs the query. Instead, Elena creates a parameter query.

For a **parameter query**, Access displays a dialog box and prompts you to enter your criteria, or parameters, when you run the query. Access then creates the dynaset just as if you had changed the criteria in the Query Design window.

REFERENCE WINDOW

Creating a Parameter Query

- Create a select query that includes all the fields that will appear in the dynaset. Also choose the sort keys and set the criteria that do not change when you run the query.

- Decide on the fields that will have prompts when you run the query. For each of them, type the prompt you want in the field's Criteria box and enclose the prompt in brackets.

- Highlight the prompt, but do not highlight the brackets. Click Edit and then click Copy to copy the prompt to the Clipboard.

- Click Query and then click Parameters... to open the Query Parameters dialog box.

- Press [Ctrl][V] to paste the contents of the Clipboard into the Parameter text box. Press [Tab] and select the field's data type.

- Click the OK button to close the Query Parameters dialog box.

Elena opens the query saved under the name Article Type Query in the Query Design window and changes its design.

To open a saved query and modify its design:

❶ Be sure that the Database window is active and the Query object button is selected. Click **Article Type Query** in the Queries list box and then click the **Design command button** to open the Query Design window.

❷ To remove the sort key for the Type field, click its Sort text box, click the **down arrow button**, and then click **(not sorted)**.

❸ To add a sort key for the Article Title field, click its **Sort text box**, click the **down arrow button**, and then click **Ascending**.

Elena has completed the changes to the select query. She now changes the query to a parameter query.

To create a parameter query:
➊ Click the **Criteria text box** for the Type field and type **[Enter an Article Type:]**. See Figure 4-49.

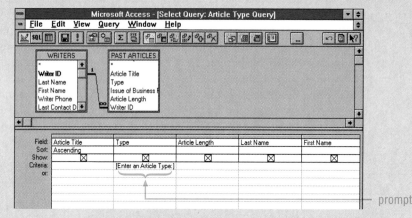

Figure 4-49
Entering a
prompt for a
parameter query

➋ Highlight the prompt, including the colon, but do not highlight the brackets. The parameter query will not work unless "Enter an Article Type:" is exactly what you highlight. Click **Edit** and then click **Copy** to copy the prompt to the Clipboard.
➌ Click **Query** and then click **Parameters...** to open the Query Parameters dialog box.
➍ Press **[Ctrl][V]** to paste the prompt from the Clipboard into the Parameter text box and then press **[Tab]**. See Figure 4-50.

Figure 4-50
The Query
Parameters
dialog box

➎ Your selection in the Data Type text box must be of the same data type as that of the Type field. Because the data type of the Type field is text, which is the default, click the **OK button** to close the Query Parameters dialog box.

Elena runs the parameter query, saves it with the name Article Type Parameter Query, and closes the dynaset. Elena wants to keep the saved version of the query named Article Type Query, as well as save the new parameter query. When she saves the parameter query, therefore, Elena uses the File menu's Save Query As... command instead of the Save Query command. If she were to use the Save Query command, Access would save the parameter query with the name Article Type Query after deleting the saved query.

To run and save a parameter query:

❶ Click the toolbar **Run button** 🔳. The Enter Parameter Value dialog box appears with your prompt above the text box.

❷ To see all the articles that are exposés, type **EXP** in the text box. See Figure 4-51.

Figure 4-51
The Enter Parameter
Value dialog box

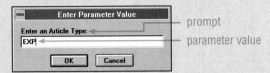

❸ Press **[Enter]**. Access runs the parameter query and displays the dynaset. See Figure 4-52. Only records of type EXP appear, and the records are in ascending order by the Article Title field.

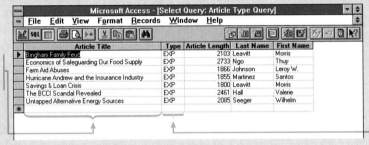

records in
ascending
sort order

Figure 4-52
The dynaset for a
parameter query

parameter value entered

❹ To save the query, click **File** and then click **Save Query As....** The Save As dialog box appears showing the query name Article Type Query, which is the name of the previously saved query. Place the insertion point just in front of the letter Q, type **Parameter**, press **[Spacebar]**, and then press **[Enter]** to name the new query.

❺ Double-click the Datasheet View window **Control menu box**. The dynaset disappears. The Database window becomes the active window and lists the newly saved query.

▪   ▪   ▪

Elena exits Access and then schedules a meeting with her colleagues to review the results of her queries.

Questions

1. What is QBE?
2. What are three methods for adding all the fields from a table to the QBE grid?
3. What is a dynaset?
4. How do you exclude from a dynaset a field that appears in the QBE grid?
5. What are the two components of a simple condition?
6. What comparison operator is used to select records based on a specific pattern?
7. When do you use the In comparison operator?
8. How must you position the fields in the QBE grid when you have multiple sort keys?
9. When do you use logical operators?
10. What is a calculated field?

11. When do you use an aggregate function?

12. When do you use the Group By operator?

E 13. Look for an example of a one-to-many relationship and an example of a many-to-many relationship in a newspaper, magazine, or everyday situation you encounter. For each one, name the entities and select the primary keys and common fields.

14. What are the two referential integrity rules?

15. What does a join line signify?

16. When do you use a parameter query?

E 17. Use Cue Cards to document for your instructor four aggregate functions that do not appear in Figure 4-34.

E 18. Suppose you create a calculated field in the Query Design window by typing NewField:[Writer ID]+50. Writer ID is a text field from the table you are using in your query and it appears in the QBE grid. When you run the query, the calculated field does not appear in the dynaset. Why did this occur?

E 19. Suppose you want to print a dynaset selection, but the Selection option is dimmed out when the Print dialog box appears. What has caused this problem, and how do you correct it?

Tutorial Assignments

Elena creates several queries using the PAST ARTICLES table that she imported into the Issue25 database. Launch Access, open the Issue25 database on your Student Disk, maximize the Database window, click the PAST ARTICLES table, click the New Query button on the toolbar, and then click the New Query button in the New Query message box.

For each of the following questions, prepare an appropriate query in the Query Design window and print its entire dynaset. Whenever you use the Issue of Business Perspective field, rename it Issue. Whenever fields are listed in the question, display the fields in the order listed. Do not save any of the queries.

1. Which articles are of type BUS? Print all fields for this query.

2. What are the article titles and article lengths for all articles that have a length greater than 2103?

3. What are the article titles, article lengths, and writer IDs for all articles written by writers with writer IDs H400 or W432?

4. What are the article titles, article lengths, writer IDs, and issues for all articles published in *Business Perspective* in the 1980s?

5. What are the article lengths, article titles, writer IDs, and issues for all articles of type EXP that have a length less than 2100?

6. What are the article titles, writer IDs, and issues for all articles of type ITV or that were written by writer L130?

7. What are the article lengths, writer IDs, issues, types, and article titles for all articles that have a length less than 2000 and are of type BUS or LAW?

8. What are the article lengths, writer IDs, issues, types, and article titles for all articles that have a length less than 2000 and are of type BUS or LAW? Print in ascending order by length.

9. What are the article lengths, writer IDs, issues, types, and article titles for all articles in descending order by length?

10. What are the writer IDs, article titles, issues, types, and article lengths for all articles? Display the dynaset in ascending order with writer ID as the primary sort key and article length as the secondary sort key.

11. What are the article titles, writer IDs, issues, types, article lengths, and costs per article for all articles, based on a cost per article of three cents per word? Use the name CostPerArticle for the calculated field, assume that the Article Length field gives the number of words in the article, and use ascending sort order for the Article Length field.

12. What is the total cost, average cost, lowest cost, and highest cost for all articles? Assume that the Article Length field gives the number of words in an article and that the cost per article is three cents per word.

13. What is the total cost, average cost, lowest cost, and highest cost for all articles by type? Assume that the Article Length field gives the number of words in an article and that the cost per article is three cents per word.

E   14. Using the PAST ARTICLES and WRITERS tables, list the article titles, article types, issues, writer last names, and writer first names in ascending order by article length for all articles of type BUS, LAW, or POL. Do not print the Article Length field in the dynaset. Be sure that there is no Total row in the QBE grid.

15. Using the PAST ARTICLES and WRITERS tables, list the article titles, issues, writer last names, and writer first names in ascending order by article length for a selected article type. This query should be a parameter query.

Case Problems

1.   Walkton Daily Press Carriers

Grant Sherman has created and updated his Press database and is now ready to query it. Launch Access and do the following:

1. Open the Press database on your Student Disk and maximize the Database window.
2. Delete the BILLINGS table.
3. Import the BILLINGS table from the Walkton database on your Student Disk.

Grant creates several queries using the CARRIERS table. For each of the following questions, prepare an appropriate query in the Query Design window and print its entire dynaset. Whenever you use one of the carrier name fields, rename it omitting the word "Carrier." Whenever fields are listed in the question, display the fields in the order listed.

4. What is all the carrier information on Ashley Shaub?
5. What is all the information on those carriers whose last names begin with the letter S?
6. What are the birthdates, phone numbers, first names, and last names of carriers born in 1981 or later?
7. What are the birthdates, phone numbers, last names, and first names of carriers whose phone numbers end with the digits 4 or 7?
8. What are the birthdates, carrier IDs, first names, and last names of those carriers born prior to 1980 who have a carrier ID either less than 5 or greater than 10?
9. What are the birthdates, carrier IDs, first names, last names, and phone numbers of all carriers in descending order by birthdate?

Close the dynaset to return to the Database window without saving your queries. Complete the following queries using the BILLINGS table.

E   10. What is the total, average, lowest, and highest balance amount for all carriers? Your four calculated fields should use the Balance Amount field as is. Note that Balance Amount is the table field name and Balance is the Caption property name.

E   11. What is the total, average, lowest, and highest balance amount, grouped by carrier?

12. Create a parameter query to display all the fields in the BILLINGS table based on a selected Carrier ID.

2.   Lopez Used Cars

Maria and Hector Lopez have created and updated their Usedcars database and are now ready to query it. Launch Access and do the following:

1. Open the Usedcars database on your Student Disk and maximize the Database window.
2. Delete the LOCATIONS table.

3. Import the CLASSES, LOCATIONS, and TRANSMISSIONS tables from the Lopez database on your Student Disk.

Maria and Hector create several queries using the USED CARS table. For each of the following questions, prepare an appropriate query in the Query Design window and print its entire dynaset. Whenever fields are listed in the question, display the fields in the order listed. If a field has a Caption property, rename the field to match the name in the Query Design window.

4. What are the manufacturers, models, years, and selling prices for all cars?

5. What are the manufacturers, models, years, and selling prices for cars manufactured by Ford?

6. What are the manufacturers, models, years, costs, and selling prices for cars manufactured prior to 1989?

7. What are the manufacturers, models, years, costs, and selling prices for cars having a manufacturer that starts with the letter C or the letter N?

8. What are the manufacturers, models, classes, years, costs, and selling prices for cars manufactured prior to 1990 and having either an S2 or an S3 class?

9. What are the manufacturers, models, classes, years, costs, and selling prices for all cars in descending sequence by selling price?

10. Create a field that calculates the difference (profit) between the Selling Price and the Cost and name it Diff. What are the manufacturers, models, classes, years, costs, selling prices, and profits for all cars?

E   11. What is the total cost, total selling price, total profit, and average profit for all the cars?

E   12. What is the total cost, total selling price, total profit, and average profit grouped by year?

13. Create a parameter query to display all the fields from the USED CARS table based on a selected manufacturer.

Close the dynaset to return to the Database window without saving your query, and then complete the following problem.

E   14. Add a one-to-many relationship between the LOCATIONS and USED CARS tables using Location Code as the common field. Create a query to find the manufacturers, models, selling prices, location names, and manager names for all cars in descending sequence by manager name.

3.   Tophill University Student Employment

Olivia Tyler has created and updated her Parttime database and is now ready to query it. Launch Access and do the following:

1. Open the Parttime database on your Student Disk and maximize the Database window.

2. Delete the EMPLOYERS table.

3. Import the EMPLOYERS table from the Tophill database on your Student Disk.

Olivia creates several queries using the JOBS table. For each of the following questions, prepare an appropriate query in the Query Design window and print its entire dynaset. Whenever fields are listed in the question, display the fields in the listed order. If a field has a Caption property, rename the field to match the name in the Query Design window.

4. What is all the job information on job order 7?

5. What is all the information on jobs having job titles that begin with Computer?

6. What are the job titles, hours per week, and wages of jobs paying wages greater than or equal to $7.05?

7. What are the job titles, hours per week, employer IDs, and wages of jobs requiring between 20 and 24 hours per week, inclusive?

8. What are the job titles, hours per week, employer IDs, and wages of jobs requiring between 20 and 24 hours per week, inclusive, and paying wages less than or equal to $6.75?

9. What are the job titles, hours per week, employer IDs, and wages of all jobs in order by ascending hours per week (the primary sort key) and by descending job title (the secondary sort key)?

10. Create a calculated field that is the product of hours per week and wage, and name it Weekly. What are the hours per week, wages, weekly wages, and job titles for all jobs?

E 11. What is the total, average, lowest, and highest weekly wage for all the jobs listed in the JOBS table?

E 12. What is the total, average, lowest, and highest weekly wage for all jobs grouped by employer ID?

13. Create a parameter query to display all the fields in the JOBS table based on a selected employer ID.

4. Rexville Business Licenses

Chester Pearce has created and updated his Buslic database and is now ready to query it. Launch Access and do the following:

1. Open the Buslic database on your Student Disk and maximize the Database window.

2. Delete the LICENSES table.

3. Import the LICENSES and ISSUED LICENSES tables from the Rexville database on your Student Disk.

Chester creates several queries using the BUSINESSES table. For each of the following questions, prepare an appropriate query in the Query Design window and print its entire dynaset. Whenever fields are listed in the question, display the fields in the listed order. If a field has a Caption property, rename the field to match the name in the Query Design window.

4. What is all the information for business ID 11?

5. What is all the information on those businesses that have the word "avenue" in the street-name field?

6. What are the business names, street numbers, street names, and proprietors for businesses having street numbers greater than 5100?

7. What are the business names, street numbers, street names, proprietors, and phone numbers for businesses having phone numbers starting 243 or 942?

8. What are the proprietors, business names, street numbers, street names, and phone numbers of all businesses in ascending sequence by business name?

Close the dynaset to return to the Database window without saving your query. Complete the following queries using the ISSUED LICENSES table.

E 9. What is the total amount, total count, and average amount for all issued licenses?

E 10. What is the total amount, total count, and average amount for all issued licenses grouped by license type?

11. Create a parameter query to display all the fields from the BUSINESSES table based on a selected business ID.

Designing Forms

Creating Forms at Vision Publishers

CASE

Vision Publishers   At the next Issue25 database meeting Brian Murphy, Judith Rossi, and Harold Larson are pleased when Elena Sanchez presents her query results. Everyone agrees that Elena should place the Issue25 database on the company network so that everyone can access and query the data.

Because some people seek information about a single writer, Elena creates a form to display one writer at a time on the screen. The form will be easier to read than a datasheet or dynaset and Elena can use the form to correct a writer's data.

Using a Form

A **form** is an object you use to maintain, view, and print records of data from a database. In Access, you can design your own form or use a Form Wizard to automate the form creation process. A **Form Wizard** is an Access tool that asks you a series of questions and then creates a form based on your answers. Whether you use a Form Wizard or design your own form, you can change a form's design after it is created.

Access has five different Form Wizards. Four of these Form Wizards are shown in Figure 5-1.

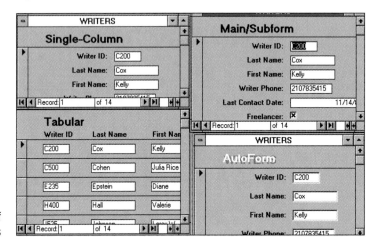

Figure 5-1
Four types of
Form Wizards

- A **single-column form** displays the fields, one on a line, vertically on the form. Field values appear in boxes. Labels, which are the table field names, appear to the left of the field values.
- A **tabular form** displays multiple records and field values in a row-and-column format. Field values appear in boxes with the table field names as column headings.
- A **main/subform form** displays data from two or more related tables. One record from the primary table appears in single-column format in the main form at the top. Access displays one or more records in datasheet format from the related tables in the subforms at the bottom.
- An **AutoForm form** is a special single-column form that Access creates immediately without asking you further questions about the form's content and style. Access includes in the form all the fields from the underlying table or query.
- A **graph form** displays a graph of your designated data.

Each Form Wizard offers you a choice of five different form styles, as shown in Figure 5-2.

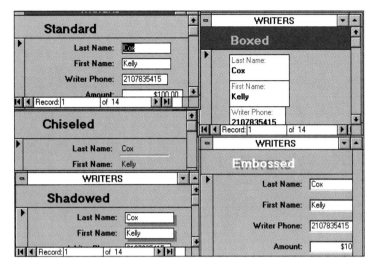

Figure 5-2
Form style options

- The **standard style** displays field values in white boxes on a light gray background.
- The **chiseled style** displays field values with sculpted underlines on a light gray background.
- The **shadowed style** is the same as the standard style with the addition of dark rectangles attached to the field-value boxes to give a shadowed, three-dimensional effect.
- The **boxed style** pairs field values and their labels inside white boxes on a light gray background with each label above its field value.
- The **embossed style** displays field values inside white boxes with a sunken, three-dimensional effect on a blue-green background.

Although you might find the last four styles to be more elegant, you should choose the standard style when you first begin working with forms. Some printers have problems printing colored forms, and changing a form's design by moving or resizing fields is easier when you use the standard style.

Access has a set of Cue Cards you can use while working with forms. Although we will not use these Cue Cards in this tutorial, you might find they enhance your understanding of forms. At any time during this tutorial, therefore, select Design a Form from the Cue Card menu window to launch the appropriate Cue Cards.

Creating Forms Using the AutoForm Wizard

The quickest way to create a form is to use the toolbar AutoForm button, which launches the AutoForm Wizard. When you click the **AutoForm button**, the AutoForm Wizard selects all the fields from the highlighted table or query in the Database window, creates a single-column form for these fields, and displays the form on the screen.

To create a form to display all the fields from the TYPES table, Elena uses the AutoForm button. If you have not done so, place your Student Disk in the appropriate drive, launch Access, and open the Issue25 database on your Student Disk.

To create a form using the AutoForm button:

❶ Click **TYPES** in the Tables list box. Access will place the fields from the TYPES table, which is now highlighted, into the form it creates when you click the toolbar AutoForm button 🖾.

❷ Locate 🖾 on the toolbar. See Figure 5-3.

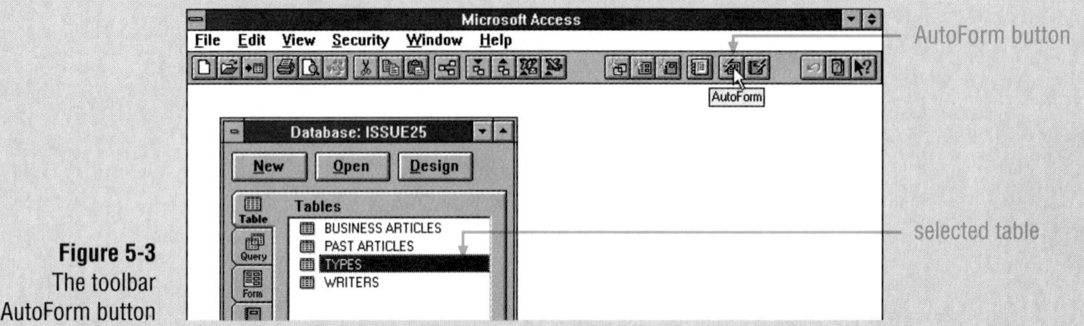

Figure 5-3
The toolbar
AutoForm button

❸ Click 🖾. Access constructs and displays a form that contains the two fields from the TYPES table. See Figure 5-4.

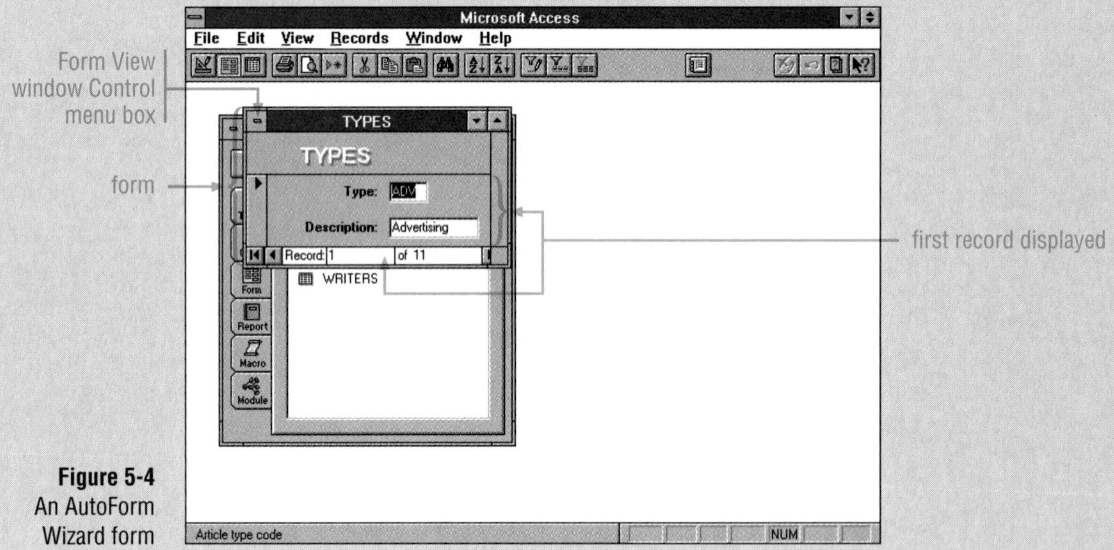

Figure 5-4
An AutoForm
Wizard form

Access displays the first record from the TYPES table in the new form. If you want to view other records from the TYPES table, click the form navigation buttons or type a record number between the navigation buttons. You might need to resize the form to see all four navigation buttons.

Saving a Form

Elena saves the form so that she and others can use it for future work with data from the TYPES table. Elena saves the form, using the name TYPES form, and then closes the Form View window.

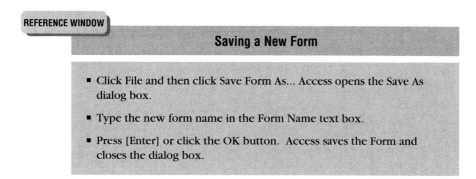

REFERENCE WINDOW

Saving a New Form

- Click File and then click Save Form As... Access opens the Save As dialog box.
- Type the new form name in the Form Name text box.
- Press [Enter] or click the OK button. Access saves the Form and closes the dialog box.

Let's save Elena's form.

To save and close a new form:
❶ Click **File**, and then click **Save Form As...**. The Save As dialog box appears.
❷ Type **TYPES form** in the Form Name text box.
❸ Press **[Enter]**. The Save As dialog box disappears, and Access saves the form.
❹ Double-click the Form View window **Control menu box**. The Form View window disappears, and the Database window becomes the active window.
❺ Click the **Form object button**. Access lists the newly saved form. See Figure 5-5.

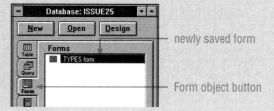

Figure 5-5
Listing a new form

newly saved form

Form object button

Creating Forms Using Form Wizards

For her next form, Elena uses a Form Wizard to display data from the WRITERS table. She chooses to display all the fields from the table in a single-column form with the standard style.

Creating Single-Column Forms

Let's use a Form Wizard to create a single-column form type with the standard style.

To activate Form Wizards and select a form type:
❶ Click the toolbar **New Form button** 🔳. The New Form dialog box appears.
❷ Click the Select A Table/Query drop-down list box **down arrow button** to display the list of the Issue25 database tables and queries.

❸ Scroll through the Select A Table/Query drop-down list box and then click **WRITERS**. The drop-down list disappears and WRITERS appears highlighted in the box. See Figure 5-6.

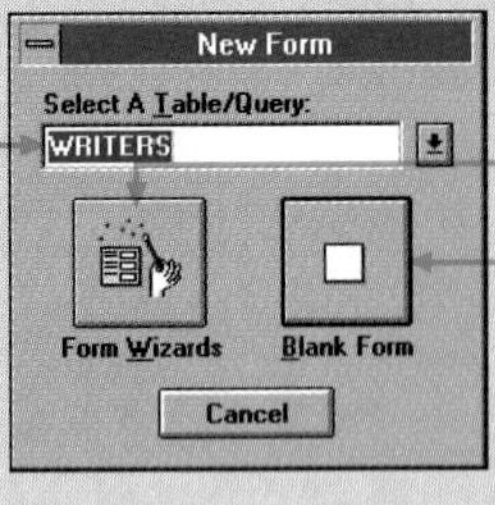

table or query selected for the new form

a Form Wizard-created form

a form of your own design

Figure 5-6
The New Form
dialog box

❹ Click the **Form Wizards button**. The Form Wizards dialog box appears. This dialog box lists the five form types available through Form Wizards. See Figure 5-7.

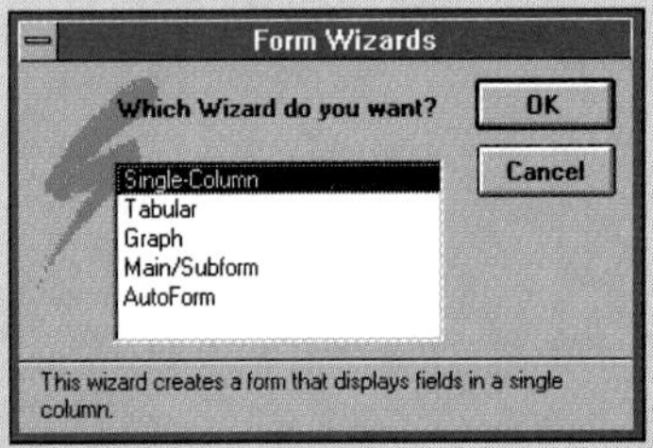

Figure 5-7
Choosing the
form type

❺ If Single-Column is not highlighted, click it, and then click the **OK button**. The first Single-Column Form Wizard dialog box appears. See Figure 5-8.

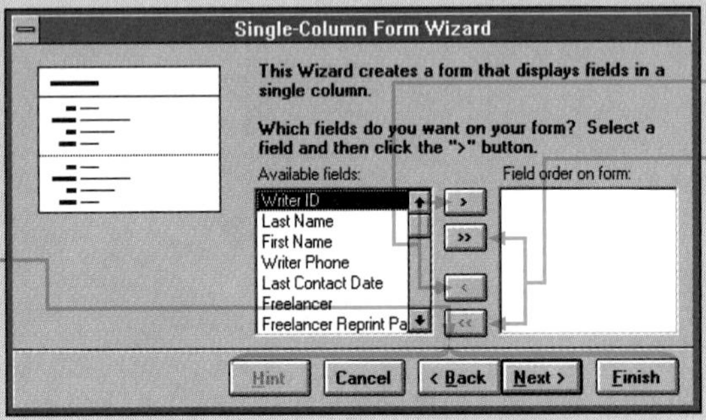

move/remove
highlighted field

move/remove all fields

command buttons

Figure 5-8
Selecting fields
for a form

In this Single-Column Form Wizard dialog box, you select fields in the order you want them to appear on the form. If you want to select fields one at a time, highlight a field by clicking it, and then click the > button. If you want to select all fields, click the >> button. The selected fields move from the box on the left to the box on the right as you select them. If you make a mistake, click the << button to remove all fields from the box on the right or highlight a field and click the < button to remove fields one at a time.

Each Form Wizards dialog box displays command buttons on the bottom that allow you to move quickly to the other Form Wizards dialog boxes. You can go to the previous or next Form Wizards dialog box. You can also cancel the form creation process to return to the Database window; you can prematurely finish the form and accept the Form Wizards defaults for the remaining form options; and you can ask for hints about the Form Wizards options.

Elena wants her form to display all the fields from the WRITERS table in the order in which they appear in the table.

To finish creating a form using the Single-Column Form Wizards:

❶ Click the **>> button**. Access removes all the fields from the box on the left and places them in the same order in the box on the right.

❷ Click the **Next > button** to display the next Single-Column Form Wizard dialog box, in which you choose the form's style.

❸ Click the **Standard radio button** and then click the **Next > button**. Access displays the final Single-Column Form Wizard dialog box and shows the table name as the default for the title that will appear in the Form Header section. Elena wants to use the default form title. See Figure 5-9.

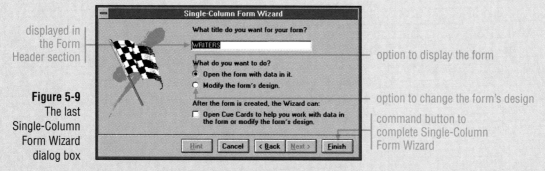

displayed in the Form Header section

option to display the form

option to change the form's design

command button to complete Single-Column Form Wizard

Figure 5-9
The last Single-Column Form Wizard dialog box

❹ Click the **Finish button**. The Form View window opens and displays the completed form. See Figure 5-10.

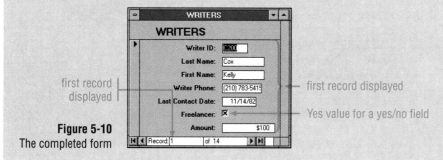

first record displayed

first record displayed

Yes value for a yes/no field

Figure 5-10
The completed form

Notice that Freelancer is a yes/no field and that Form Wizards automatically creates a check box for it. An empty check box indicates a value of No, and an ✕ in the check box indicates a value of Yes.

Elena saves the form, using the name WRITERS form, and then closes the Form View window.

To save and close a new form:

❶ Click **File**, and then click **Save Form As…**. The Save As dialog box appears.

❷ Type **WRITERS form** in the Form Name text box.

❸ Press **[Enter]**. The Save As dialog box disappears, and Access saves the form.

❹ Double-click the Form View window **Control menu box**. The Form View window disappears, and the Database window becomes the active window.

Creating Main/Subform Forms

Elena next creates a form to show a specific writer and his or her articles. Elena will use this form to enter the writer and article data for the first two new articles written for the 25th-anniversary issue.

Because the main/subform form type allows you to work with data from two or more tables, Elena chooses this form type for her new form. The WRITERS table has a one-to-many relationship with the PAST ARTICLES table. Elena selects the WRITERS table for the main form because it is the primary table and the PAST ARTICLES table for the subform because it is the related table. Elena again uses a Form Wizard to create the form.

Because the Form object button is selected, Elena can create the new form by clicking either the toolbar New Form button or the New command button.

To activate Form Wizards and create a main/subform form type:

❶ Click the **New command button**. The New Form dialog box appears.

❷ Click the Select A Table/Query drop-down list box **down arrow button** to display the list of the Issue25 database tables and queries.

❸ Scroll down the list and then click **WRITERS**. The drop-down list disappears and WRITERS appears highlighted in the box.

❹ Click the **Form Wizards button**. The Form Wizards dialog box appears.

❺ Click **Main/Subform** in the list box and then click the **OK button**. Access displays the first Main/Subform Wizard dialog box, in which you select the table or query for the subform. See Figure 5-11.

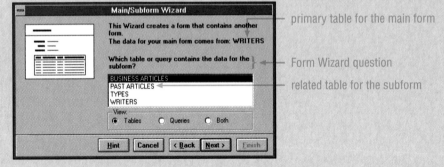

Figure 5-11
Selecting the
subform table
or query

❻ Click **PAST ARTICLES** in the list box, and then click the **Next > button**. Access displays the next Main/Subform Wizard dialog box, in which you select the fields for the main form. Elena wants to display all the fields from the WRITERS table on the main form.

❼ Click the **>> button** to select all fields and move them to the box on the right, and then click the **Next > button**. Access displays the next Main/Subform Wizard dialog box, in which you select the fields for the subform.

The Writer ID field will appear in the main form, so it is not needed in the subform. Otherwise, Elena wants to place all the fields from the PAST ARTICLES table on the subform.

To select the subforms fields and a main/subform style:
❶ Click the **>>button** to select all fields. If Writer ID is not highlighted in the box on the right, click it. Then click the **< button** to remove Writer ID from the box on the right. See Figure 5-12.

field not selected
for the subform

Figure 5-12
Selecting fields
for a subform

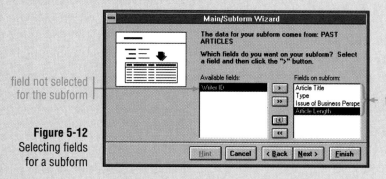

fields selected for the subform

❷ Click the **Next > button**. Access displays the next Main/Subform Wizard dialog box, in which you select the form style.
❸ Click the **Standard button** and then click the **Next > button**. Access displays the final Main/Subform Wizard window and shows the primary table name as the default form title.

Elena enters the form title WRITERS and PAST ARTICLES. This form title appears at the top of the form in the Form View window. The form itself is saved as two separate forms when you create a main/subform form type. You first save the subform and then you save the form/subform combination.

To title a form and save a subform:
❶ Type **WRITERS and PAST ARTICLES**, and then click the **Finish button**. Access displays the "Save the subform" dialog box. You must save the subform before the Main/Subform Wizard can continue.
❷ Click the **OK button**. The dialog box disappears, and the Save As dialog box appears.
❸ Type **PAST ARTICLES subform** in the Form Name box and then press **[Enter]**. Access saves the subform and displays the completed main/subform window. See Figure 5-13.

form title

main form
navigation
buttons

subform

Figure 5-13
The completed
main/subform
form type

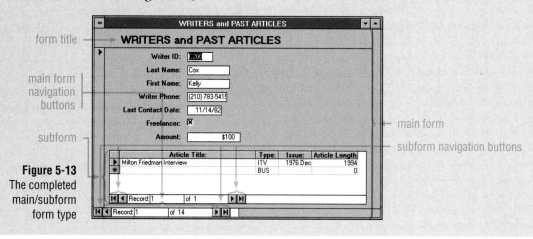

main form

subform navigation buttons

Access displays the fields from the first record in the WRITERS table in single-column format. The records in this main form appear in primary-key sequence. The writer Kelly Cox has one record in the PAST ARTICLES table that is shown at the bottom in datasheet format.

Elena wants to view the data for a writer who has more than one record in the PAST ARTICLES table. Two sets of navigation buttons appear at the bottom of the form. You use the top set of navigation buttons to select records from the related table in the subform and the bottom set to select records from the primary table in the main form.

To navigate to different main and subform records:

❶ Click the main form **Next Record button** ▶ three times. Access displays the record for Valerie Hall in the main form and her three articles in the subform.

❷ Click the subform ▶ once. Access changes the current record to the second article in the subform.

In addition to viewing data in a form and in a subform, you can also add, change, and delete field values and records. If a writer has four or more articles, Access adds a scroll bar on the right side of the subform.

Elena saves the main/subform combination using the name WRITERS and PAST ARTICLES form. This form name will appear in the Database window when you click the Form object button to display a list of the database's forms.

To save a new form/subform:

❶ Click **File**, and then click **Save Form As...**. The Save As dialog box appears.

❷ Type **WRITERS and PAST ARTICLES form**.

❸ Press **[Enter]**. The Save As dialog box disappears, and Access saves the form.

Maintaining Table Data Using a Form

Elena needs to make two field value changes to one of Valerie Hall's articles. Then she will add two new articles to the database. The database modifications involve three articles and three writers, as shown in Figure 5-14.

Action	Table	Record and Fields
Change	PAST ARTICLES	Article Title: The BBCI Scandal Revealed (by Valerie Hall) Issue: from 1991 Jul to 1991 Aug Article Length: from 2461 to 2779
Add	PAST ARTICLES	Article Title: Advertising Over the Past 25 Years (by Thuy Ngo) Type: ADV Issue: 1994 Dec Article Length: 3285
Add	WRITERS	Writer ID: L350 Last Name: Lawton First Name: Pat Writer Phone: (705) 677–1991 Last Contact Date: 9/4/94 Freelancer: No Amount: $0
	PAST ARTICLES	Article Title: Law Over the Past 25 Years (by Pat Lawton) Type: LAW Issue: 1994 Dec Article Length: 2834

Figure 5-14
Maintenance changes
to the Issue25
database

To maintain table data using a form, you must know how to move from field to field and from record to record. The mouse movement, selection, and placement techniques to do this are the standard Windows techniques that you used in Tutorial 3. If you are maintaining data in a subform, the keyboard techniques are also the same as those described in Tutorial 3. For other form types, you use the same keyboard deletion techniques that you use in editing mode and the same data entry and editing shortcut keys. The form navigation and editing mode keyboard movement techniques, however, differ slightly, as shown in Figure 5-15 on the following page.

Press	To Move the Selection Point in Navigation Mode	To Move the Insertion Point in Editing Mode
[Left Arrow]	To the previous field value	Left one character at a time
[Right Arrow] or [Tab] or [Enter]	To the next field value	Right one character at a time
[Home]	To the first field value in the record	Before the first character in the field value
[End]	To the last field value in the record	After the last character in the field value
[Up Arrow] or [Down Arrow]	To the previous or next field value	The insertion point does not move
[PgUp]	To the same field value in the previous record	To the same field value in the previous record and switch to navigation mode
[PgDn]	To the same field value in the next record	To the same field value in the next record and switch to navigation mode
[Ctrl][Left Arrow] or [Ctrl][Right Arrow]	To the previous or next field value	Left or right one word at a time
[Ctrl][Up Arrow] or [Ctrl][Down Arrow]	To the same field value in the first or last record	Before the first character or after the last character in the field value
[Ctrl][PgUp]	To the same field value in the previous record	Before the first character in the field value
[Ctrl][PgDn]	To the same field in the next record	After the last character in the field value
[Ctrl][Home]	To the first value in the first record	Before the first character in the field value
[Ctrl][End]	To the first subform field value for the last main form record	After the last character in the field value

Figure 5-15
Form navigation and editing mode keyboard movement techniques

Elena first makes the two changes to one of Valerie Hall's articles. Because the article she wants to change is already selected, Elena just moves to the field values in the subform and changes them.

To change table field values using a form:
❶ Press **[Tab]** twice. The Issue field value 1991 Jul is highlighted.
❷ Double-click Jul and then type **Aug** as the changed month value for the Issue field.
❸ Press **[Tab]** to move to and highlight the Article Length field.
❹ Type **2779** as the changed field value for the Article Length field.

Elena next adds records to the Issue25 database. She first adds one article for Thuy Ngo. There is already a record for Thuy Ngo in the WRITERS table, record number 10.

To add a record in a subform:

❶ Click the record number that is displayed between the main form navigation buttons **(4)** and then press **[F2]** to highlight the number. Type **10** and then press **[Enter]**. Thuy Ngo's record appears, and the Article Title field is selected in the subform.

❷ Press **[Down Arrow]** once to move to the Article Title field for the next available record in the subform.

❸ Type **Advertising Over the Past 25 Years**, press **[Tab]**, type **ADV**, press **[Tab]**, type **1994 Dec**, press **[Tab]**, type **3285**, and then press **[Tab]**. See Figure 5-16. Access has added this record to the PAST ARTICLES table for Thuy Ngo.

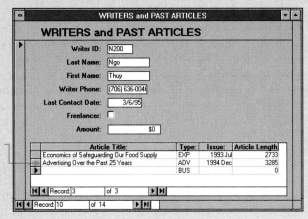

record added

Figure 5-16
Adding a record
in a subform

Elena's last change is to add one record to the WRITERS table and one record to the PAST ARTICLES table. To add a record to the WRITERS table, Elena navigates to the next available record in the table. You use the bottom set of navigation buttons to change which record Access displays in the main WRITERS form.

To add a new writer and a new article using a form:

❶ Click the main form's **Last Record button** . Access displays the record for Shinjiro Yamamura in the main form and his one article in the subform.

❷ Click the main form's **Next Record button** . Access moves to record 15 in the main form and to record 1 in the subform, clears all field values, and positions the insertion point in the subform's Article Title field.

❸ Click the **field-value box** for the Writer ID field in the main form to position the insertion point there.

❹ Type **L350**, press **[Tab]**, type **Lawton**, press **[Tab]**, type **Pat**, press **[Tab]**, type **7056771991**, press **[Tab]**, type **9/4/94**, and then press **[Tab]** to enter the first five field values. An ×, which indicates a value of Yes, appears in the Freelancer field value box.

❺ Press **[Spacebar]** to change the Freelancer field value to No, and then press **[Tab]** to move to the Amount field.

❻ Press **[Tab]**. Access saves the new record in the WRITERS table and positions the insertion point in the Article Title field in the subform.

❼ Type **Law Over the Past 25 Years**, press **[Tab]**, type **LAW**, press **[Tab]**, type **1994 Dec**, press **[Tab]**, and then type **2834**. See Figure 5-17.

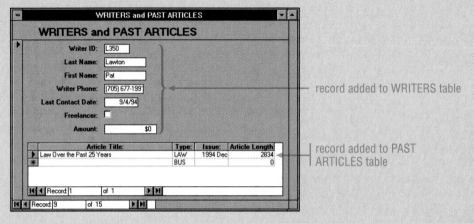

Figure 5-17
Adding records
in a main form
and a subform

❽ Press **[Tab]**. Access saves the new record in the PAST ARTICLES table and positions the insertion point in the Article Title field for the next available record in the subform.

When you created the WRITERS and PAST ARTICLES form, you selected all fields from the WRITERS table for the main form. However, you did not select the Writer ID field for the subform. Because the Writer ID field is the common field between the two tables, Access uses the Writer ID field value from the main form when it saves the subform record in the PAST ARTICLES table.

Elena has completed her maintenance tasks, so she closes the Form View window and maximizes the Database window to see a list of the forms in the Issue25 database.

To close the Form View window and list the forms for a database:
❶ Double-click the Form View window **Control menu box**. The Form View window disappears.

❷ Click the Database window **maximize button**. Access displays a full list of the forms you created. See Figure 5-18.

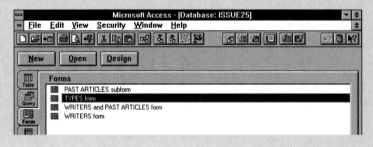

Figure 5-18
The Forms list in the
Database window

If you want to take a break and resume the tutorial at a later time, you can exit Access by double-clicking the Microsoft Access window Control menu box. When you resume the tutorial, place your Student Disk in the appropriate drive, launch Access, open the Issue25 database on your Student Disk, maximize the Database window, and click the Form object button.

■   ■   ■

Finding and Sorting Records in a Form

Later that same day, Harold calls Elena to ask for the phone number of the freelance writer Chong Kim. Elena answers Harold's question by searching in the WRITERS and PAST ARTICLES form.

Using the Find Command

To find Chong Kim's phone number, Elena uses the toolbar Find button. Elena first opens the WRITERS and PAST ARTICLES form.

To open a form:
❶ If it is not already selected, click **WRITERS and PAST ARTICLES form** in the Database window's Forms list box.

❷ Click the **Open command button**. The Form View window that appears is maximized because you had maximized the Database window.

The left side of the toolbar in the Form View window has several buttons, as shown in Figure 5-19. You have already used some of these buttons. You will use the six buttons on the right side of Figure 5-19 in the next few steps of this tutorial.

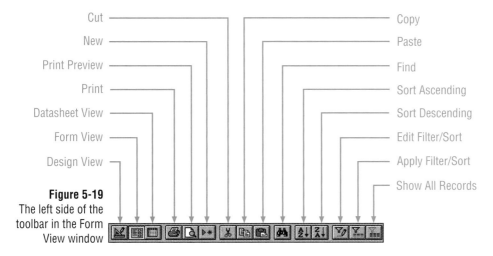

Cut — Copy
New — Paste
Print Preview — Find
Print — Sort Ascending
Datasheet View — Sort Descending
Form View — Edit Filter/Sort
Design View — Apply Filter/Sort
Show All Records

Figure 5-19
The left side of the toolbar in the Form View window

To find Chong Kim's record, Elena uses the Find button to search for a match on the Last Name field.

To find data in the Form View window:

❶ Click the main form's **field-value box** for the Last Name field to make it the search field for the Find command.

❷ Click the toolbar **Find button** 🔍. The Find dialog box appears.

❸ Click the title bar of the Find dialog box and drag the Find dialog box to the lower right to get a better view of the main form's field values and navigation buttons.

❹ Type **Kim** in the Find What text box, and then click the **Find First button** in the Find dialog box. Access finds the first Chong Kim and displays the sixth WRITERS table record. This Chong Kim is not a freelancer, so Elena searches for the next Chong Kim.

❺ Click the **Find Next button** in the Find dialog box. Access displays the next Chong Kim, whose record is the seventh WRITERS table record. His article is titled Cola Advertising War. This Chong Kim is a freelancer, so Elena has completed her search. She jots down the phone number.

❻ Click the **Close button**. The Find dialog box disappears.

Elena gives Chong Kim's phone number to Harold. Harold next asks Elena for the phone number and name of the writer with the oldest last contact date.

Quick Sorting in a Form

To find the writer with the oldest last contact date, Elena uses the toolbar Sort Ascending button to do a quick sort. She first selects the Last Contact Date field, so that the records will appear in the form in increasing order by this field.

To quick sort records in a form:

❶ Click the main form's **field-value box** for the Last Contact Date field to make it the selected field for the quick sort.

❷ Click the toolbar **Sort Ascending button** ⬆️. Access displays the record for Shinjiro Yamamura, who has the earliest Last Contact Date field value, 9/26/72.

You can use the main form's Next Record navigation button to display the writer records, one at a time, in ascending order by last contact date. If you want Access to display the records in the default order by Writer ID, which is the primary key, click the toolbar's Show All Records button, and then use the navigation buttons.

Elena gives Shinjiro Yamamura's phone number to Harold. Harold next asks Elena for the phone numbers of all freelance writers.

Using a Filter

You use the Find command in a form when you want to see records that match a specific field value, and you use the quick sort buttons if you want Access to display all records in order by a single field. If you want Access to display selected records, display records sorted by two or more fields, or display selected records and sort them, you use a filter.

A **filter** is a set of criteria that describes the records you want to see in a form and their sequence. You enter record selection criteria in the Filter window in the same way you specify record selection criteria for a query. Elena wants to view only records for freelancers in her form, so she uses a filter to specify this criterion. Elena chooses a descending sort of the records based on the Last Contact Date field.

To open the Filter window and specify selection and sorting criteria:

❶ Click the toolbar **Edit Filter/Sort button** 🔲. The Filter window appears.

❷ Scroll the WRITERS field list to display the Freelancer field. Double-click **Freelancer** in the WRITERS field list. Access adds the Freelancer field to the second column of the Filter window grid. Because you selected the Last Contact Date field for the previous quick sort, it appears in the Filter window grid in the first column.

❸ Click the **Criteria text box** in the Freelancer column and then type **Yes**.

❹ Click the **Sort text box** in the Last Contact Date column, click the **down arrow button**, and click **Descending**. See Figure 5-20.

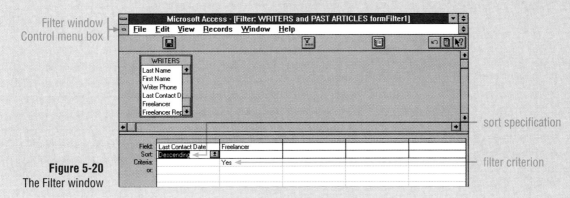

Figure 5-20
The Filter window

Elena has defined the filter; next she saves it as a query. By doing this, she can reuse the filter in the future by opening the saved query.

To save a filter as a query:

❶ Click the toolbar **Save button** 🔲. The Save As Query dialog box appears.

❷ Type **Freelancers and PAST ARTICLES** in the Query Name box and then press **[Enter]**. Access saves the filter as a query, and the Save As Query dialog box disappears.

Elena closes the Filter window and applies the filter. Applying the filter selects the records based on your selection criteria in the order specified by the sort criteria.

To close the Filter window and apply a filter:
❶ Double-click the Filter window **Control menu box**. The Filter window disappears and Access displays the Form View window.

TROUBLE? If you accidentally exit Access, launch Access, open the Issue25 database, maximize the Database window, click the Form object button, double-click the WRITERS and PAST ARTICLES form, click the Edit Filter/Sort button [⊽], click File, click Load From Query..., double-click Freelancers and PAST ARTICLES, and double-click the Filter window Control menu box. Then continue to Step 2.

❷ Click the toolbar **Apply Filter/Sort button** [⊻]. Access selects records based on the filter criteria and displays records in sort-key sequence. The record for Wilhelm Seeger is the first record to appear in the main form. His three articles appear in the subform.

❸ Click the main form **Last Record button** [▶|]. Access displays the record for Tonya Nilsson in the main form and her two articles in the subform.

The last record is record six. Because you view only the freelancer records when you apply the filter, you see only six of the 15 records in the table.

Elena gives Harold the phone numbers for all the freelancers. She then removes the filter. You remove a filter by clicking the Show All Records button on the toolbar.

To remove a filter:
❶ Click the toolbar **Show All Records button** [▦]. Access displays the record from the WRITERS table with the lowest primary-key value. This is the record for Kelly Cox, who has a Writer ID of C200.

❷ Click the main form **Last Record button** [▶|]. Access displays the record from the WRITERS table with the highest primary key value. This is the record for Shinjiro Yamamura, who has a Writer ID of Y556.

When the filter is applied, Access displays one of the six records for freelancers from the WRITERS table. When you remove the filter, Access displays one of the 15 records stored in the WRITERS table.

Elena closes the Form View window and checks to be sure the filter was saved as a query.

To close the Form View window and view the query list:
❶ Double-click the Form View window **Control menu box**. Access closes the Form View window and activates the Database window.

❷ Click the **Query object button**. The Queries list box appears. See Figure 5-21.

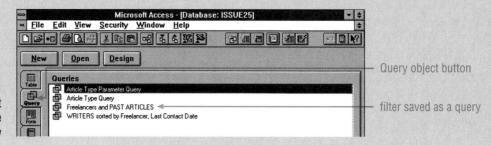

Figure 5-21
The Queries list box in the Database window

Query object button

filter saved as a query

Elena wants to be sure she remembers how to apply a filter that she saved as a query. She opens the WRITERS and PAST ARTICLES form and applies the Freelancers and PAST ARTICLES query as a filter.

To apply a filter that was saved as a query:

❶ Click the **Form object button** in the Database window and double-click **WRITERS and PAST ARTICLES form** in the Forms list box. The Form View window appears.

❷ Click the toolbar **Edit Filter/Sort button** ⊞. Access displays the Filter window.

❸ Click **File**, and then click **Load From Query...**. The Applicable Filter dialog box appears. See Figure 5-22.

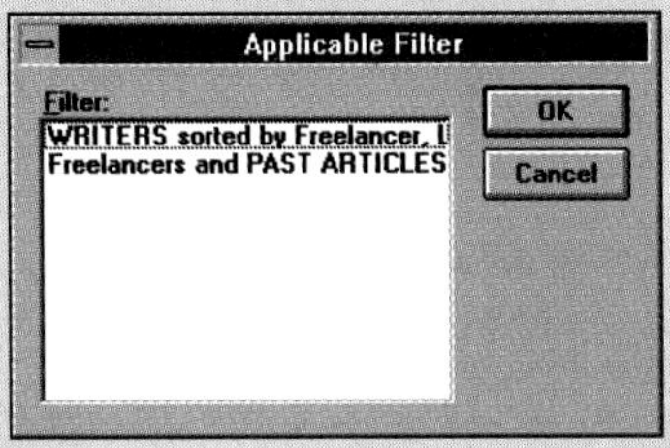

Figure 5-22
The Applicable
Filter dialog box

Applicable Filter

Filter:
WRITERS sorted by Freelancer, L
Freelancers and PAST ARTICLES

OK
Cancel

❹ Double-click **Freelancers and PAST ARTICLES**. The Applicable Filter dialog box disappears, and Access loads the saved query into the Filter grid.

❺ Double-click the Filter window **Control menu box** to close the Filter window.

❻ Click the toolbar **Apply Filter/Sort button** ⊞. Access applies the filter.

❼ Click the main form **Last Record button** ⊞. Access displays the sixth freelancer record, which is for Tonya Nilsson.

❽ Double-click the Form View window **Control menu box**. The Form View window disappears, and the Database window becomes the active window.

If you want to take a break and resume the tutorial at a later time, you can exit Access by double-clicking the Microsoft Access window Control menu box. When you resume the tutorial, place your Student Disk in the appropriate drive, launch Access, open the Issue25 database on your Student Disk, maximize the Database window, and click the Form object button.

Creating a Custom Form

Elena places the Issue25 database on the company network, and Harold, Judith, and Brian use it to answer their questions. The most popular query proves to be the Article Type Query, which lists the article title, type, and length, and the writer's first and last names. Harold tells Elena that he would like the option of viewing the same information in a form, and Elena designs a custom form based on the query.

If you modify a form created by a Form Wizard, or if you design and create a form without using a Form Wizard, you have developed a **custom form**. You might create a custom form, for example, to match a paper form, to display some fields side by side and others top to bottom, to highlight the form with color, or to add special buttons and list boxes.

Designing a Custom Form

Although Elena's custom form is relatively simple, she first designs the form's content and appearance on paper. Elena's finished design is shown in Figure 5-23.

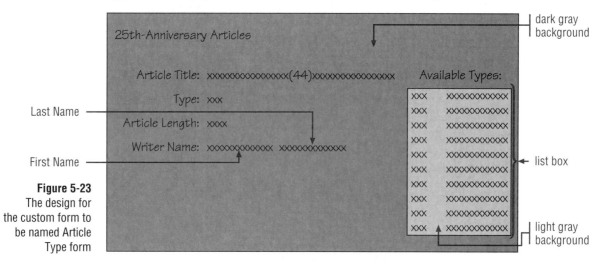

Figure 5-23
The design for
the custom form to
be named Article
Type form

The title for the designed form is 25th-Anniversary Articles. The designed form displays all fields from the Article Type Query in single-column format, except for the writer's First Name and Last Name fields, which are side by side.

Each field value will appear in a text box and will be preceded by a label. Elena indicates the locations and lengths of each field value by a series of ×s. The three ×s that follow the Type field label indicate that the field value will be three characters wide.

Because many of her coworkers are unfamiliar with all the article type codes, a list box containing both the article types and their full descriptions will appear on the right. Elena plans to add background colors of light gray to the list box and dark gray to the rest of the form to make the form easier to read.

All the data Elena needs for her custom form is contained in the Article Type Query. Thus, unlike her previous Form Wizard forms that were based on tables, Elena will use a query to create the custom form and will use all the fields from the Article Type Query. This query obtains data from both the PAST ARTICLES and WRITERS tables and displays records in ascending order by Article Type. The form, which Elena plans to name Article Type form, will likewise display records in ascending Article Type.

The Form Design Window

You use the **Form Design window** to create and modify forms. To create the custom form, Elena creates a blank form based on the Article Type Query in the Form Design window.

To create a blank form in the Form Design window:
❶ Click the toolbar **New Form button** ⬚. The New Form dialog box appears.
❷ Click the Select A Table/Query drop-down list box **down arrow button**. Scroll if necessary, click **Article Type Query**, and then click the **Blank Form button**. The Form Design window appears. See Figure 5-24.

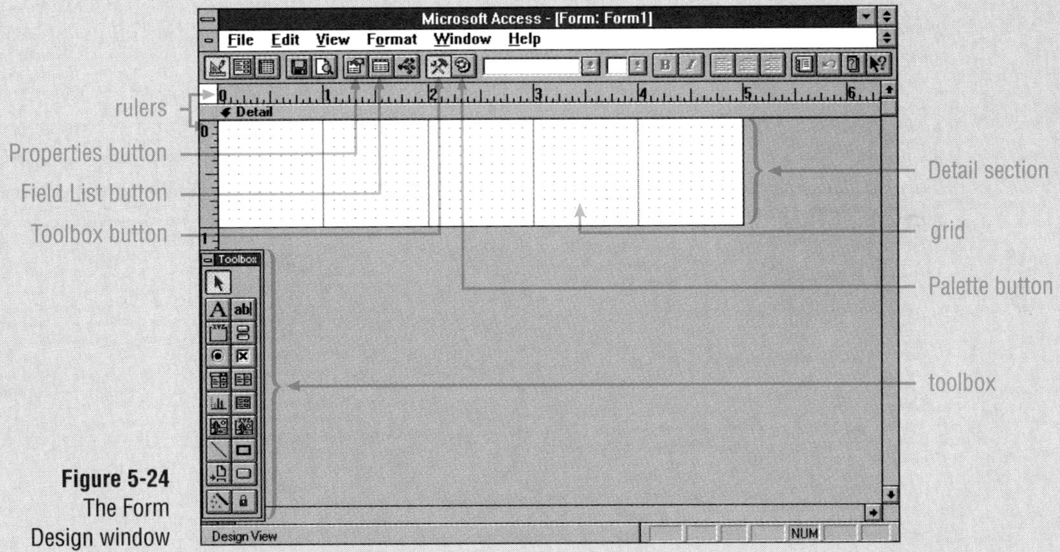

Figure 5-24
The Form
Design window

TROUBLE? If the rulers, grid, or toolbox do not appear, click the View menu and then click Ruler, Grid, or Toolbox to display the missing component in the Form Design window. A check mark appears in front of these View menu commands when the components are displayed in the Form Design window. If the grid is still invisible, see your technical support person or instructor for assistance. If the Palette appears in the Form Design window, click the toolbar Palette button ⬚ to close it until later in the tutorial. If the toolbar Properties button ⬚ is selected, click it to close the property sheet.

The Form Design window contains four new components and four new toolbar buttons. The new components are the rulers, the Detail section, the grid, and the toolbox; the new toolbar buttons are the Properties button, the Field List button, the Toolbar box and the Palette button.

The **rulers** show the horizontal and vertical dimensions of the form and serve as a guide to the placement of controls on the form. A **control** is a graphical object, such as a text box, a list box, a rectangle, or a command button, that you place on a form or a report to display data, perform an action, or make the form or report easier to read and use. Access has three types of controls: bound controls, unbound controls, and calculated controls. A **bound control** is linked, or bound, to a field in the underlying table or query. You use a bound control to display or update a table field value. An **unbound control** is not linked to a field in the underlying table or query. You use an unbound control to display text, such as a form title or instructions, or to display graphics and pictures from other applications. If you use an unbound control to display text, the unbound control is called a **label**. You can have a label relate to a bound control—a field-name label and a field-value text box can be paired as a bound control, for example. A **calculated control** displays a value calculated from data from one or more fields.

When you want to create a bound control, click the toolbar **Field List button** to display a list of fields available from the underlying table or query. You click and drag fields from the field list box to the Form Design window, placing the bound controls where you want them to appear on the form. Clicking the Field List button a second time closes the field list box.

To place other controls on a form, you use the tool buttons on the toolbox. The **toolbox** is a specialized toolbar containing buttons that represent the tools you use to place controls on a form or a report. When you hold the mouse pointer on a tool, Access displays a ToolTip for that tool. If you want to show or hide the toolbox, click the toolbar **Toolbox button**. A summary of the tools available in the toolbox is shown in Figure 5-25.

Icon	Tool Name	Control Purpose on a Form or Report
	Select objects	Select, move, size, and edit controls
	Label	Display text, such as a title or instructions; an unbound control
	Text Box	Display a label attached to a text box that contains a bound control or a calculated control
	Option Group	Display a group frame containing toggle buttons, option buttons, or check boxes; can use Control Wizards to create
	Toggle Button	Signal if a situation is true (button is selected or pushed down) or false
	Option Button	Signal if a situation is true (black dot appears in the option button's center) or false; also called a radio button
	Check Box	Signal if a situation is true ($\times$ appears in the check box) or false
	Combo Box	Display a drop-down list box, so that you can either type a value or select a value from the list; can use Control Wizards to create
	List Box	Display a list of values from which you can choose one value; can use Control Wizards to create
	Graph	Display a graph that can be editd with Microsoft Graph; uses Graph Wizard
	Subform/Subreport	Display both a main form or report from a primary table and a subform or subreport form a related table
	Object Frame	Display a picture, graph, or other OLE object that is stored in an Access database table
	Bound Object Frame	Display a picture, graph, or other OLE object that is stored in an Access database table
	Line	Display a horizontal, vertical, or diagonal line
	Rectangle	Display a rectangle
	Page Break	Mark the start of a new screen or printed page
	Command Button	Display a command button that runs a macro or calls an Access Basic event procedure when the button is clicked; can use Control Wizards to create
	Control Wizards	When selected, activates Control Wizards for certain other toolbox tools
	Tool Lock	Keeps a toolbox tool selected when clicked after target tool is selected; clicking another toolbox tool deactivates

Figure 5-25
Summary of tools available in the toolbox for a form or a report

To open and close the property sheet for a selected control, a section of the form, or the entire form, click the toolbar **Properties button**. You use the **property sheet** to modify the appearance, behavior, and other characteristics of the overall form, a section of a form, or the controls on a form. For example, you can change a control's size or position on the form. The properties shown in the property sheet differ depending on the type of control selected.

When you click the toolbar Palette button, you open or close the Palette. You use the **Palette** to change the appearance and color of a form and its controls. **Appearance** options are normal, raised, or sunken. Colors can be chosen for text, background, and borders from a color palette. You can also use the Palette to control the thickness of lines drawn on the form.

The **Detail section**, which appears in white in the Form Design window, is the area in which you place the fields, labels, and most other controls for your form. You can change the default Detail section size, which is 5" wide by 1" high, by dragging the edges. The **grid** consists of the dots that appear in the Detail section. These dots help you to position controls precisely on a form.

You can add four other sections to a form by clicking the Format menu. The other four sections are the Form Header, Form Footer, Page Header, and Page Footer. Use the **Form Header** and **Form Footer sections** for information such as titles, dates, and instructions that you want to appear only at the top or bottom of a form on the screen or in print. Use the **Page Header** and **Page Footer sections** for information such as column headings or page numbers that you want to appear at the top or bottom of each page in a printed form.

Adding Fields to a Form

Elena's first task in the Form Design window is to add bound controls to the form Detail section for all the fields from the Article Type Query. When you add a bound control to a form, Access adds a label and, to its right, a field-value text box. You create a bound control by selecting one or more fields from the field list box and dragging them to the form. You select a single field by clicking the field. You select two or more fields by holding down [Ctrl] and clicking each field, and you select all fields by double-clicking the field-list title bar.

Because Elena wants to place all the fields from the field list box on the form, she adds bound controls to the form Detail section for all the fields in the field list.

To add bound controls for all the fields in the field list:
❶ Click the toolbar **Field List button** ▦. The field list box appears.
❷ Double-click the **field-list title bar** to select all the fields in the field list. Access highlights the field list box.
❸ Click anywhere in the highlighted area of the field list box and drag to the form's Detail section. Release the mouse button when the ▱ is positioned at the top of the Detail section and at the 1.25" mark on the horizontal ruler. Access adds bound controls for the five selected fields. Each bound control consists of a text box and, to its left, an attached label. See Figure 5-26.

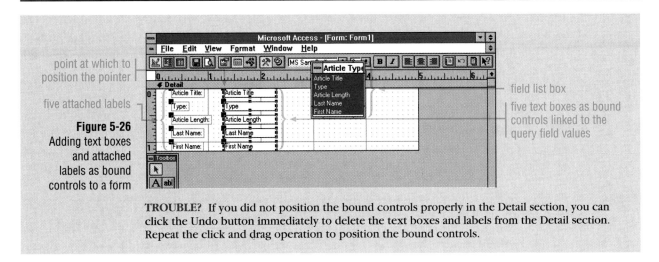

Figure 5-26
Adding text boxes and attached labels as bound controls to a form

point at which to position the pointer

five attached labels

field list box

five text boxes as bound controls linked to the query field values

TROUBLE? If you did not position the bound controls properly in the Detail section, you can click the Undo button immediately to delete the text boxes and labels from the Detail section. Repeat the click and drag operation to position the bound controls.

Performing operations in the Form Design window might seem awkward for you at first. With practice you will become comfortable with creating a custom form. Remember that you can always click the Undo button immediately after you make a form adjustment that has undesired results.

Selecting, Moving, and Deleting Controls

Five text boxes now appear in a column in the form Detail section. Each text box is a bound control linked to a field in the underlying query and has an attached label box to its left. Because she is done with the field list box, Elena closes it by clicking the Field List button. Elena next compares the form Detail section with her design and arranges the Last Name and First Name text boxes side by side to agree with her form design, as shown in Figure 5-23.

To close the field list box and select a single bound control:
❶ Click the toolbar **Field List button** 📋 to close the field list box.
❷ Two boxes in the Detail section have Last Name inside them. The box on the left is the label box, and the box on the right is the field-value text box. Click in the gray area outside the Detail section to deselect any previous selection and then click inside the Last Name **field-value text box**. Move handles appear on the field-value text box and its attached label box; in addition, sizing handles appear, but only on the field-value text box. See Figure 5-27.

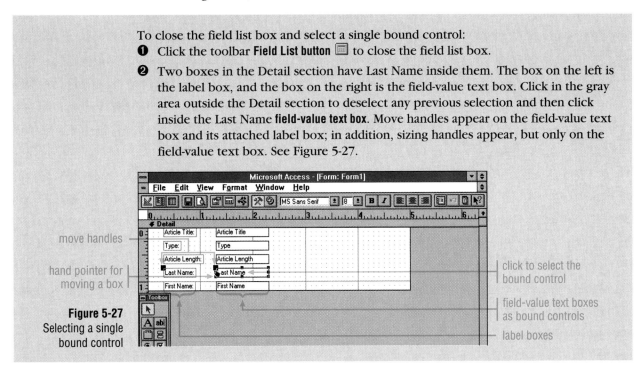

Figure 5-27
Selecting a single bound control

move handles

hand pointer for moving a box

click to select the bound control

field-value text boxes as bound controls

label boxes

You can move a field-value text box and its attached label box together. To move them, place the pointer anywhere on the border of the field-value text box, but not on a move handle or a sizing handle. When the pointer changes to ✋, drag the field-value text box and its attached label box to the new location. As you move the boxes, their outline moves to show you the changing position.

You can also move either the field-value text box or its label box individually. If you want to move the field-value text box but not its label box, for example, place the pointer on the text box's move handle. When the pointer changes to ✋, drag the field-value text box to the new location. You use the label box's move handle in a similar way to move just the label box.

You can also delete a field-value text box and its attached label box or delete just the label box. To delete both boxes together, click inside the field-value text box to select both boxes, click the right mouse button inside the text box to open its Shortcut menu, and then click Cut on the menu. To delete just the label box, perform the same steps, clicking inside the label box instead of the field-value text box.

Elena moves the Last Name field-value text box to the right without moving its label box. She moves the First Name field-value text box (without its label box) up beside the Last Name box. Then she deletes the First Name label box.

To move field-value text boxes and delete labels:

❶ Move the pointer to the Last Name field-value text box move handle. When the mouse pointer changes to ✋, drag the text box horizontally to the right, leaving enough room for the First Name field-value text box to fit in its place. An outline of the box appears as you change its position to guide you in the move operation. Be sure to take advantage of the grid dots in the Detail section to position the box outline.

TROUBLE? If you move the box incorrectly, click the Undo button immediately and then repeat the step.

❷ Click the **field-value text box** for the First Name field and then move the pointer to its move handle. When the mouse pointer changes to ✋, drag the box up to the position previously occupied by the Last Name field-value text box.

❸ Click the **label box** for the First Name field to select it. Click the First Name **label box** with the right mouse button to open its Shortcut menu and click **Cut**. The First Name label box disappears. See Figure 5-28.

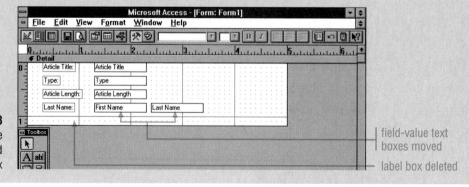

Figure 5-28
Moving field-value
text boxes and
deleting a label box

Resizing a Control

Elena notices that the Article Title field-value text box is too small to contain long titles, so she resizes it.

You use the seven sizing handles to resize a control. Moving the pointer over a sizing handle changes the pointer to a two-headed arrow; the pointer's direction differs depending on the sizing handle you use. When you drag the sizing handle you resize the control. Thin lines appear, which guide you as you drag the control. You can also resize a label box by selecting the label and using the sizing handles that appear.

Let's resize the Article Title field-value text box by stretching it to the right.

To resize a field-value text box:

❶ Click the field-value **text box** for the Article Title field to select it. Move handles and sizing handles appear.

❷ Move the pointer to the right side of the box over the middle handle. The pointer changes to ↔.

❸ Drag the right border horizontally to the right until the right edge is just past the 3.75" mark on the horizontal ruler. The text box will now accommodate longer Article Title field values.

Changing a Label's Caption and Resizing a Label

Elena now compares the form to her design and notices that she needs to change the name in the Last Name label box to Writer Name. Elena uses the label's property sheet to change the label's Caption property.

To change the Caption property for a label:

❶ Click in an unoccupied area of the grid to deselect all the control boxes.

❷ Click the Last Name **label box** to select it.

❸ Click the toolbar **Properties button** ▣. The property sheet for the Last Name label appears.

❹ Click the **Caption text box** in the property sheet and then press [F2] to select the entire value. See Figure 5-29 on the following page.

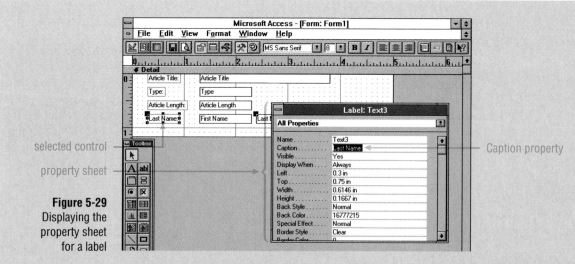

selected control

property sheet

Caption property

Figure 5-29
Displaying the
property sheet
for a label

TROUBLE? If the property sheet is not positioned as shown in Figure 5-29, click the title bar of the property sheet and drag the property sheet to the position shown. If some of the property values on your screen differ from those shown in the figure, do not be concerned. Property values will be different if you completed prior operations in a slightly different way.

❺ Type **Writer Name:**. Be sure to type a colon at the end of the caption.

❻ Click ▣ to close the property sheet. The label box contents change from Last Name: to Writer Name:.

Only part of the new caption is visible in the label box, so Elena resizes the label box.

To resize a label box:
❶ The Writer Name **label box** is still the selected control, so move the pointer to the left side of the control over the middle handle. When the pointer changes to ↔, drag the left border horizontally to the left one entire set of grid dots. You might need to try a few times to get it right. If you change the vertical size of the box by mistake, just click the Undo button and try again.

Aligning Labels

Elena next notices that the top three label boxes are left-justified; that is, they are aligned on their left edges. She wants all four label boxes aligned on their right edges. This is an individual preference on her part. Some people prefer left justification for the labels and others prefer right justification. To align several label boxes on the right simultaneously, you must first select all the label boxes by clicking inside each label box while holding down [Shift]. In the following steps be sure you select the label boxes only. If you select the field-value text boxes by mistake, click Undo.

To align all label boxes on the right:
❶ While pressing and holding **[Shift]**, click each of the four label boxes, and then release [Shift]. This action selects the four label boxes.

❷ Click any one of the selected label boxes with the right mouse button to display the Shortcut menu.

❸ Click **Align** in the Shortcut menu to open the Align list box, and then click **Right**. Access aligns the label boxes on their right edges. See Figure 5-30.

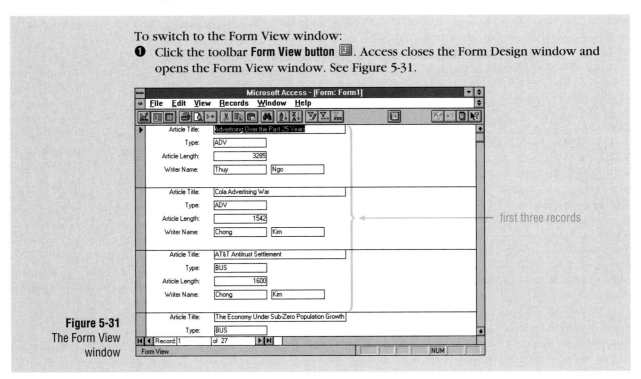

label boxes aligned on the right

Figure 5-30
Aligning label boxes on the right

Viewing a Form in the Form View Window

Before Elena makes further changes in the Form Design window, she switches to the Form View window to study her results. The first three buttons on the left of the toolbar allow you to switch at any time among the Form Design, Form View, and Datasheet View windows. When you create a form, you should periodically check your progress in the Form View window. You might see adjustments you want to make on your form in the Form Design window.

Let's switch to the Form View window.

To switch to the Form View window:
❶ Click the toolbar **Form View button** 🖫. Access closes the Form Design window and opens the Form View window. See Figure 5-31.

first three records

Figure 5-31
The Form View window

Your form uses the Article Type Query to sort the records in ascending order by the Type Field. Access displays the first three records from the query and part of the fourth record. You can use the scroll bars and navigation buttons to view other records from the query on the form.

Elena sees some adjustments she wants to make to her design. By default, Access displays as many form records as it can on the screen at one time. Elena wants to display only one record at a time. She also needs to add a form title and add the list box for the article types and descriptions.

Using Form Headers and Footers

Elena next adds a title to the form so that others can easily identify the form when they see it. To do this, she chooses the Form Header/Footer command from the Format menu to add header and footer sections to the form. She then places the title in the Form Header section and deletes the Form Footer section by decreasing its height to zero.

The Form Header and Footer sections allow you to add titles, instructions, command buttons, and other information to your form. You add the Form Header and Footer as a pair. If your form needs one of them but not the other, decrease the height of the unwanted one to zero. This is a way you delete any section on a form.

Elena adds the Form Header and Footer sections to the form.

To add Form Header and Footer sections to a form:

❶ Click the toolbar **Design View button** 🖾. Access closes the Form View window and opens the Form Design window.

❷ Click **Format**, and then click **Form Header/Footer**. Access inserts a Form Header section above the Detail section and a Form Footer section below the Detail section. See Figure 5-32.

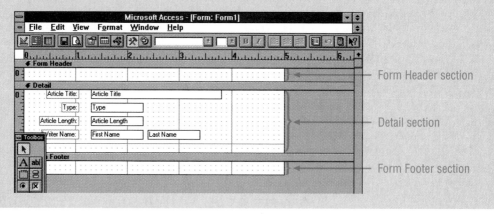

Figure 5-32
Adding the Form
Header and Form
Footer sections

When you change the width of one section of a form, all sections of the form are affected—the sections all have the same width. Each section, however, can have a different height. You change the width of a form by dragging the right edge of any section, and you change the height of a section by dragging its bottom edge.

Elena deletes the Form Footer section by dragging its bottom edge upward until it disappears.

To delete a Form Footer section:

❶ Move the pointer to the bottom edge of the Form Footer section. When the pointer changes to ↕, click and drag the bottom edge upward until it disappears. Even though the words Form Footer remain, the white area defining the section is gone and the section will not appear in the form.

Elena now adds the form title to the Form Header section with the toolbox Label tool. You use the toolbox **Label tool** to add an unbound control to a form or report for the display of text, such as a title or instructions.

To add a label to a form:

❶ Click the toolbox **Label tool** Ⓐ.

❷ Move the pointer into the Form Header section. As you move the pointer into the form, the pointer changes to ⁺A. See Figure 5-33. Position the pointer as shown in Figure 5-33.

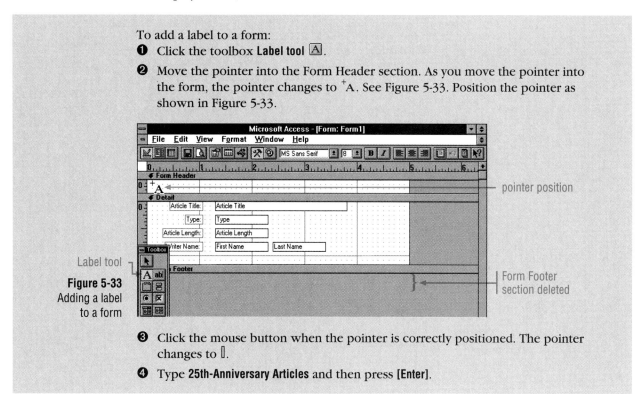

Figure 5-33
Adding a label
to a form

❸ Click the mouse button when the pointer is correctly positioned. The pointer changes to Ⅰ.

❹ Type **25th-Anniversary Articles** and then press **[Enter]**.

Adding a List Box Using Control Wizards

Because many of her coworkers are unfamiliar with the various article type codes, Elena adds a list box to the form's Detail section. The list box will display all the article types and their full descriptions from the TYPES table. A **list box** is a control that displays a list of values. You can use a list box when a field, such as the Type field, contains a limited set of values. The list box eliminates the need to remember all the Type field values. When you click one of the list box values, Access replaces the form's Type field value with the value you clicked. Thus, you can eliminate the need to keyboard a Type field-value. When you add a list box to a form, Access by default adds a label box to its left.

You use the toolbox List Box tool to add a list box to a form. Depending on whether the toolbox Control Wizards tool is selected, you can add a list box with or without using Control Wizards. A **Control Wizard** is an Access tool that asks you a series of questions and then creates a control on a form or report based on your answers. Access offers Control Wizards for the toolbox Combo Box tool, List Box tool, Option Group tool, and Command Button tool.

Elena will use the List Box Wizard to add the list box for the article types and descriptions. Before she adds the list box, Elena increases the width and the height of the Detail section to make room for the list box. She first moves the toolbox, so that it is out of the way.

To move the toolbox and resize the Detail section:
❶ Click the **toolbox title bar** and drag it to the right to the ruler 1" mark.
❷ Drag the right edge of the Detail section to the horizontal ruler's 6" mark.
❸ Drag the bottom edge of the Detail section to the vertical ruler's 2.25" mark.
❹ Drag the **toolbox title bar** to the lower-right corner of the screen. See Figure 5-34.

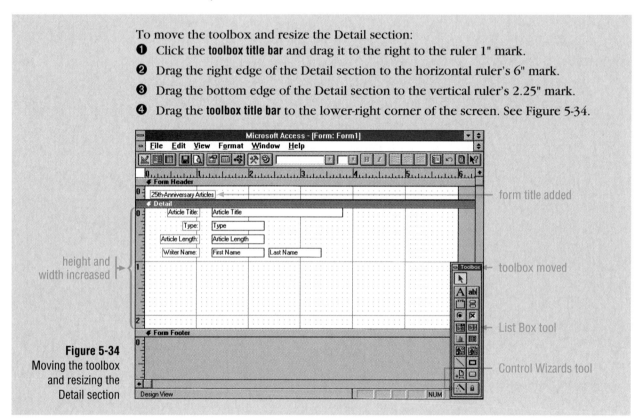

Figure 5-34
Moving the toolbox and resizing the Detail section

Elena adds a list box to the Detail section using the List Box Wizard.

To activate the List Box Wizard:
❶ Click the toolbox **Control Wizards tool** ▨.
❷ Click the toolbox **List Box tool** ▦. As you move the pointer away from the toolbox, the pointer changes to ⁺▦. See Figure 5-35.

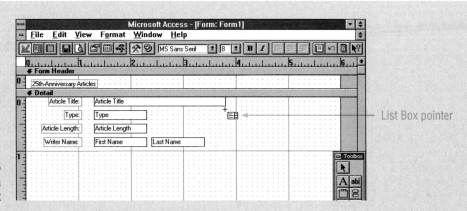

Figure 5-35
Positioning a
list box

❸ Click when the list box pointer is positioned as shown in Figure 5-35. After a few seconds, the first List Box Wizard dialog box appears.

Elena tells the List Box Wizard to display two fields from the TYPES table: the Type field and the Description field. She also uses the List Box Wizard dialog box to size the two fields' column widths and to add the label Article Types.

To add a list box using the List Box Wizard:

❶ The TYPES table will supply the values for the list box, so click the **top radio button**, which is labeled "I want the list box to look up the values in a table or query." Then click the **Next > button**. The second List Box Wizard dialog box appears.

❷ Click **TYPES** as the source table for the list box and then click the **Next > button**. The third List Box Wizard dialog box appears.

❸ Because you want both the Type and Description fields to appear in the list box, click the **>> button** to select both fields and then click the **Next > button**. The fourth List Box Wizard dialog box appears.

❹ For both columns, double-click the right edge of each column selector to get the best column fit and then click the **Next > button**. The fifth List Box Wizard dialog box appears.

❺ If Type is not highlighted, click it to select it. Then click the **Next > button**. The sixth List Box Wizard dialog box appears.

❻ Because you want to be able to select a Type field value from the list box and store it in the form's Type field-value text box, click the bottom radio button, which is labeled "Store that value in this field:." Next, click the **down arrow button**, click **Type**, and then click the **Next > button**. The seventh and final List Box Wizard dialog box appears.

❼ For a label, type **Article Types:** in the text box and then click the **Finish button**. Access closes the List Box Wizard dialog box and displays the completed list box in the Detail section of the form. See Figure 5-36.

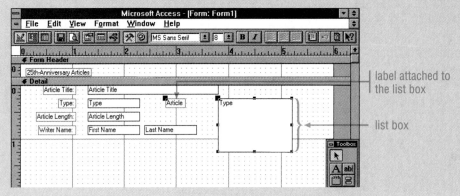

Figure 5-36
Adding a list box
to a form

label attached to the list box

list box

The attached label appears to the left of the list box. Elena resizes the label and then moves it above the list box.

To resize and move a label:
❶ Click the label box attached to the list box to select it.
❷ Click **Format**, click **Size**, and then click **to Fit.** The label's entire caption is now visible.
❸ Click and drag the **label box's move handle** to position the label box above the list box. See Figure 5-37.

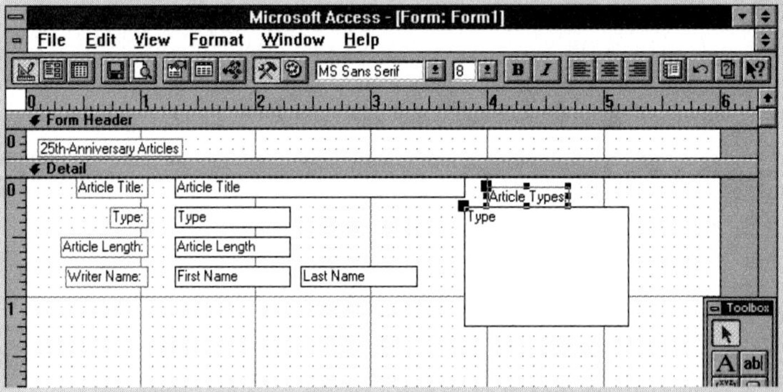

Figure 5-37
Resizing and
moving a label

Adding Background Colors to a Form

Elena's final tasks are to add background colors to the list box and to the Form Header and Detail sections and to change the form property sheet to display a single record at a time. The Default View property for a form, Continuous Forms, displays as many records as possible on a form. To show a single record on a form, you change the Default View property to Single Form.

To display a single record at a time on a form:

❶ Click anywhere in the area below the Form Footer bar. This action makes the form itself the selected control.

❷ Click the toolbar **Properties button** 🖼 to display the property sheet for the form.

❸ Click the **Default View box** in the property sheet, click the **down arrow button**, and then click **Single Form**.

❹ Click 🖼 to close the property sheet.

Elena changes the background colors on the form. She changes the list box background to light gray and the background of the Detail and Form Header sections to a darker gray.

Adding Colors to a Form

- Click the control you want to color.
- Click the toolbar Palette button to display the Palette.
- Select the appearance, color, or other special effect from the Palette.
- Click the Palette button to close the Palette.

Let's change the colors of the list box and the two form sections.

To change the colors of a list box and the form sections:

❶ Click the list box to select it.

❷ Click the toolbar **Palette button** 🖫 to display the Palette. See Figure 5-38.

dark gray —

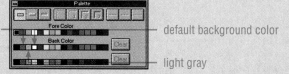

— default background color

Figure 5-38
The Palette

— light gray

❸ Click the **light gray color box** on the Back Color line. This is the third box from the left.

❹ Click the Detail section, but do not click any of the controls in that section. This makes the Detail section the selected control.

❺ Click the **dark gray color box** on the Back Color line. This is the second box from the left.

❻ Click the Form Header section, but do not click the label box. This makes the Form Header section the selected control.

❼   Click the **dark gray color box** on the Back Color line again. See Figure 5-39.

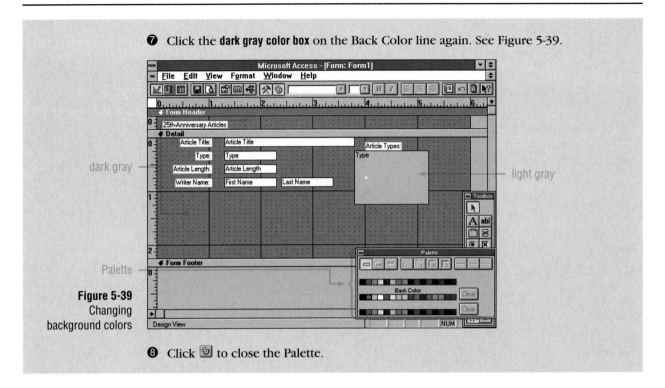

Figure 5-39
Changing
background colors

dark gray

light gray

Palette

❽   Click 🔲 to close the Palette.

Making Final Revisions to a Custom Form

Elena switches to the Form View window to review the custom form. She wants to see if there are any further changes she needs to make to the form.

To switch to the Form View window to review a custom form:
❶   Click the toolbar **Form View button** 🔲. Access closes the Form Design window and opens the Form View window. See Figure 5-40.

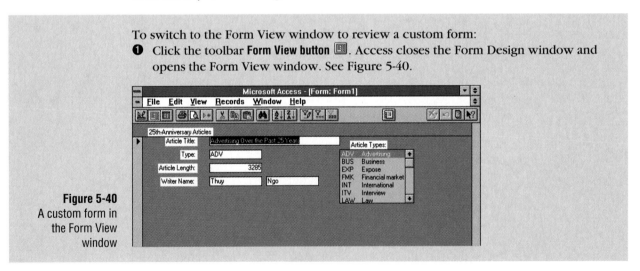

Figure 5-40
A custom form in
the Form View
window

Elena sees that the list box is not tall enough to show the entire list of article types and descriptions. She switches back to the Form Design window to resize the list box.

To switch to the Form Design window and resize a list box:

❶ Click the toolbar **Design View button** 🔲. Access closes the Form View window and opens the Form Design window.

❷ Click the list box to select it. Drag the middle sizing handle on the bottom border to the 2.00" mark on the vertical ruler to increase the height of the list box. Switch back and forth between the Form View window and the Form Design window until the list box is large enough to show all the article types. See Figure 5-41.

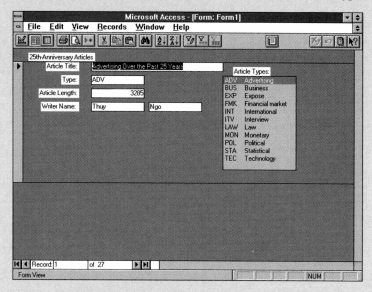

Figure 5-41
The final version
of a custom
form in the Form
View window

❸ When you have completed the custom form, switch to the Form Design window to view the form's final design. See Figure 5-42.

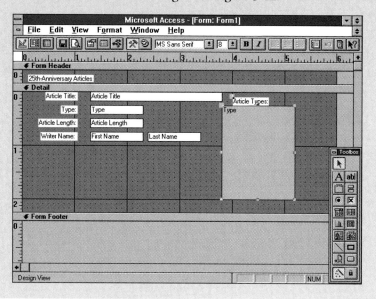

Figure 5-42
The final version
of a custom form
in the Form
Design window

Elena saves the custom form, naming it Article Type form, and closes the Form Design window.

To save a custom form and close the Form Design window:
❶ Click the toolbar **Save button** 🖫. The Save As dialog box appears.
❷ Type **Article Type form** and then press [Enter]. Access saves the custom form.
❸ Double-click the Form Design window **Control menu box**. Access closes the Form Design window and activates the Database window.

Elena now has five forms displayed in the Forms list box. Having completed her work with forms for the Issue25 database, Elena exits Access.

Questions

1. What type of Form Wizard form displays data from two related tables?
2. Which Form Wizard style should you select when you first start working with forms?
3. What is the quickest way to create a form?
4. How does a Form Wizard display the value for a yes/no field?
5. What formats do Form Wizards use to display records in a main/subform form?
6. How many sets of navigation buttons appear in a main/subform form, and what does each set control?
7. When should you use a filter instead of the Find button or the quick sort buttons?
8. If you want to reuse a filter in the future, you save the filter as what type of object?
9. What is the difference between a bound and an unbound control?
10. What five different sections can a form have?
11. How do you move a control and its label together, and how do you move each separately?
12. How do you change a label name?
13. What form property do you change so that Access displays a single record at a time?

Tutorial Assignments

Elena uses a Form Wizard to create a form named PAST ARTICLES form for the Issue25 database. Launch Access, open the Issue25 database on your Student Disk, and do the following:
1. Use Form Wizards to create a single-column form type with the standard style based on the PAST ARTICLES table. Select all the fields from the table in the order in which they are stored in the table, and use the default form title PAST ARTICLES.
2. Open the Form View window and then print the first page.
3. Change the form's design so that the Article Length text box and its attached label box are to the right of, and on the same line as, the Issue field.
4. Move the Writer ID text box and its attached label box up to the position previously occupied by the Article Length bound control.
5. Change the Caption property for the Article Length label box to Length followed by a colon.
6. Resize the Article Title text box so that the field value for each record is completely displayed.

7. Verify your design changes in the Form View window by navigating through all records.

8. Print the first page.

9. Save the form, using the name PAST ARTICLES form, and close the form window on your screen.

Elena next creates a custom form and names it PAST ARTICLES by Issue and Length form. Use the Issue25 database on your Student Disk to do the following:

10. Create a query by selecting the PAST ARTICLES and WRITERS tables and selecting the following fields in the order given here: Article Title, Type, Issue of Business Perspectives, Article Length, Last Name, and First Name. Rename the Issue of Business Perspectives field simply Issue. Then sort the records based on Issue as the primary sort key in descending order and Article Length as the secondary sort key in ascending order. Print the entire dynaset for this query. Finally, save the query, naming it ARTICLES sorted by Issue, Length, and close the active window to activate the Database window.

11. Create a custom form by selecting the query named ARTICLES sorted by Issue, Length and then clicking the Blank Form button.

12. Add all the fields from the query named ARTICLES sorted by Issue, Length to the Detail section and print the first page of the form.

13. Change the Caption property for the Article Length label box to Length, right align all the label boxes, resize the Article Title text box so that the field-value for each record is completely displayed, and print the first page of the form.

14. Move the First Name text box to the right of, and on the same line as, the Last Name text box; delete the First Name label; change the Caption property for the Last Name label to Writer Name; resize the Writer Name label; and print the first page of the form.

E 15. Use the Format menu's to Fit option under the Size command for the five labels and then right align all the labels. Print the first page of the form.

E 16. Change the form width to 4.5" and then move the Issue text box and its attached label to the right of, and on the same line as, the Type field. Move all the lines that follow the Type and Issue fields up to eliminate blank lines. If necessary, right align all the labels that appear on the left of the form and then left align the field-value text boxes to their immediate right. Print the first page of the form.

E 17. Add Form Header and Footer sections; delete the Form Footer section; add to the Form Header section the form title PAST ARTICLES by Issue, Length; change the height of the Detail section to 3"; and print the first page of the form.

E 18. Use the List Box Wizard to create a list box to display all the article types and their descriptions. Position the list box under all the fields. Use the TYPES table for the list box, and display both table fields. Add the label Types to the form and position it just to the left of the list box. Resize the list box to display all types and descriptions. Finally, change the form's Default View to Single Form, and then print the first and last pages of the form.

19. Save the form as PAST ARTICLES by Issue and Length form.

Case Problems

1. Walkton Daily Press Carriers

Grant Sherman uses a Form Wizard to create a form for his Press database. Launch Access, open the Press database on your Student Disk, and do the following:

1. Use Form Wizards to create a single-column form type with the standard style based on the CARRIERS table. Select all the fields from the table in the order in which they are stored in the table. Use the form title CARRIERS data.

2. Open the Form View window and then print the second page.

3. Save the form with the name CARRIERS form and close the form window on your screen.

Grant creates a custom form named CARRIERS by Name, Route ID form. Use the Press database on your Student Disk to do the following:

4. Create a query by selecting the BILLINGS and CARRIERS tables. Create a join line for the Carrier ID fields and select these fields in the order given here: Carrier Last Name, Carrier First Name, Carrier Phone, Route ID, and Balance Amount. Rename the Balance Amount field simply Balance, and then sort the records based on Carrier Last Name as the primary sort key in ascending order and on Route ID as the secondary sort key in ascending order. Print the entire dynaset for this query. Finally, save the query, naming it CARRIERS sorted by Name, Route ID. Close the active window to activate the Database window.

E 5. Create a custom form by selecting the query named CARRIERS sorted by Name, Route ID and then clicking the Blank Form button.

E 6. To the Detail section of the form, add all the fields from the query named CARRIERS sorted by Name, Route ID. Print the first page of the form.

E 7. Move the Carrier Last Name text box without its attached label to the right on the same line, leaving room to move the Carrier First Name text box from the line below up in front of it. Then move the Carrier First Name text box without its attached label up between the Carrier Last Name label box and the Carrier Last Name text box. Delete the Carrier First Name label box, change the Caption property for the Carrier Last Name label box to Carrier Name, resize the Carrier Name label box to accommodate the shorter caption, and print the first page of the form.

E 8. Move the Carrier Phone text box and its attached label up one line, and move the Route ID text box and its attached label up one line. Move the Balance text box and its attached label to the right of, and on the same line as, the Route ID bound control. Print the first page of the form.

9. Move the Balance label to the right, so that it is closer to its attached text box.

10. Right align all the labels on the left side of the form.

11. Change the form's Default View to Single Form and change the Detail section background color to blue-green (third color from the right in the Back Color row of the Palette).

12. Add Form Header and Footer sections. Add to the Form Header section the form title CARRIERS by Name and Route ID. Add to the Form Footer section the label Press Database, and print the first page of the form.

13. Save the form as CARRIERS by Name, Route ID form.

2. Lopez Used Cars

Hector Lopez uses a Form Wizard to create a form for his Usedcars database. Launch Access, open the Usedcars database on your Student Disk, and do the following:

1. Use Form Wizards to create a single-column form type with the standard style based on the USED CARS table. Select all the fields from the table in the order in which they are stored in the table. Use the form title USED CARS data.

2. Open the Form View window and then print the first two pages.

3. Save the form with the name USED CARS form and close the form window on your screen.

Maria Lopez creates a custom form, naming it USED CARS by Manufacturer and Model form. Use the Usedcars database on your Student Disk to do the following:

4. Create a query by selecting the CLASSES, LOCATIONS, USED CARS, and TRANSMISSIONS tables. You need join lines between the two Transmission Type fields, between the two Location Code fields, and between Class Type and Class. If any of these join lines are not shown, then create them. Select these fields in the order given here: Manufacturer, Model, Class Description, Transmission Desc, Year, Location Name, Manager Name, Cost, and Selling Price. Sort the records based on Manufacturer as the primary sort key in ascending order and on Model as the secondary sort key in ascending order. Print the entire dynaset for this query. Finally, save the query, naming it USED CARS by Manufacturer, Model.

E 5. Create a custom form by selecting the query named USED CARS by Manufacturer, Model and then clicking the Blank Form button.

E 6. Add to the Detail section all the fields from the query named USED CARS by Manufacturer, Model. Print the fourth page of the form.

E 7. Resize the field-value text boxes, as necessary, so that, in the Form View window, all the field values for each record are completely displayed without unnecessary extra space. Navigate through the records in the Form View window to be sure the box sizes are correct. The Class Description and Transmission Desc text boxes should be widened, for example, and the Year, Cost, and Selling Price text boxes should be narrowed.

E 8. Change the form's Default View to Single Form and then change the width of the Detail section to 5.75" and its height to 3.75".

9. Move the Model text box and its attached label to the right of, and on the same line as, the Manufacturer bound control. Then move the Model text box to the left to be one grid dot away from its related label.

10. Move the Year text box and its attached label to the right of, and on the same line as, the Model bound control. Then move the Year label to the right to be one grid dot away from its related text box.

11. Move the Manager Name text box and its attached label to the right of, and on the same line as, the Location Name bound control.

12. Move the Selling Price text box and its attached label to the right of, and on the same line as, the Cost bound control.

13. Eliminate blank lines by moving text boxes and their attached labels up, and then print the fourth page of the form.

14. Change the Captions properties for these labels: Class Description to Class, Transmission Desc to Trans, and Location Name to Location.

E 15. Apply the Format menu's to Fit option under the Size command for the labels on the left side of the form labels, right align these labels, and then print the fourth page of the form.

E 16. Use the List Box Wizard to add two list boxes to the form—one for class types and descriptions and one for location codes and names. Position the list boxes side by side below all the control boxes in the Detail Section, placing the one containing class types and descriptions on the left. For the class list box, use the CLASSES table, display both table fields, and enter Classes for the label. For the location list box, use the LOCATIONS table, display the Location Code and Location Name fields, and enter Locations as the labels. Resize and move the labels and list boxes to display as much of each record and as many records as possible.

E 17. Print the fourth page of the form.

18. Save the form as USED CARS by Manufacturer and Model form.

3.   Tophill University Student Employment

Olivia Tyler uses a Form Wizard to create a form for her Parttime database. Launch Access, open the Parttime database on your Student Disk, and do the following:

1. Use Form Wizards to create a main/subform form type with the standard style based on the EMPLOYERS table as the primary table for the main form and the JOBS table as the related table for the subform. Select all the fields from the EMPLOYERS table in the order in which they are stored in the table. Select all the fields from the JOBS table, except for the Employer ID field, in the order in which they are stored in the table. Use the form title EMPLOYERS and JOBS data.

2. Open the Form View window, save the subform with the name JOBS subform, and then print the first page.

3. Save the form as EMPLOYERS and JOBS form and close the form window on your screen.

Olivia creates a custom form named JOBS by Employer and Job Title form. Use the Parttime database on your Student Disk to do the following:

E   4. Create a query by selecting the EMPLOYERS and JOBS tables and, if necessary, create a join line for the Employer ID fields. Select all the fields from the EMPLOYERS table in the order in which they are stored in the table, and then select these fields from the JOBS table in the order given here: Hours/Week, Job Title, and Wage. Sort the records based on Employer Name as the primary sort key in ascending order and on Job Title as the secondary sort key in ascending order. Print the entire dynaset for this query. Finally, save the query, naming it JOBS sorted by Employer, Job Title.

E   5. Create a custom form by selecting the query named JOBS sorted by Employer, Job Title and then clicking the Blank Form button.

E   6. Add all the fields from the query named JOBS sorted by Employer, Job Title to the Detail section and then print the first page of the form.

E   7. Resize the Employer Name and Job Title text boxes and print the first page of the form.

8. Right align all the labels.

9. Change the form's Default View to Single Form, change the Detail section background color to light gray (third color from the left in the Back Color row on the Palette), and then print the first page of the form.

10. Add Form Header and Footer sections, add to the Form Header section the form title JOBS by Employer and Job Title, add to the Form Footer section the label Parttime Database, and print the first page of the form.

11. Save the form as JOBS by Employer and Job Title form.

4.   Rexville Business Licenses

Chester Pearce uses a Form Wizard to create a form for his Buslic database. Launch Access, open the Buslic database on your Student Disk, and do the following:

1. Use Form Wizards to create a single-column form type with the standard style based on the BUSINESSES table. Select all the fields from the table in the order in which they are stored in the table. Use the form title BUSINESSES data.

2. Open the Form View window and then print the first two pages.

3. Save the form as BUSINESSES form and close the form window on your screen.

Chester"creates a custom form, naming it BUSINESSES by License Type and Business Name form. Use the Buslic database on your Student Disk to do the following:

E   4. Create a query by selecting the BUSINESSES, ISSUED LICENSES, and LICENSES tables and, if necessary, create join lines for the Business ID fields and the License Type fields. Select all the fields, except the Business ID field, from the BUSINESSES table in the order in which they are stored in the table; select the License Number, License Type, Amount, and Date Issued fields (in the order given here) from the ISSUED LICENSES table; and then select the License

Description and Basic Cost fields from the LICENSES table. Rename the License Description field simply License. Sort the records based on License Type as the primary sort key in ascending order and on Business Name as the secondary sort key in ascending order, but do not show the License Type field in the dynaset. Print the entire dynaset for this query. Finally, save the query, naming it BUSINESSES sorted by License Type, Business Name.

E   5. Create a custom form by selecting the query named BUSINESSES sorted by License Type, Business Name and then clicking the Blank Form button.

E   6. Add all the fields from the query named BUSINESSES sorted by License Type, Business Name to the Detail section and then print the first page of the form.

7. Resize the Business Name and License text boxes, and print the first page of the form.

8. Right align all the labels.

9. Change the form's Default View to Single Form, change the Detail section background color to blue-green (third color from the right in the Back Color row on the Palette), and then print the first page of the form.

E   10. Add Form Header and Footer sections, add to the Form Header section the form title BUSINESSES by License Type and Business Name, add to the Form Footer section the label Buslic Database, and print the first page of the form.

11. Save the form as BUSINESSES by License Type and Business Name form.

Creating Reports

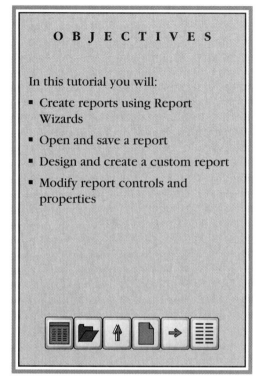

OBJECTIVES

In this tutorial you will:

- Create reports using Report Wizards
- Open and save a report
- Design and create a custom report
- Modify report controls and properties

Creating a Marketing Report at Vision Publishers

CASE

Vision Publishers Harold Larson plans a meeting with several advertisers in New York for the special 25th-anniversary issue of *Business Perspective*. He asks Elena Sanchez to produce a report of all the articles and authors to help him describe their contents to potential advertisers.

Using a Report

A **report** is a formatted hardcopy of the contents of one or more tables from a database. Although you can print data from datasheets, queries, and forms, reports allow you the greatest flexibility for formatting hardcopy output. Reports can be used, for example, to print membership lists, billing statements, and mailing labels.

The Sections of a Report

Figure 6-1 shows a sample report produced from the Issue25 database.

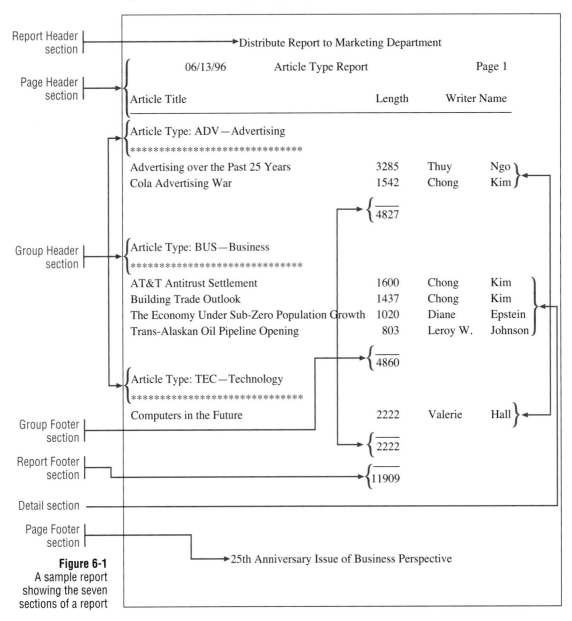

Figure 6-1
A sample report showing the seven sections of a report

The report is divided into **sections**. Each Access report can have seven different sections, which are described in Figure 6-2. You do not need to use all seven report sections in a report. When you design your report, you determine which sections to use and what information to place in each section.

Report Section	Description
Report Header	Appears once at the beginning of a report. Use it for report titles, company logos, report introductions, and cover pages.
Page Header	Appears at the top of each page of a report. Use it for column headings, report titles, page numbers, and report dates. If your report has a Report Header section, it precedes the first Page Header section.
Group Header	Appears once at the beginning of a new group of records. Use it to print the group name and the field value that all records in the group have in common. A report can have up to 10 grouping levels.
Detail	Appears once for each record in the underlying table or query. Use it to print selected fields from the table or query and to print calculated values.
Group Footer	Appears once at the end of a group of records. It is usually used to print totals for the group.
Report Footer	Appears once at the end of the report. Use it for report totals and other summary information.
Page Footer	Appears at the bottom of each page of a report. Use it for page numbers and brief explanations of symbols or abbreviations. If your report has a Report Footer section, it precedes the Page Footer section on the last page of the report.

Figure 6-2
Descriptions of Access
report sections

Elena has never created an Access report, so she first familiarizes herself with the Report Wizards tool.

Using Report Wizards

In Access, you can create your own report or use Report Wizards to create one for you. **Report Wizards** ask you a series of questions about your report requirements and then create a report based on your answers. Whether you use Report Wizards or create your own report, you can change a report design after it is created.

Access has seven different Report Wizards. Six of these Report Wizards are shown in Figure 6-3 on the following page.

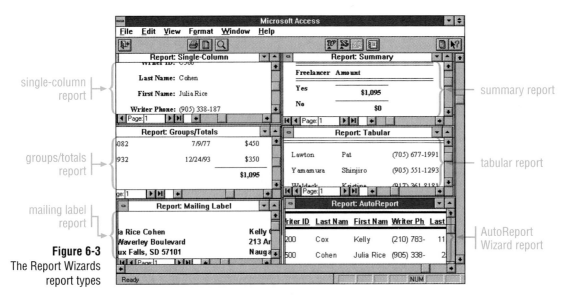

single-column report → (pointing to Report: Single-Column)

groups/totals report → (pointing to Report: Groups/Totals)

mailing label report → (pointing to Report: Mailing Label)

summary report ← (pointing to Report: Summary)

tabular report ← (pointing to Report: Tabular)

AutoReport Wizard report ← (pointing to Report: AutoReport)

Figure 6-3
The Report Wizards
report types

- A **single-column report** prints the fields, one to a line, vertically on the report. Table field names appear as labels to the left of the field values.
- A **groups/totals report** prints record and field values in a row-and-column format with the table field names used as column heads. You can group records according to field values and calculate totals for each group and for all groups. For example, Elena might create a groups/totals report that shows freelancers and then staff writers, with total payment amounts for freelancers, for staff writers, and for all writers.
- A **mailing label report** prints names and addresses that are positioned to fit your company's mailing label forms.
- A **summary report** organizes data into groups and prints both a subtotal for each group and a grand total for all the groups in a tabular format. No detail lines appear in a summary report.
- A **tabular report** prints field values in columns with field names at the top of each column. Each row is a separate record. It is like a groups/totals report, but does not contain totals.
- An **AutoReport Wizard report** is a tabular report of all the fields in the selected table or query. Access automatically produces an AutoReport without asking you questions.
- An **MS Word Mail Merge report** allows you to merge data from a table or query to a Microsoft Word for Windows 6.0 document. You can use the merged data to create form letters or envelopes, for example.

Report Wizards offer you a choice of three different report styles, as shown in Figure 6-4. The main difference between the **executive style** and the **presentation style** is the font in which the report is printed. The executive style uses the serif Times New Roman font, and the presentation style uses the sans serif Arial font. Use either style for the majority of your reports; they both produce easy-to-read text with ample open space. Because it packs more information into a page, the **ledger style** is suitable for long, detailed reports, such as financial reports, especially when they are intended for internal use.

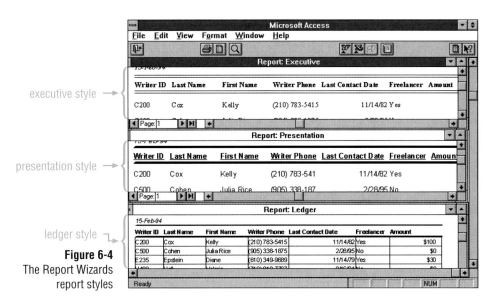

executive style →

presentation style →

ledger style

Figure 6-4
The Report Wizards
report styles

Access has a set of Cue Cards you can use while working with reports. Although we will not use these Cue Cards in this tutorial, you might find they enhance your understanding of reports. At any time during this tutorial, select Design a Report or Mailing Labels from the Cue Card menu window to launch the appropriate Cue Cards.

Creating a Report Using the AutoReport Wizard

The quickest way to create a report is to use the toolbar AutoReport button, which launches the **AutoReport Wizard**. The AutoReport Wizard selects all the fields from the highlighted table or query in the Database window, creates a single-column report for these fields, and displays the report on the screen in the Print Preview window.

Elena uses the AutoReport Wizard to create a report containing all the fields from the TYPES table. If you have not done so, place your Student Disk in the appropriate drive, launch Access, and open the Issue25 database on your Student Disk.

To create a report using the AutoReport button:

❶ Click **TYPES** in the Tables list box. Access will place the fields from the TYPES table, which is now highlighted, into the report it creates when you click the toolbar AutoReport button 📝.

❷ Click 📝 on the toolbar. Access creates a report that contains the two fields from the TYPES table and displays the report in the Print Preview window.

❸ You can use the vertical scroll bar buttons and the navigation buttons on the Print Preview window to view the entire report. See Figure 6-5 on the following page.

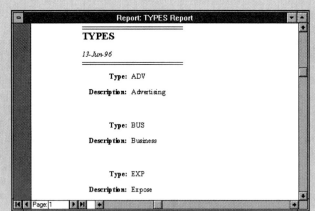

Figure 6-5
An AutoReport
Wizard report
in the Print
Preview window

Saving a Report

After viewing the first several lines of the report based on the TYPES table in the Print Preview screen, Elena saves the report so that she and others can print it whenever they need an updated copy. She saves the report using the name TYPES Report and then closes the Print Preview window.

To save and close a new report:
❶ Click **File** and then click **Save As...**. The Save As dialog box appears.
❷ Type **TYPES Report** in the Report Name text box and then press **[Enter]**. The Save As dialog box disappears, and Access saves the report.
❸ Double-click the Print Preview window **Control menu box**. The report disappears, and the Database window becomes the active window.

Creating Reports Using Report Wizards

Elena next uses Report Wizards to create a report containing all the fields from the WRITERS table. Because she wants space on the report to make notes, she chooses the single-column report type and the presentation style.

Creating Single-Column Reports

Let's use Report Wizards to create a single-column report in the presentation style.

To activate Report Wizards and select a report type:
❶ Locate the toolbar New Report button ▦. It is to the right of the New Form button and to the left of the Database Window button.
❷ Click ▦. The New Report dialog box appears. Click the Select A Table/Query box **drop-down list box arrow button** to display the list of the Issue25 database tables and queries. Scroll through the list if necessary and click **WRITERS** in the drop-down list box.

❸ Click the **Report Wizards button**. The first Report Wizards dialog box appears. See Figure 6-6. This dialog box displays the list of report types available through Report Wizards.

Figure 6-6
Choosing the
report type

❹ If it is not already highlighted, click **Single-Column**, and then click the **OK button**. The first Single-Column Report Wizard dialog box appears.

In the first Single-Column Report Wizard dialog box, you select fields in the order you want them to appear on the report. Elena wants the report to contain all the fields in the WRITERS table in the order in which they appear in the table, and she wants Freelancer to be the primary sort key and Last Contact Date to be the secondary sort key. She will include the report title WRITERS by Last Contact Date Within Freelancer.

To finish creating a report using the Single-Column Report Wizard:
❶ Click the **>> button**. Access removes all the fields from the box on the left and places them in the same order in the box on the right.
❷ Click the **Next > button**. The second Single-Column Report Wizard dialog box appears. In this dialog box, you select the primary and secondary sort keys.
❸ Click **Freelancer** and then click the **> button**. Access moves the Freelancer field to the list box on the right, designating the Freelancer field as the primary sort key. Click **Last Contact Date** and then click the **> button**. Access moves the Last Contact Date field under the Freelancer field in the list box on the right, designating it as the secondary sort key. See Figure 6-7.

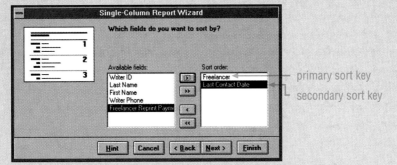

Figure 6-7
Selecting sort
keys for a report

❹ Click the **Next > button**. The third Single-Column Report Wizard dialog box appears. In this dialog box, you choose the style for your report.

⑤ If it is not already selected, click the **Presentation radio button**; then click the **Next > button**. Access displays the final Single-Column Report Wizard dialog box and shows the table name WRITERS as the default report title.

⑥ To change the default report title that will appear at the beginning of the report, type **WRITERS by Last Contact Date Within Freelancer**. See Figure 6-8.

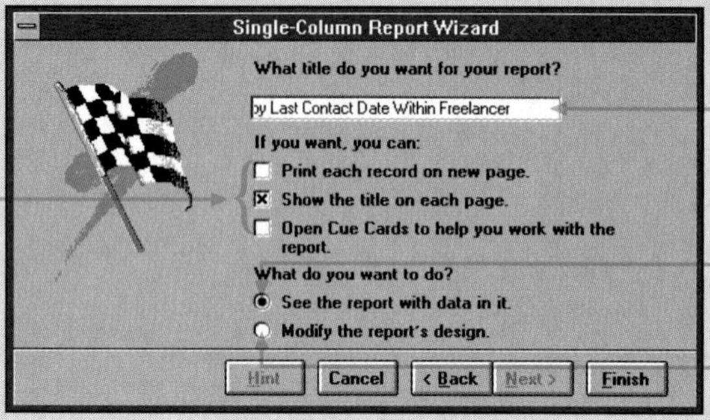

check-box options

Figure 6-8
The last
Single-Column
Report Wizards
dialog box

report title

Print Preview window
as next window

Report Design window
as next window

The three check boxes in the last Report Wizards dialog box let you do the following:
- Print each record on a new page
- Change the report title that prints once at the beginning of each report to a page title that prints on the top of each page
- Use Cue Cards

Printing the report title on each page is usually preferred, so make sure that the first and third boxes are unchecked and the second box is checked.

Previewing a Report

Now that she has made her report selections, Elena checks the overall report layout. She views the new report in the Print Preview window to see what the report will look like when it's printed.

To view a report in the Print Preview window:

❶ In the last Report Wizard dialog box, be sure that only the middle check box is checked and the top radio button is on.

❷ Click the **Finish button**. The Print Preview window opens, and Access displays the new report.

❸ Click the Print Preview window **maximize button**. See Figure 6-9.

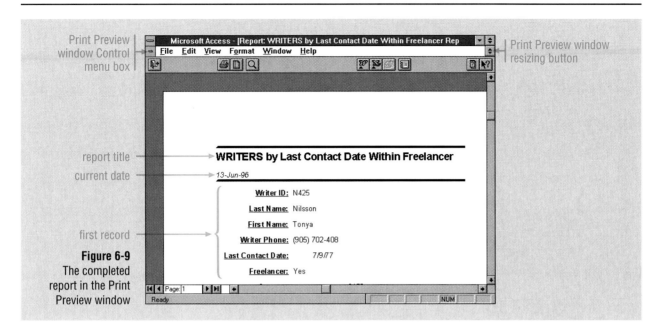

Print Preview window Control menu box

Print Preview window resizing button

report title

current date

first record

Figure 6-9
The completed report in the Print Preview window

Access displays the report title and current date at the top of the report page. These are preceded and followed by lines that serve to separate this section visually from the rest of the report page.

Below the title section, the record for the freelance writer having the earliest Last Contact Date in the WRITERS table appears as the first record on the report. You can use the vertical scroll bar and the navigation buttons to view the other records in the report.

Printing a Report

Next, Elena prints the first page of the report from the Print Preview window as a sample.

To print the first page of a report from the Print Preview window:
❶ Make sure your printer is on line and ready to print. Click the toolbar **Print button** to open the Print dialog box.

❷ Check the Printer section of the Print dialog box to make sure your computer's printer is selected.

❸ Click the **Pages button** to choose the range of pages to print.

❹ Type **1** in the From box, press **[Tab]**, and then type **1** in the To box.

❺ Press **[Enter]** to initiate printing. After a printing dialog box appears briefly and then disappears, Access prints the first page of the report and returns you to the Print Preview window.

Elena saves the report as WRITERS by Last Contact Date Within Freelancer Report and then closes the Print Preview window.

To save and close a new report:

❶ Click **File**, and then click **Save As....** The Save As dialog box appears.

❷ Type **WRITERS by Last Contact Date Within Freelancer Report** in the Report Name text box and then press **[Enter].** The Save As dialog box disappears, and Access saves the report.

❸ Double-click the Print Preview window **Control menu box.** The report disappears, and the Database window becomes the active window.

❹ Click the **Report object button.** Access lists the two reports that have been created and saved. See Figure 6-10.

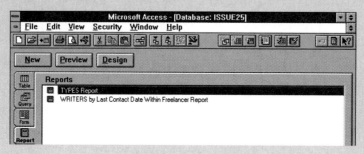

Figure 6-10
List of reports

Creating a Groups/Totals Report

After viewing, printing, and saving the single-column report, Elena decides that a groups/totals report of the same data would be more useful to her and her colleagues. A **group** is a set of records that share common values for one or more fields. Grouping records is a way for you to organize and sequence printed information. When you use a groups/totals report, you can select up to three different grouping fields. The first grouping field is the primary sort key, and any subsequent grouping fields are secondary sort keys.

Elena groups her report using the Freelancer field. This means that all the freelancer records will be printed first, then all the staff writer records. Because Access can print headers before each group and footers after each group, Elena's report includes a **Group Header section** that introduces each group and a **Group Footer section** that concludes each group. The Group Header section prints the value of the Freelancer field, and the Group Footer section prints the total of the Amount field values for the group. Elena's report also has a **Report Footer section** to print the grand total of the Amount field values for both groups.

When you create a groups/totals report, Access asks you to choose a grouping method for each grouping field. A **grouping method** uses either an entire field value or a portion of a field value upon which to base the record grouping process. **Normal grouping** uses the entire field value to group records and is the default grouping method. You can also base groups on a portion of a grouping field. For a date/time field, for example, you can group records based on the year, quarter, month, week, day, hour, or minute portions of the grouping field. For number or currency fields, you can group based on 10s, 50s, 100s, 500s, 1000s, 5000s, or 10000s. For text fields, you can group on the first character, first two characters, first three characters, first four characters, or first five characters. Because yes/no fields have just two values, normal grouping is the only possible option for them.

Elena again uses Report Wizards to create this report. Because the Report object button is selected, Elena can start creating the new report by clicking either the toolbar New Report button or the New command button.

To activate Report Wizards and create a groups/totals report:

❶ Click the **New command button**. The New Report dialog box appears. Click the Select A Table/Query **drop-down list box arrow button** to display the list of the Issue25 database tables and queries and scroll until WRITERS appears. Click **WRITERS** in the list box.

❷ Click the **Report Wizards button**. Access displays the first Report Wizards dialog box, in which you select the report type.

❸ Click **Groups/Totals** in the list box, and then click the **OK button**. Access displays the first Group/Totals Report Wizard dialog box, in which you select the fields for the report. Elena wants the report to contain all the WRITERS table fields in the order in which they appear in the table.

❹ Click the **>> button**. Access removes all the fields from the box on the left and places them in the same order in the box on the right.

❺ Click the **Next > button**. Access displays the second Group/Totals Report Wizard dialog box, in which you choose the grouping field. Elena groups the records from the WRITERS table by the Freelancer field.

❻ Click **Freelancer** in the Available fields list box, and then click the **> button** to move it to the list box on the right. See Figure 6-11.

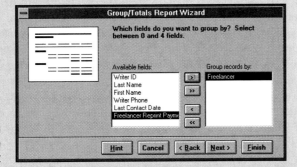

Figure 6-11
Selecting a field
on which to
group a report

❼ Click the **Next > button**. Access displays the third Group/Totals Report Wizard dialog box, in which you select the grouping method. The only grouping choice for the yes/no Freelancer field is Normal. See Figure 6-12.

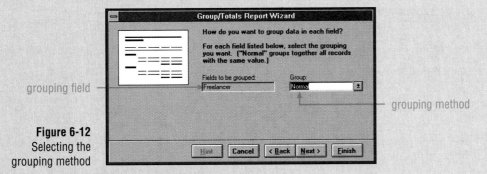

grouping field

grouping method

Figure 6-12
Selecting the
grouping method

❽ Click the **Next > button**. Access displays the next Group/Totals Report Wizard dialog box, in which you choose the report's sort keys.

Elena chooses Last Contact Date to be a sort key. Because the Freelancer field is a grouping field, Access uses it as the primary sort key and uses Last Contact Date as the secondary sort key.

To choose a report sort key:
❶ Click **Last Contact Date** in the Available fields list box, and then click the **> button** to move it to the list box on the right.
❷ Click the **Next > button**. Access displays the next Group/Totals Report Wizard dialog box, in which you choose the report style.
❸ If it is not already selected, click the **Executive button**, and then click the **Next > button**. Access displays the final Group/Totals Report Wizard dialog box and shows the table name WRITERS as the default title that will appear at the beginning of the report. Elena changes the default report title.
❹ Type **WRITERS With Freelancer Group Totals**.

In the final Group/Totals Report Wizard dialog box, Access displays three check boxes. Access uses the first check box, "See all the fields on one page," for reports that have too many columns to fit on one page using the standard column widths. If the box is checked, Access narrows the report columns so that all the fields can fit on one page. If the box is unchecked, Access prints multiple pages for groups of columns. You should check this option box unless you have so many fields that they cannot be read clearly when printed on one page.

Use the other two check boxes if you want to print percentages of the totals for each report group or if you want to use Cue Cards. Elena makes sure that the first box is checked and the other two are unchecked and then opens the Print Preview window to preview the report.

To finish and preview a groups/totals report:
❶ Be sure that, in the final Group/Totals Report Wizard dialog box, the first check box is checked and the other two check boxes are unchecked. See Figure 6-13.

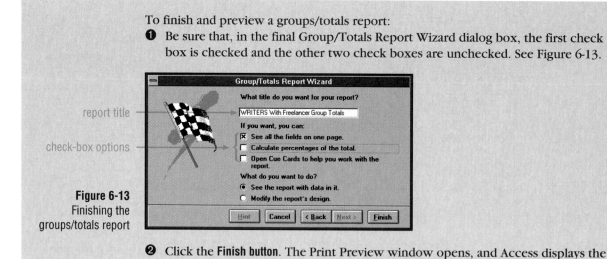

report title

check-box options

Figure 6-13
Finishing the
groups/totals report

❷ Click the **Finish button**. The Print Preview window opens, and Access displays the groups/totals report.

❸   Click the Print Preview window **maximize button**, click the **right arrow scroll button** three times, and then click the **down arrow scroll button** three times. See Figure 6-14.

Report Header section
Page Header section →

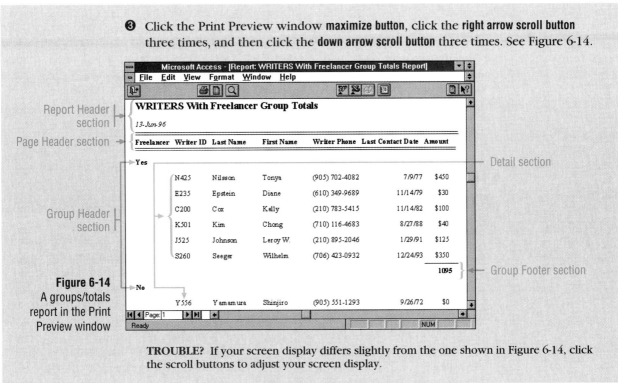

Detail section
Group Header section
Group Footer section

Figure 6-14
A groups/totals report in the Print Preview window

TROUBLE? If your screen display differs slightly from the one shown in Figure 6-14, click the scroll buttons to adjust your screen display.

Elena previews the rest of the report by using the down arrow scroll button.

To preview the end of a groups/totals report:

❶   Click the **down arrow scroll button** until you see the bottom of the first page of the report. If you do not see the grand totals at the end of the report, click the navigation **Next Record button** ▶ and click the **up arrow scroll button** until the grand totals are in view.

As she previews the report, Elena notices that it contains each of the seven different sections that a report can contain. Elena saves the groups/totals report and closes the Print Preview window.

To save and close a new report:

❶   Double-click the Print Preview window **Control menu box**. The "Save changes to 'Report1'" dialog box appears.

❷   Click the **Yes button**. The Save As dialog box appears.

❸   Type **WRITERS With Freelancer Group Totals Report** and then press **[Enter]**. The Save As dialog box disappears, Access saves the report, and the Database window becomes the active window.

If you want to take a break and resume the tutorial at a later time, you can exit Access by double-clicking the Microsoft Access window Control menu box. When you resume the tutorial, place your Student Disk in the appropriate drive, launch Access, open the Issue25 database on your Student Disk, maximize the Database window, and click the Report object button.

■   ■   ■

Creating a Custom Report

Elena and Harold discuss his report requirements and decide that the report should contain the following:
- A Detail section that lists the title, type, and length of each article, and the name of each writer. Records should appear in ascending order based on Type and in descending order based on Article Length, and the records should be grouped by the Type field value
- A Page Header section that shows the current date, report title, page number, and column headings for each field
- A Group Footer section that prints subtotals of the Article Length field for each Type group
- A Report Footer section that prints the grand total of the Article Length field

From her work with Report Wizards, Elena knows that Access places the report title and date in the Report Header section and the page number in the Page Footer section. Harold prefers all three items at the top of each page, so Elena needs to place that information in the Page Header section. To do this, Elena will create a custom report.

If you modify a report created by Report Wizards or if you design and create your own report, you have produced a **custom report**. You should create a custom report whenever Report Wizards cannot automatically create the specific report you need.

Designing a Custom Report

Before she creates the custom report, Elena designs the report's contents and appearance. Elena's completed design is shown in Figure 6-15.

The report title is Article Type Report. Descriptive column heads appear at the bottom of the Page Header section. The Page Header section also contains the current date and page number on the same line as the report title.

Elena indicates the locations and lengths of the field values by a series of ✕'s. The three ✕'s under the Type field label indicate that the field value will be three characters wide. The Type field value will appear only with the first record of a group.

The subtotals for each group and an overall total will appear in the report. The Article Length is the only field for which totals will appear.

Group Footer section

Page Header section

Detail section

Report Footer section

Figure 6-15
The design for the
custom report named
Article Type Report

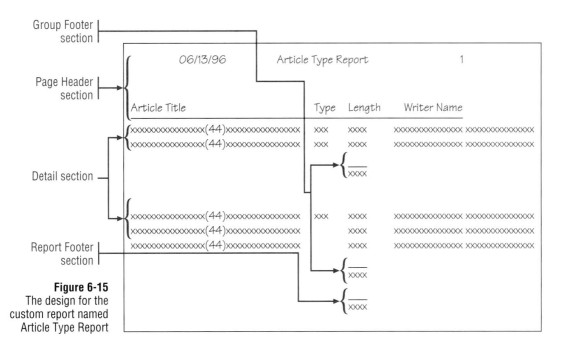

Elena's report design contains four different report sections: the Page Header section, the Detail section, the Group Footer section, and the Report Footer section. Her report will not include Report Header, Group Header, or Page Footer sections.

The data for a report can come from either a single table or from a query based on one or more tables. Because Elena's report will contain data from the WRITERS and PAST ARTICLES tables, Elena must use a query for this report. She will use the Article Type Query because it contains the fields she needs from the two tables.

The Report Design Window

Elena could use Report Wizards to create a report based on the Article Type Query and then modify the report to match her report design. Report Wizards would construct the majority of the report, so Elena would save time and reduce the possibility for errors. However, Elena creates her custom report without using Report Wizards so that she can control the precise placement of fields and labels and become more skilled at constructing reports. Elena's first step is to create a blank report in the Report Design window. You use the **Report Design window** to create and modify reports.

> **REFERENCE WINDOW**
>
> ### Creating a Blank Report
>
> - Click the toolbar New Report button. The New Report dialog box appears.
>
> - Select the table or query you want to use for the new report and then click the Blank Report button. Access opens the Report Design window.

Elena creates a blank report based on the Article Type Query and opens the field list box.

To create a blank report in the Report Design window and open the field list box:

❶ Click the toolbar **New Report button** 📧 to open the New Report dialog box.

❷ Click the Select A Table/Query **drop-down list box arrow button** to display the list of the Issue25 database tables and queries.

❸ Click **Article Type Query** and then click the **Blank Report button**. The Report Design window appears.

❹ Click the toolbar **Field List button** 🔳. The field list box appears. See Figure 6-16.

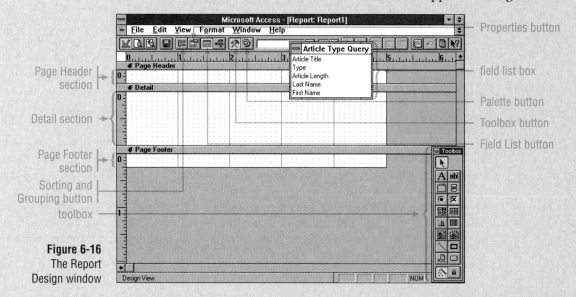

Figure 6-16
The Report Design window

TROUBLE? If the rulers, grid, or toolbox do not appear, click the View menu and then click Ruler, Grid, or Toolbox to display the missing component in the Report Design window. A check mark appears in front of these View menu commands when the components are displayed in the Report Design window. If the grid is still invisible, see your technical support person or instructor for assistance. If the Palette appears, click the View menu and then click Palette to close the Palette.

The Report Design window has several components in common with the Form Design window. The toolbar for both windows has a Properties button, a Field List button, and a Palette button. Both windows also have horizontal and vertical rulers, a grid, and a toolbox.

The Report Design window displays one new toolbar button, the Sorting and Grouping button. Recall that for a form you use a filter to display records in a specific order. In reports, you use the **Sorting and Grouping button** to establish sort keys and grouping fields. A maximum of 10 fields can serve as sort keys, and any number of them can also be grouping fields.

Unlike the Form Design window, which initially displays only the Detail section on a blank form, the Report Design window displays a Page Header section and a Page Footer section in addition to the Detail section. Reports often contain these sections, so Access automatically includes them in a blank report.

Adding Fields to a Report

Elena's first task is to add bound controls to the report Detail section for all the fields from the Article Type Query. You use bound controls to print field values from a table or query on a report. You add bound controls to a report the same way you added them to a form. In fact, every task you accomplished in the Form Design window is done in a similar way in the Report Design window.

To add bound controls for all the fields in the field list:

❶ If the toolbox Control Wizards tool ▨ is selected, click it to deselect it.

❷ Double-click the **field list title bar** to highlight all the fields in the Article Type Query field list.

❸ Click anywhere in the highlighted area of the field list and drag to the report Detail section. Release the mouse button when the 🖱 is positioned at the top of the Detail section and at the 1.25" mark on the horizontal ruler. Access resizes the Detail Section and adds bound controls for the five selected fields. Each bound control consists of a text box and, to its left, an attached label. See Figure 6-17. Notice that the text boxes align at the 1.25" mark.

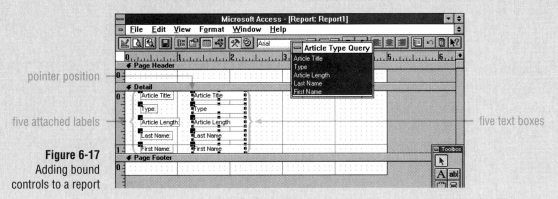

pointer position

five attached labels

five text boxes

Figure 6-17
Adding bound
controls to a report

TROUBLE? If you did not position the bound controls properly in the Detail section, click the Undo button immediately and then repeat the drag operation.

Performing operations in the Report Design window will become easier with practice. Remember, you can always click the Undo button immediately after you make a report design change that has undesired results.

You can also click the toolbar Print Preview button at any time to view your progress on the report and return to the Report Design window by clicking the toolbar Close Window button in the Print Preview window.

Selecting, Moving, Resizing, and Deleting Controls

Five text boxes now appear in a column in the Detail section. Each text box is a bound control linked to a field in the underlying query and has an attached label box to its left. Because she is done with the field list box, Elena closes it by clicking the toolbar Field List button. Elena next compares the report Detail section with her design and moves all the label boxes to the Page Header section. She then repositions the label boxes and text boxes so that they agree with her report design, shown in Figure 6-15.

To close the field list and move all label boxes to the Page Header section:

❶ Click the toolbar **Field List button** ▢ to close the field list.

❷ Click anywhere in the Page Footer section to deselect the five text boxes and their attached label boxes. While pressing and holding [**Shift**], click each of the five label boxes in the Detail section. This action selects all the label boxes in preparation for cutting them from the Detail section and pasting them in the Page Header section.

❸ With the ✋ positioned inside any one of the selected label boxes click the right mouse button to display the Shortcut menu.

❹ Click **Cut** in the Shortcut menu. Access deletes the label boxes from the Detail section and places them in the Windows Clipboard. See Figure 6-18.

Figure 6-18
Label boxes
cut from the
Detail Section

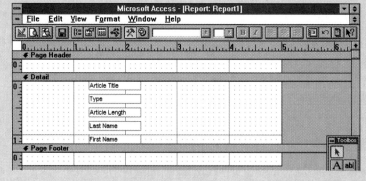

TROUBLE? If you selected both the label boxes and the text boxes, click Undo and try again, selecting only the label boxes.

❺ Click anywhere in the Page Header section, click the right mouse button in the Page Header section to open the Shortcut menu, and then click **Paste**. Access resizes the Page Header section and pastes all the label boxes from the Windows Clipboard into that section. See Figure 6-19.

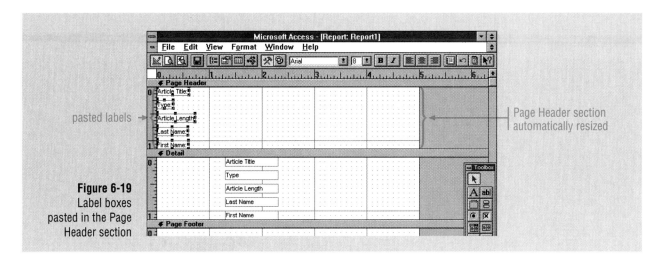

Figure 6-19
Label boxes
pasted in the Page
Header section

Moving the label boxes has unlinked them from their attached text boxes. You can now select and move either a label box or a text box, but not both at once.

Elena needs to reposition the text boxes and label boxes. She first drags the Article Title text box to the left into the corner of the Detail section and resizes it. She then moves and resizes the other four text boxes and resizes the Detail section.

To move and resize text boxes and resize the Detail section:

❶ Click the Article Title field-value **text box** in the Detail section, move the pointer to the move handle in the upper-left corner of the field-value text box, and click and drag the 🖑 to the upper-left corner of the Detail section.

❷ Next, move the pointer to the middle sizing handle on the right side of the Article Title field-value text box. When the pointer changes to ↔, drag the right border horizontally to the right to the 2.5" mark on the horizontal ruler. See Figure 6-20.

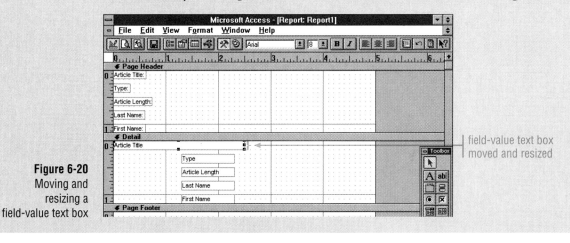

Figure 6-20
Moving and
resizing a
field-value text box

❸ Select each of the other four field-value text boxes in the Detail section, and move and resize them separately, following the report design. See Figure 6-21.

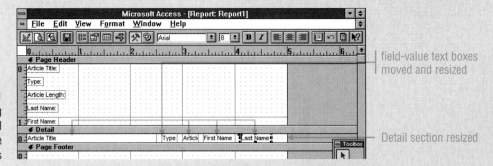

Figure 6-21
After moving
and resizing all
the field-value
text boxes

field-value text boxes
moved and resized

Detail section resized

❹ Move the pointer to the bottom edge of the Detail section. When the pointer changes to ⬍, drag the bottom edge upward to align with the bottom of the field-value text boxes. See Figure 6-21. When the Detail section height is the same as the text-box height, the lines in the Detail section of the report will be single spaced.

TROUBLE? If Access widens the report too much while you are moving and resizing the text boxes, wait until you are finished with these operations and then reduce the width of the report. To reduce the report's width, start by moving the pointer to the right edge of the Detail section. When the pointer changes to ⬌, drag the right edge to the left to narrow the report's width to 5".

Elena deletes the First Name label and changes the Caption property for all other labels in the Page Header section. She changes the Last Name Caption property to Writer Name and the Article Length Caption property to Length. She also deletes the colons in the Caption properties for the Article Title label and the Type label.

To delete a label and change label Caption properties:
❶ Click the First Name **label box** to select it. Click the First Name **label box** with the right mouse button to open the Shortcut menu and then click **Cut**. The First Name **label box** disappears.
❷ Click the Last Name **label box** to select it, and then click the toolbar **Properties button** 🔲. The property sheet for the Last Name label appears.
❸ Click the **Caption text box** in the property sheet, press **[F2]** to select the entire value, and then type **Writer Name**.
❹ Click the Article Length **label box** to select it. The property sheet changes to show the properties for the Article Length field. Click the **Caption text box** in the property sheet, press **[F2]**, and then type **Length**.
❺ Click the Type **label box** to select it. Click near the end of the **Caption text box** in the property sheet and press **[Backspace]** to remove the colon from the caption.
❻ Click the Article Title **label box** to select it. Click near the end of the **Caption text box** in the property sheet and press **[Backspace]** to remove the colon from the caption.
❼ Click 🔲 to close the property sheet.

After checking her report design, Elena resizes the Length and Writer Name label boxes and rearranges the label boxes in the Page Header section.

To resize and move labels:

❶ Click in an unoccupied area of the grid to deselect the Article Title **label box**. While holding **[Shift]**, click the Length **label box** and then click the Writer Name **label box** to select them.

❷ Click **Format**, click **Size**, and then click **to Fit**. Access resizes the two label boxes to fit around the captions. See Figure 6-22.

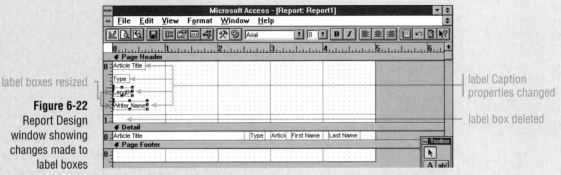

label boxes resized

label Caption properties changed

label box deleted

Figure 6-22
Report Design window showing changes made to label boxes

❸ Individually select and move each of the label boxes in the Page Header section, following the report design. See Figure 6-23.

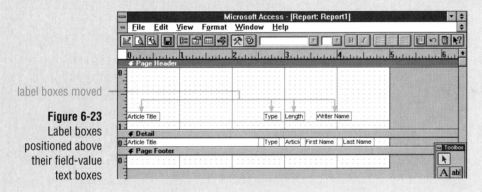

label boxes moved

Figure 6-23
Label boxes positioned above their field-value text boxes

Adding a Title, Date, and Page Number to a Report

Elena's report design includes the title Article Type Report. She places this report title in the Page Header section using the toolbox Label tool.

To add a report title to the Page Header section:

❶ Click the toolbox **Label tool** [A].

❷ Move the pointer into the Page Header section. As you move the pointer into the report, the pointer changes to $^+$A. Click the mouse button when the pointer's plus symbol (+) is positioned at the top of the Page Header section at the 2" mark on the horizontal ruler. The pointer changes to ⌐.

❸ Type **Article Type Report** and then press **[Enter]**. See Figure 6-24.

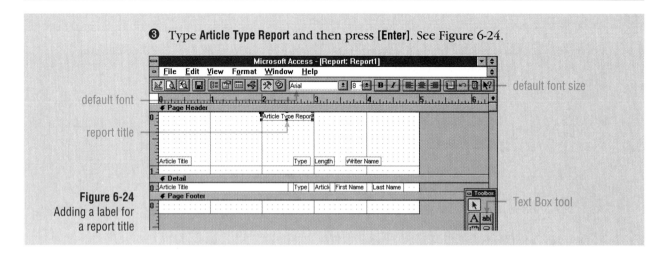

Figure 6-24
Adding a label for
a report title

Elena increases the report title font size from 8, the default, to 10 (the default type-face is Arial), and adds a text box to the Page Header section. Here she will insert the Date function. You use the toolbar **Text Box tool** to add a text box with an attached label to a report or form. Text boxes are mostly used to contain bound controls or calculated controls. You use the **Date function**, which is a type of calculated control, to print the current date on a report. Let's do this now.

To change font size and use the Text Box tool to add the Date function:

❶ Click the Font Size **drop-down list box arrow button** and click **10**. Access changes the font size of the report title from 8 to 10. The text box is now too small to display the entire report title. The text box needs to be resized and recentered in the Page Header section.

❷ Resize the height and width of the report title **text box**, so that the entire report title is visible. Next, move the report title text box one grid mark to the left, so it is centered in the Page Header section.

❸ Click the toolbar **Text Box tool** [abl] . Move the pointer into the Page Header section. As you move the pointer into the report, the pointer changes to ⁺[abl]. Click the mouse button when the pointer's plus symbol is positioned at the top of the Page Header section just to the right of the .75" mark on the horizontal ruler. Access adds a text box with an attached label box to its left. Inside the text box is the description Unbound.

❹ Click the Unbound **text box**, type **=Date()**, and then press **[Enter]**. See Figure 6-25.

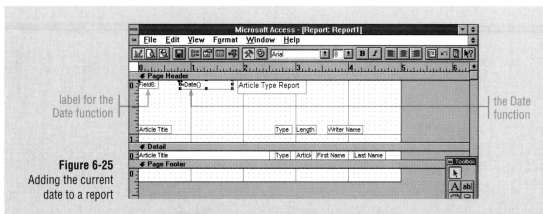

label for the
Date function

the Date
function

Figure 6-25
Adding the current
date to a report

TROUBLE? If your text box and attached label box are too close together, resize and reposition the text box using Figure 6-25 as a guide. Also, the attached label box on your screen might have a Caption other than Field6. This causes no problem.

When Access prints your report, the current date replaces the Date function you entered in the Unbound text box. Because a current date in a Page Header section does not usually need a label, Elena deletes the label box. She then changes the Date text box to font size 10 and moves it to the upper-left corner of the Page Header section. Finally, Elena uses the Text Box tool to add the Page property to the upper-right corner of the Page Header section. The **Page property** automatically prints the correct page number on each page of a report.

To finish formatting the current date and add a page number in the Page Header section:

❶ Click the Date **label box**, which is located in the upper-left corner of the Page Header section. Click the Date **label box** with the right mouse button to open the Shortcut menu and then click **Cut** to delete the label.

❷ Click the Date **text box** and then drag its move handle to the upper-left corner of the Page Header section.

❸ Click the Font Size **drop-down list box arrow button** and click **10** to change the font size of the Date text box.

❹ Click the toolbox **Text Box tool** [abl]. Move the pointer into the Page Header section. The mouse pointer changes to ⁺[abl]. Click the mouse button when the pointer's plus symbol is positioned at the top of the Page Header section at the 4.5" mark on the horizontal ruler. Access adds an Unbound text box with an attached label box to its left.

❺ Click the label box with the right mouse button to open the Shortcut menu, and then click **Cut**. The label box disappears.

❻ Click the Unbound text box, type **=Page**, press **[Enter]**, click the Font Size **drop-down list box down arrow button**, and then click **10**. See Figure 6-26 on the following page.

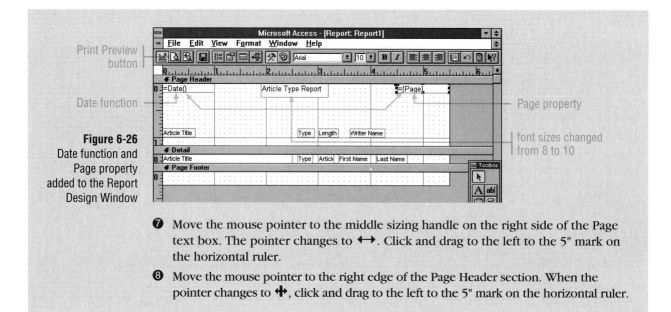

Figure 6-26
Date function and
Page property
added to the Report
Design Window

❼ Move the mouse pointer to the middle sizing handle on the right side of the Page text box. The pointer changes to ↔. Click and drag to the left to the 5" mark on the horizontal ruler.

❽ Move the mouse pointer to the right edge of the Page Header section. When the pointer changes to ✛, click and drag to the left to the 5" mark on the horizontal ruler.

Elena switches to the Print Preview window. She wants to check the report against her design.

To view a report in the Print Preview window:
❶ Click the toolbar **Print Preview button** 🔍 to open the Print Preview window. See Figure 6-27.

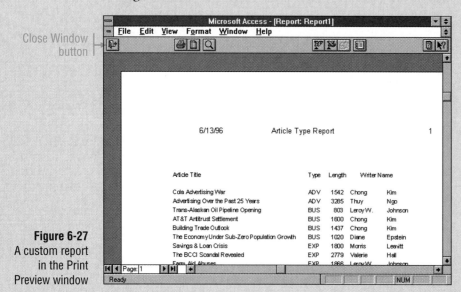

Figure 6-27
A custom report
in the Print
Preview window

TROUBLE? If your report shows a gap between the first and second records in the Detail section, you need to reduce the height of the Detail section. The bottom of the Detail section should align with the bottom of the text boxes in that section. Reduce the height during the next series of steps.

Adding Lines to a Report

Elena adds a horizontal line to the Page Header section below the column heads. Before doing this, she repositions the column heading labels just below the report title line and decreases the height of the Page Header section.

To move labels and decrease the Page Header section height:

❶ Click the toolbar **Close Window button** 🖳 to return to the Report Design window.

❷ While pressing and holding **[Shift]**, click each of the four label boxes in the Page Header section to select them. Click one of the label boxes when the pointer changes to ✋ and drag the label boxes straight up so they are positioned just below the report title. Position the labels so that the top of each label box is at the .25" mark on the vertical ruler.

   TROUBLE? If the label boxes do not move, the Page text box is probably selected along with the label boxes. Click in any unoccupied portion of the Page Header section to deselect all boxes, then repeat Step 2.

❸ Move the pointer to the bottom edge of the Page Header section. When the pointer changes to ✛, drag the bottom edge upward to reduce the height of the Page Header section. Align the bottom edge with the grid marks that are just below the .5" mark on the vertical ruler.

Elena now adds a medium-thick horizontal line to the bottom of the Page Header section. You use the **toolbox Line tool** to add a line to a report or form.

To add a line to a report:

❶ Click the toolbox **Line tool** ╲. Move the pointer into the Page Header section; the pointer changes to ⁺╲. Position the Pointer's plus symbol at the left edge of the Page Header section and at the .5" mark on the vertical ruler.

   TROUBLE? If the toolbox is too low for you to see the Line tool, drag the toolbox title bar straight up until the Line tool is visible.

❷ Click and hold the mouse button, drag a horizontal line from left to right ending just after the 4.25" mark on the horizontal ruler, and then release the mouse button.

❸ To increase the thickness of the line, click the toolbar **Properties button** 🖻. The property sheet appears. The Border Width property controls the line's width, or thickness.

❹ Click the **Border Width text box** in the property sheet, click the **down arrow button** that appears, and then click **3 pt**. The line's width increases. See Figure 6-28 on the following page.

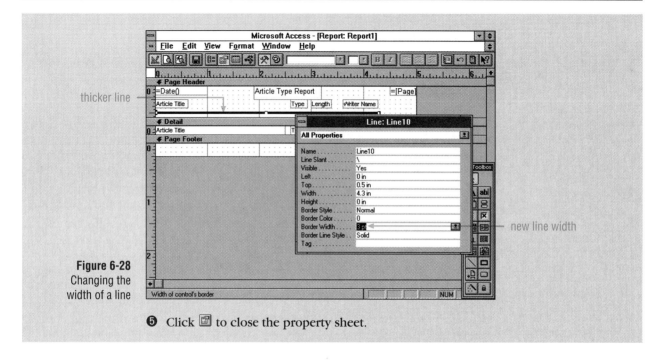

Figure 6-28
Changing the
width of a line

❺ Click ▣ to close the property sheet.

Elena has finished her design of the Page Header section. She next chooses the sort fields and the grouping field for the report.

Sorting and Grouping Data in a Report

Elena wants Access to print records in ascending order based on the Type field and to print subtotals for each set of Type field values. Thus, the Type field is both the primary sort key and the grouping field. Elena wants the records within a Type to be printed in descending order based on the Article Length field. This makes Article Length the secondary sort key. Because Elena does not want subtotals for each Article Length value, Article Length is not a grouping field.

You use the toolbar **Sorting and Grouping button** to select sort keys and grouping fields. Each report can have up to 10 sort fields, and any of the 10 sort fields can also be grouping fields.

To select sort keys and grouping fields:
❶ Click the toolbar **Sorting and Grouping button** ▣. The Sorting and Grouping dialog box appears.

❷ Click the **down arrow button** in the first Field/Expression box in the Sorting and Grouping dialog box and then click **Type**. Ascending is the default sort order in the Sort Order box.

❸ Click anywhere in the second Field/Expression box in the Sorting and Grouping dialog box, click the **down arrow button** that appears, and then click **Article Length**. Ascending, the default sort order, needs to be changed to Descending in the Sort Order box.

❹ Click anywhere in the second Sort Order box, click the **down arrow button** that appears, and then click **Descending**. See Figure 6-29.

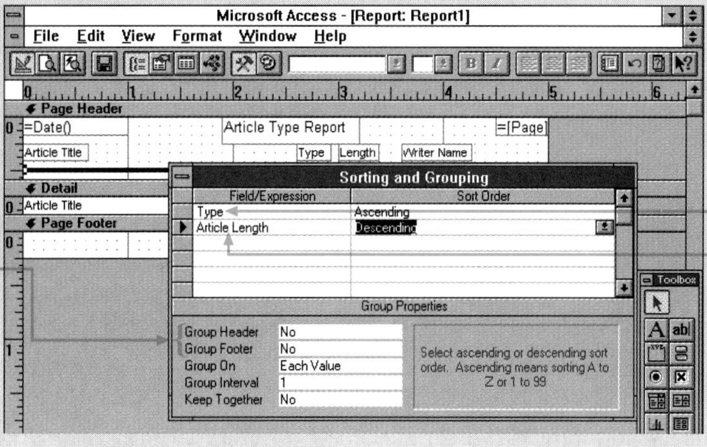

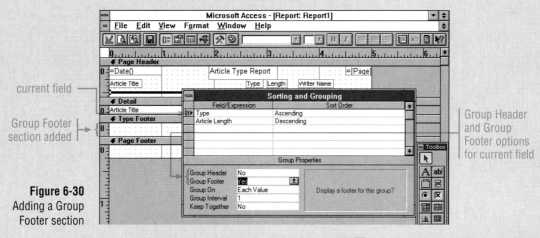

Figure 6-29
The Sorting and
Grouping dialog box

Elena notices that adding the two sort keys did not cause any new sections to be added to the report. To add a Group Footer, she must choose the Group Footer option for the Type field in the Sorting and Grouping dialog box.

To add a Group Footer to a report:
❶ Click the **Field/Expression box** for the Type field in the Sorting and Grouping dialog box, click the **Group Footer box**, click the **down arrow button** that appears, and then click **Yes**. Access adds a Group Footer section called Type Footer to the Report Design window. See Figure 6-30.

Figure 6-30
Adding a Group
Footer section

❷ Click the toolbar **Sorting and Grouping button** to close the Sorting and Grouping dialog box.

Adding a Report Header and Footer

Elena compares her progress against her report design again and sees that she is almost done. She next adds a Report Footer section to her report. To add this new section, Elena adds the Report Header and Footer sections to the report. Because she does not need the Report Header section, she deletes it. She also deletes the Page Footer section that was automatically included when the Report Design window was opened.

REFERENCE WINDOW

Adding Report Header and Footer Sections

- Click Format, then click Report Header/Footer. Access adds a Report Header section and a Report Footer section to the report.

Let's add Report Header and Footer sections to the report and then delete the Page Footer section.

To add and delete sections from a report:

❶ Click **Format** and then click **Report Header/Footer**. Access creates a Report Header section at the top of the report and a Report Footer section at the bottom of the report.

❷ Move the pointer to the bottom edge of the Report Header section. When the pointer changes to ✛, drag the bottom edge upward until the section disappears. Repeat this process for the Page Footer section. See Figure 6-31.

Figure 6-31
Adding and deleting report sections

sections resized to zero

Report Footer section added

Calculating Group Totals and Overall Totals

Elena wants the report to print subtotals for each Type group and an overall grand total. She adds calculations to produce these totals for the Article Length field. To calculate a total for a group of records or for all records, you use the **Sum function**. You place the Sum function in a Group Footer section to print a group total and in the Report Footer section to print an overall total. The format for the Sum function is =Sum([field name]). When you enter the function, you replace "field name" with the name of the field you want to sum. Use the toolbox Text Box tool to create appropriate text boxes in the footer sections.

In the Type Footer and Report Footer sections, Elena adds text boxes, deletes the attached labels for both, and adds the Sum function to each text box. She also draws lines above each Sum function so that the totals will be visually separated from the Detail section field values.

To add text boxes to footer sections and delete labels:

❶ Increase the height of the Type Footer section so that you see four rows of grid dots, and increase the height of the Report Footer section so that you see three rows of grid dots.

❷ Click the toolbox **Text Box tool** [abl]. Move the pointer into the Type Footer section. Click the mouse button when the pointer's plus symbol is positioned in the second row of grid lines and vertically aligned with the right edge of the Type field-value text box. Access adds a text box with an attached label box to its left.

❸ Click [abl]. Move the pointer into the Report Footer section. Click the mouse button when the pointer's plus symbol is positioned in the second row of grid lines and vertically aligned with the right edge of the Type field-value text box. Access adds a text box with an attached label box to its left. See Figure 6-32.

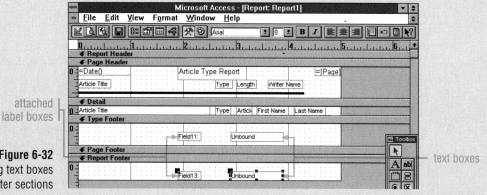

Figure 6-32
Adding text boxes
in footer sections

attached
label boxes

text boxes

❹ Click anywhere in the Type Footer section, outside both boxes to deselect all boxes.

❺ While you press and hold **[Shift]**, click the label box in the Type Footer section, and then click the label box in the Report Footer section. You have selected both boxes.

❻ Click either label box with the right mouse button to open the Shortcut menu and then click **Cut**. The two label boxes disappear.

Elena now adds the Sum function to the two footer section text boxes.

To add the Sum function to calculate group and overall totals:

❶ Click the text box in the Type Footer section, type **=Sum([Article Length])**, and then press **[Enter]**. The text box in the Type Footer section needs to be narrower.

❷ Click the middle **sizing handle** on the right side of the text box and drag it to the left until the right edge of the box lines up with the right edge of the Article Length field-value text box in the Detail section.

❸ Click the text box in the Report Footer section, type **=Sum([Article Length])**, and then press **[Enter]**. See Figure 6-33.

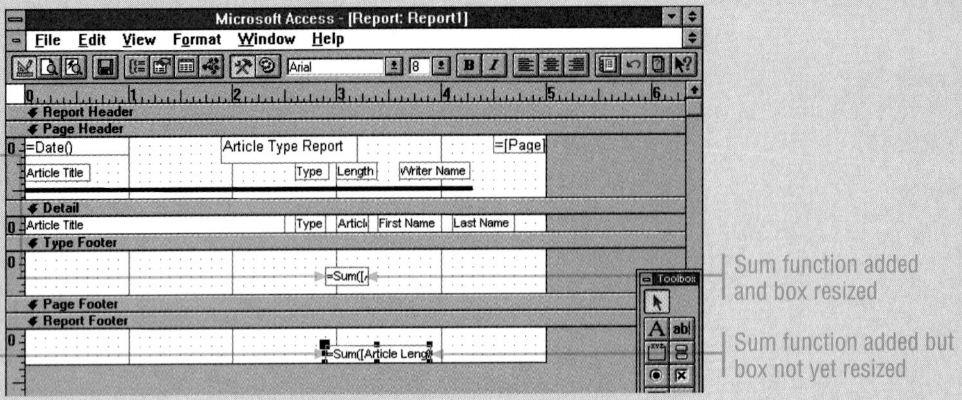

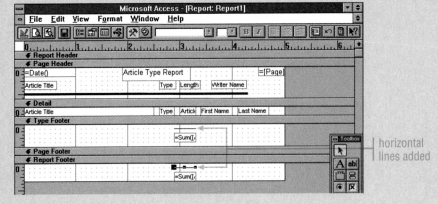

group total

overall total

Figure 6-33
Adding a group total
and overall total

Sum function added
and box resized

Sum function added but
box not yet resized

❹ To resize the text box in the Report Footer section, click the middle **sizing handle** on the right side of the text box and drag it to the left until the right edge of the box lines up with the right edge of the Article Length field-value text box in the Detail section.

Elena next adds lines above each Sum function.

To add lines above totals:

❶ Click the toolbox **Line tool** ▢. Move the pointer into the Type Footer section; the pointer changes to ⁺◥. Position the pointer's plus symbol in the top row of grid lines and vertically align it with the right edge of the Type field-value text box in the Detail section above.

❷ Click and hold the mouse button, and drag a horizontal line to the right until the right end of the line is below the right edge of the Article Length field-value text box.

❸ Repeat Steps 1 and 2 for the Report Footer section. See Figure 6-34.

Figure 6-34
Adding horizontal
lines above group
and overall totals

horizontal
lines added

Elena's report is almost finished. There is, however, still one change she can make to improve its appearance.

Hiding Duplicate Values in a Group Report

Elena's final change is to display the Type value only in the first record in a group. Within a group, all Type field values are the same, so if you display only the first one, you simplify the report and make it easier to read.

To hide duplicate values:

❶ Click the Type **text box** in the Detail section and then click the toolbar **Properties button** 📷. The property sheet for the Type field appears.

❷ If necessary, scroll through the property sheet, then click the **Hide Duplicates text box** in the property sheet, click the **down arrow button**, and click **Yes**. See Figure 6-35.

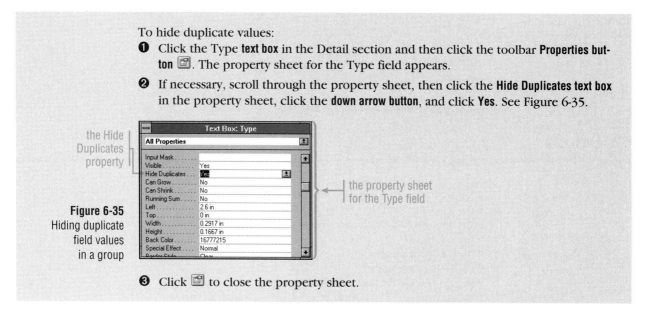

the Hide Duplicates property

Figure 6-35
Hiding duplicate field values in a group

the property sheet for the Type field

❸ Click 📷 to close the property sheet.

Elena views the report in the Print Preview window and then saves the report.

To view and save a report:

❶ Click the toolbar **Print Preview button** 🔍. Access displays the first page of the report. See Figure 6-36.

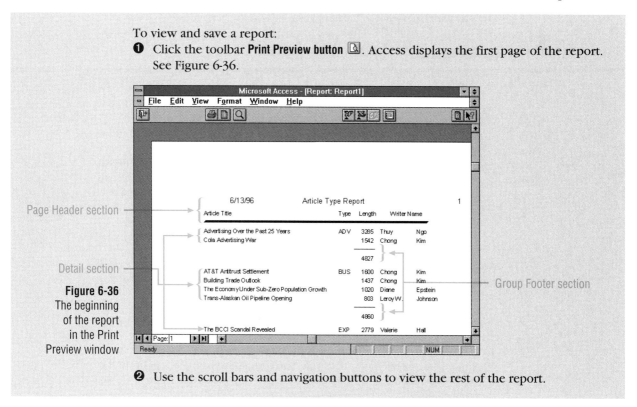

Page Header section

Detail section

Figure 6-36
The beginning of the report in the Print Preview window

Group Footer section

❷ Use the scroll bars and navigation buttons to view the rest of the report.

❸ Double-click the Print Preview window **Control menu box**. The "Save changes to 'Report1'" dialog box appears.

❹ Click the **Yes button**. The dialog box disappears, and Access displays the Save As dialog box.

❺ Type **Article Type Report** in the Report Name text box and then press **[Enter]**. Access saves the custom report, closes the dialog box, and activates the Database window.

▓   ▓   ▓

Elena exits Access and brings her report to Harold.

Questions

1. What are the seven Access report sections, and when is each printed?
2. What types of reports can the Report Wizards tool create?
3. What three different styles does Report Wizards offer you?
4. What is a group?
5. What is normal grouping?
6. What is a custom report?
7. When do you use the toolbox Text Box tool?
8. What do you type in a text box to tell Access to print the current date?
9. What do you type in a text box to tell Access to print the page number?
10. How do you add a Report Footer section to a report without adding a Report Header section?
11. Why might you want to hide duplicate values in a group report?

Tutorial Assignments

Elena uses Report Wizards to create a report named PAST ARTICLES Report for the Issue25 database. Launch Access, open the Issue25 database on your Student Disk, and do the following:

1. Use Report Wizards to create a groups/totals report based on the PAST ARTICLES table. Use the executive style for the report. Select all the fields from the table in the order in which they are stored in the table, group the records by Writer ID, select Normal grouping, select no sort key fields, check the "Calculate percentages of the total" box, and enter PAST ARTICLES Report as the report title.
2. Display the report in the Print Preview window and then print the last report page.
3. Save the report, naming it PAST ARTICLES Report, and return to the Database window.

Elena next creates a custom report. Use the Issue25 database on your Student Disk to do the following. Use the report shown in Figure 6-14 as a basis for your report design.

E   4. Create a blank report using the WRITERS table.

E   5. Include in your report these sections: Page Header, Freelancer Header, Detail, Freelancer Footer, Page Footer, and Report Footer.

E   6. In the Page Header section at the beginning of the first line, enter Freelancer Group Totals as the report title. Enter the current date at the beginning of the second line. Position the labels under these lines, as shown in Figure 6-14. Add a single line, instead of a double line, below the column heads line. Do not place any lines above the column heads or above the report title.

E   7. Use Freelancer for the grouping field. There are no sorting fields in this report. In the Freelancer Header section, include the Freelancer field value.

E   8. In the Detail section, include the field values, as shown in Figure 6-14.

E   9. In the Freelancer Footer section, include the group total for the Amount field.

E   10. In the Page Footer section, include a page number aligned with the right edge of the Amount field.

E   11. In the Report Footer section, include the overall total for the Amount field.

E   12. When you finish creating the report, print the entire report.

E   13. Save the report, naming it Freelancer Group Totals Report, and then exit Access.

Case Problems

1. Walkton Daily Press Carriers

Grant Sherman uses Report Wizards to create a report for his Press database. Launch Access, open the Press database on your Student Disk, and do the following:

   1. Use Report Wizards to create a groups/totals report in the executive style based on the CARRIERS table. Select all the fields from the table in the order in which they are stored in the table. Do not select a grouping field, sort by Carrier ID, do not check the "Calculate percentages of the total" box, and enter CARRIERS Report as the report title.

   2. Display the report in the Print Preview window and then print the entire report.

   3. Save the report, naming it CARRIERS Report, then close the Print Preview window, and return to the Database window.

Grant next modifies the design of this report. Open the newly created CARRIERS Report in the Report Design window and do the following:

   4. In the Report Footer section, delete the two Sum function text boxes, delete the two sets of double lines, and delete the Report Footer section.

   5. Click the Print Preview button to display the report and then print the entire report.

   6. Save the report, naming it CARRIERS Report #2, and return to the Database window.

Grant next creates a custom report. Use the Press database on your Student Disk to do the following:

E   7. Create a blank report using the query named Carriers sorted by Name, Route ID.

E   8. Sketch a design for the report based on the requirements described in the next five steps, and then create the report following these same steps.

E   9. Include in your report these sections: Page Header, Detail, Group Footer, and Report Footer.

E   10. In the Page Header section at the beginning of the first line, enter CARRIERS sorted by Name, Route ID Report as the report title. Enter the current date at the beginning of the second line and the page number at the end of the second line. Position under these elements a row of column heads with these labels: Last Name, First Name, Carrier Phone, Route ID, and Balance. Add a single horizontal line under the column heads.

E   11. In the Detail section, include the field values for Last Name, First Name, Carrier Phone, Route ID, and Balance. Hide duplicates for the Last Name, First Name, and Carrier Phone fields.

E   12. In the Group Footer section, print the group total for the Balance field. Select Last Name as the primary sort key, and use this field as a grouping field. Select Route ID as the secondary sort key, but do not use it as a grouping field. Choose ascending sort order for each sort key.

E   13. In the Report Footer section, print the overall total for the Balance field.

E   14. When you finish creating the report, print the entire report.

E   15. Save the report, naming it CARRIERS sorted by Name and Route ID Report, and then exit Access.

2.   Lopez Used Cars

Maria Lopez uses Report Wizards to create a report for her Usedcars database. Launch Access, open the Usedcars database on your Student Disk, and do the following:

1. Use Report Wizards to create a groups/totals report in the executive style based on the USED CARS table. Select all the fields from the table in the order in which they are stored in the table. Do not select a grouping field, sort by Year, do not check the "Calculate percentages of the total" box, and enter USED CARS by Year as the report title.

2. Display the report in the Print Preview window and then print the entire report.

3. Save the report, naming it USED CARS by Year Report, and return to the Database window.

Maria next modifies the design of this report. Open the newly created report named USED CARS by Year Report in the Report Design window and do the following:

4. In the Report Footer section, delete the Sum function text box for the Year field, and delete its set of double lines.

5. Click the Print Preview button to display the report and then print the entire report.

6. Save the report, naming it USED CARS by Year Report #2, and return to the Database window.

Maria next creates a custom report. Use the Usedcars database on your Student Disk and do the following:

E   7. Create a blank report using the USED CARS table.

E   8. Sketch a design for the report based on the requirements described in the next five steps, and then create the report following these same steps.

E   9. Include in your report these sections: Page Header, Detail, Group Footer, and Report Footer.

E   10. In the Page Header section at the beginning of the first line, enter USED CARS sorted by Manufacturer, Model, Year as the report title. Enter the current date at the beginning of the second line and the page number at the end of the second line. Position under these elements a row of column heads with these labels: Manufacturer, Model, Year, Cost, and Selling Price. Add a single horizontal line under the column heads.

E   11. In the Detail section, include the field values for Manufacturer, Model, Year, Cost, and Selling Price. Hide duplicates for the Manufacturer field.

E   12. In the Group Footer section, print the group total for the Cost and Selling Price fields. Select Manufacturer as the primary sort key and as the grouping field. Select Model, and then Year, as the secondary sort keys, but do not use them as grouping fields. Choose ascending sort order for each sort key.

E   13. In the Report Footer section, print the overall totals for the Cost and Selling Price fields.

E   14. When you finish creating the report, print the entire report.

E   15. Save the report, naming it USED CARS by Manufacturer, Model, and Year Report, and then exit Access.

3. Tophill University Student Employment

Olivia Tyler uses Report Wizards to create a report for her Parttime database. Launch Access, open the Parttime database on your Student Disk, and do the following:

1. Use Report Wizards to create a groups/totals report in the executive style based on the JOBS table. Select all the fields from the table in the order in which they are stored in the table. Do not select a grouping field, sort by Job Order, do not check the "Calculate percentages of the total" box, and enter JOBS as the report title.
2. Display the report in the Print Preview window and then print the entire report.
3. Save the report, naming it JOBS Report, and return to the Database window.

Olivia next modifies the design of this report. Open the newly created JOBS Report in the Report Design window and do the following:

4. In the Report Footer section, delete the three Sum function text boxes, delete the three sets of double lines, and delete the Report Footer section.
5. Click the Print Preview button to display the report and then print the entire report.
6. Save the report, naming it JOBS Report #2, and return to the Database window.

Olivia next creates a custom report. Use the Parttime database on your Student Disk to do the following:

E   7. Create a blank report using the query named JOBS sorted by Employer, Job Title.

E   8. Sketch a design for the report based on the requirements described in the next four steps, and then create the report following these same steps.

E   9. Include in your report a Page Header section and a Detail section.

E   10. In the Page Header section at the beginning of the first line, enter JOBS sorted by Employer, Job Title as the report title. Enter the current date at the beginning of the second line and the page number at the end of the second line. Position under these elements a row of column heads with these labels: Employer Name, Hours/Week, Job Title, and Wages. Add a single horizontal line under the column heads.

E   11. In the Detail section, include the field values for Employer Name, Hours/Week, Job Title, and Wages. Hide duplicates for the Employer Name field.

E   12. Select Employer Name as the primary sort key and Job Title as the secondary sort key. Do not select a grouping field. Choose ascending sort order for each sort key.

E   13. When you finish creating the report, print the entire report.

E   14. Save the report, naming it JOBS sorted by Employer and Job Title Report, and then exit Access.

4. Rexville Business Licenses

Chester Pearce uses Report Wizards to create a report for his Buslic database. Launch Access, open the Buslic database on your Student Disk, and do the following:

1. Use Report Wizards to create a groups/totals report in the executive style based on the BUSINESSES table. Select all the fields from the table in the order in which they are stored in the table. Do not select a grouping field, sort by Business Name, do not check the "Calculate percentages of the total" box, and enter BUSINESSES Report as the report title.

2. Display the report in the Print Preview window and then print the entire report.

3. Save the report, naming it BUSINESSES Report, and return to the Database window.

Chester next modifies the design of this report. Open the newly created BUSINESSES Report in the Report Design window and do the following:

4. In the Report Footer section, delete the Sum function text box for the two fields, delete the two sets of double lines, and delete the Report Footer section.

5. Click the Print Preview button to display the report and then print the entire report.

6. Save the report, naming it BUSINESSES Report #2, and then return to the Database window.

Chester next creates a custom report. Use the Buslic database on your Student Disk to do the following:

E 7. Create a blank report using the query named BUSINESSES sorted by License Type, Business Name.

E 8. Sketch a design for the report based on the requirements described in the next five steps, and then create the report following these same steps.

E 9. Include in your report these sections: Page Header, Detail, Group Footer, and Report Footer.

E 10. In the Page Header section at the beginning of the first line, enter BUSINESSES sorted by License Type, Business Name as the report title. Enter the current date at the beginning of the second line and the page number at the end of the second line. Position under these elements a row of column heads with these labels: License, Basic Cost, Business Name, and Amount. Add a single horizontal line under the column heads.

E 11. In the Detail section, include the field values for License (do not use License Number), Basic Cost, Business Name, and Amount. Hide duplicates for the License and Basic Cost fields.

E 12. In the Group Footer section, print the group total for the Amount field. Select License as the primary sort key and as the grouping field. Select Business Name as the secondary sort key, but do not use it as a grouping field. Choose ascending sort order for each sort key.

E 13. In the Report Footer section, print the overall totals for the Amount field.

E 14. When you finish creating the report, print the entire report.

E 15. Save the report, naming it BUSINESSES sorted by License Type and Business Name Report, and then exit Access.

Index

TASK	MOUSE	MENU	KEYBOARD
Add a field to a table structure, *A 69*	See Reference Window: *Adding a Field to a Table Structure*		
Add a label to a form or report, *A 189*	A		
Add a list box to a form, *A 189*	See *Adding a List Box Using Control Wizards*		
Add a record to a table, *A 171*	▶❙, ▶ or ▶*	Click Records, click Go To, click New	Ctrl +
Add a text box to a form or report, *(633)*	abl		
Add aggregate functions to a query, *A 138*	See *Using Record Calculations*		
Add all fields to a query's QBE grid, *A 114*	See *The Query Design Window*		
Add an input mask to a field, *A 60*	See *Using Input Mask Wizard*		
Add calculated field to a query, *A 136*	See *Using Calculated Fields*		
Add fields to a form or report, *A 182*	See *Adding Fields to a Form*		
Add Form Header and Footer sections, *A 188*		Click Format, click Form Header/Footer	Alt O , H
Add lines to a form or report, *(628)*	◻		
Add record group calculations to a query, *A 141*	See *Using Record Group Calculations*		
Add Report Header and Footer sections, *(631)*		Click Format, click Report Header/Footer	Alt O , H
Add sort keys and grouping fields to a report, *(630)*	⟮≣⟯		
Align control boxes, *A 186*	See *Aligning Labels*		
Arrange controls on a form or report, *A 183*	See *Selecting, Moving, and Deleting Controls*		
Back up a database, *A 102*	See *Backing Up a Database*		
Change a datasheet's font, *A 86*	See Reference Window: *Changing a Datasheet's Font Properties*		
Change colors on a form, *A 192*	See Reference Window: *Adding Colors to a Form*		
Change the number of decimal places for a field, *A 59*	See *Changing Decimal Places*		

TASK REFERENCE
ACCESS 2.0 FOR WINDOWS
Italicized page numbers indicate the first discussion of each task.

TASK	MOUSE	MENU	KEYBOARD
Close a database, *A 25*	, double-click Database window Control menu box	Click File, click Close, click File, click Close Database	Alt F , C , Alt F , C
Close an object window, *A 22*	Double-click the object window Control menu box	Click File, click Close	Alt F , C
Close Print Preview window, *A 22*		Click File, click Close	Alt F , C
Compact a database, *A 103*	See *Compacting a Database*		
Create a custom form, *A 179*	, select table or query, click Blank Form button		
Create a custom report, *(616)*	, select table or query, click Blank Report button		
Create a database, *A 46*	See Reference Window: *Creating a Database*		
Create a filter, *A 174*	See *Using a Filter*		
Create a form with Form Wizards, *A 163*	See *Creating Forms Using Form Wizards*		
Create a multiple-table form, *A 166*	See *Creating Main/Subform Forms*		
Create a multiple-table query, *A 149*	See *Querying More Than One Table*		
Create a new query, *A 113*	Click table name, , click New Query	Click table name, click File, click New..., click Query, click New Query	Alt F , W , Q , N
Create a parameter query, *A 152*	See Reference Window: *Creating a Parameter Query*		
Create a report with Report Wizards, *(606)*	See *Creating Reports Using Report Wizards*		
Create a table, *A 47*	Click the New command button	Click File, click New, click Table	Alt N
Create an AutoForm form, *A 162*	Click the table or query,		
Create an AutoReport report, *(605)*	Click the table or query,		
Define a relationship between tables, *A 147*	See *Adding a Relationship Between Two Tables*		
Define fields in a table, *A 50*	See *Changing the Sample Field Properties*		

TASK	MOUSE	MENU	KEYBOARD
Delete a field from a table structure, *A 68*	Right-click the field, click Delete Row	Click Edit, click Delete Row	`Alt` `E`, `D`
Delete a field from the QBE grid, *A 116*	Click field selector, right-click field selector, click Cut	Click field selector, click Edit, click Cut	Click field selector, `Del`
Delete a form or report section, *A 188*	Drag section's bottom edge to 0" height		
Delete a record in a datasheet, *A 88*	Select record, right-click record selector, click Cut, click OK	Select record, click Edit, click Delete, click OK	Select record, `Del`, `Enter`
Delete a table, *A 92*	Right-click table name, click Delete, click OK	Click table name, click Edit, click Delete, click OK	Click table name, `Del`, `Enter`
Delete an index, *A 67*	Right-click the index, click Delete Row		
Delete selection criteria from QBE grid, *A 134*	See *The Or Logical Operator*		
Display a single record on a form, *A 192*	🖻, click Default View box, click Single Form		
Display a table's indexes, *A 66*	📝	Click View, click Indexes...	`Alt` `V`, `I`
Enter a default value for a field, *A 59*	See *Assigning Default Values*		
Enter record selection criteria in a query, *A 121*	See *Defining Record Selection Criteria*		
Exit Access, *A 12*	Double-click Microsoft Access window Control menu box	Click File, Exit	`Alt` `F`, `X`
Find data in a datasheet, *A 94*	See Reference Window: *Finding Data in a Table*		
Find data in a form, *A 173*	See *Using the Find Command*		
Help screens, *A 27*		Click Help, Contents or Click Help, Search...	`Alt` `H`, `C` or `Alt` `H`, `S`
Hide duplicate values in a group report, *(635)*	See *Hiding Duplicate Values in a Group Report*		
Import an Access table, *A 90*	See Reference Window: *Importing an Access Table*		
Insert a field in the QBE grid, *A 119*	See *Inserting a Field*		
Launch Access, *A 11*	Double-click Microsoft Access icon		

TASK	MOUSE	MENU	KEYBOARD
Move a field or column, *A 117*	See *Moving a Field*		
Move the toolbar, *A 24*	See *Moving the Toolbar*		
Move to first record, *A 18*	⏮	Click Records, click Go To, click First	`Alt` `R`, `G`, `F`
Move to last record, *A 18*	⏭	Click Records, click Go To, click Last	`Alt` `R`, `G`, `L`
Move to next record, *A 18*	▶	Click Records, click Go To, click Next	`Alt` `R`, `G`, `N`
Move to previous record, *A 18*	◀	Click Records, click Go To, click Previous	`Alt` `R`, `G`, `P`
Open a database, *A 13*	See Reference Window: *Opening a Database*		
Open a filter saved as a query, *A 177*		Click File, click Load From Query...	`Alt` `F`, `L`
Open a form, *A 23*	Click Form object button, click the form name, click the Open command button		
Open a saved query, *A 132*	Click Query object button, click query name, click Open		
Open a table datasheet, *A 93*	Click Table object button, double-click the table name		
Open Cue Cards, *A 64*	📖	Click Help, click Cue Cards	`Alt` `H`, `U`
Print a datasheet, *A 20*	See Reference Window: *Printing a Hardcopy of a Datasheet*		
Print a form, *A 25*	🖨	Click File, click Print...	`Alt` `F`, `P`
Print a report, *(609)*	🖨	Click File, click Print...	`Alt` `F`, `P`
Print selected records, *A 130*	See *Printing a Dynaset Selection*		
Print table documentation, *A 101*	See *Printing Table Documentation*		
Quick sort records, *A 99*	Click field, then ⬆ or ⬇	Click field, click Records, click Quick Sort, click Ascending or Descending	Click field, `Alt` `R`, `Q`, `A` or `D`
Remove a filter, *A 176*	▦	Click Records, click Show All Records	`Alt` `R`, `S`
Rename a field in a query, *A 120*	See *Renaming Fields in a Query*		
Rename a table, *A 93*	Right-click table name, click Rename	Click table name, click File, click Rename...	Click table name, `Alt` `F`, `M`
Replace data in a datasheet, *A 97*	See Reference Window: *Replacing Data in a Table*		

TASK	MOUSE	MENU	KEYBOARD
Resize a column, *A 57*	See *Resizing Columns in a Datasheet*		
Resize a control, *A 185*	Click control box, drag sizing handle		
Save a filter as a query, *A 175*	💾	Click File, click Save As Query...	Alt F , A
Save a form, *A 163*		Click File, click Save Form As...	Alt F , A
Save a query, *A 131*		Click File, click Save Query As...	Alt F , A
Save a report, *(606)*		Click File, click Save As...	Alt F , A
Save a table's structure, *A 53*	💾	Click File, click Save	Alt F , S
Select a primary key, *A 63*	See *Selecting the Primary Key*		
Sort records in a query, *A 126*	See *Sorting Data*		
Switch to Datasheet View, *A 53*	▦	Click View, click Datasheet	Alt V , S
Switch to editing mode from navigation mode, *A 84*			F2
Switch to Form View, *A 187*	▦	Click View, click Form	Alt V , F
Switch to navigation mode from editing mode, *A 84*			F2
Switch to Table Design View, *A 54*	✎	Click View, click Table Design	Alt V , D
Undo a field change, *A 55*	↺	Click Edit, click Undo Typing	Ctrl Z
Undo a quick sort, *A 100*	▦	Click Records, click Show All Records	Alt R , S
View a query dynaset, *A 115*	❗ or ▦	Click View, click Datasheet	Alt V , S